Numerical Cognition: The Basics provides an understanding of the neural and cognitive mechanisms that enable us to perceive, process, and memorize numerical information.

Starting from basic numerical competencies that humans share with other species, the book explores the mental coding of numbers and their neural representation. It explains the strategies of mental calculation, their pitfalls, and their development, as well as the developmental steps children make while learning about numbers. The book gradually builds our understanding of the underlying mental processes of numeracy and concludes with an insightful examination of the diagnosis, etiology, and treatment of dyscalculia.

Written in an accessible manner, the book summarizes and critically evaluates the major psychological explanations for various empirical phenomena in numerical cognition. Containing a wealth of student-friendly features including end-of-chapter summaries, informative figures, further reading lists, and links to relevant websites, *Numerical Cognition: The Basics* is an essential starting point for anybody new to the field.

André Knops is a CNRS researcher at the Université de Paris. He investigates the neural and cognitive underpinnings of numerical cognition across the lifespan. André Knops has been granted funding from the European Research Council, the (stigious Emmy Noether prog   ).

THE BASICS SERIES

The Basics is a highly successful series of accessible guidebooks which provide an overview of the fundamental principles of a subject area in a jargon-free and undaunting format.

Intended for students approaching a subject for the first time, the books both introduce the essentials of a subject and provide an ideal springboard for further study. With over 50 titles spanning subjects from artificial intelligence (AI) to women's studies, *The Basics* are an ideal starting point for students seeking to understand a subject area.

Each text comes with recommendations for further study and gradually introduces the complexities and nuances within a subject.

For a full list of titles in this series, please visit www.routledge.com/The-Basics/book-series/B

NUMERICAL COGNITION

THE BASICS

André Knops

Routledge
Taylor & Francis Group
LONDON AND NEW YORK

First published 2020
by Routledge
2 Park Square, Milton Park, Abingdon, Oxon OX14 4RN

and by Routledge
52 Vanderbilt Avenue, New York, NY 10017

Routledge is an imprint of the Taylor & Francis Group, an informa business

© 2020 André Knops

British Library Cataloguing-in-Publication Data
A catalogue record for this book is available from the British Library

Library of Congress Cataloging-in-Publication Data
A catalog record for this book has been requested

ISBN: 978-0-8153-5722-3 (hbk)
ISBN: 978-0-8153-5723-0 (pbk)
ISBN: 978-1-3511-2480-5 (ebk)

Typeset in Bembo
by Apex CoVantage, LLC

To Laurianne and Hannah.

CONTENTS

ACKNOWLEDGMENTS

I want to thank Klaus Willmes and Martin Fischer for their thoughtful comments.

My thanks also go to my colleagues Arnaud Viarouge, Teresa Iuculano, and the other members of LaPsyDÉ who provided me with important input and discussions throughout the writing of this book. Last but not least, I would like to thank Nydia Vurdah for her careful reading of the manuscript.

GLOSSARY

ACC – anterior cingulate cortex; anterior part of the cingulate cortex that is located on the medial aspect of the cerebral cortex

Activation – regions in the brain where the change of blood flow is systematically more correlated with one experimental variation (condition) compared to another variation (condition)

ANS – approximate number system; cognitive system that allows the rapid and approximate estimation of the number of objects in a set; allows one to approximately compare two sets or add them up

Convex hull – smallest contour that can be drawn around a given set of items; roughly resembles a band that is put around a group of pins on a board.

DD – developmental dyscalculia; DD is a specific learning disorder that prevents the acquisition of basic arithmetic and numerical skills

dlPFC – dorso-lateral prefrontal cortex

EEG – electroencephalography; recording of the voltage changes on the scalp as a consequence of cortical activity

fMRI – functional magnetic resonance imaging; measures brain activity as changes of blood flow. Mainly exploits the blood-oxygen-level dependent (BOLD) contrast, a change of the relative levels of oxyhemoglobin and deoxyhemoglobin that alters suscep-tibility to magnetic fields.

g – Hedge's g; measure of effect size ((Mean$_{\text{group 1}}$ – Mean$_{\text{group 2}}$)/ pooled SD)

IPS – intraparietal sulcus; sulcus that separates inferior from superior parietal cortex

MNL – mental number line; spatial continuum along which numeri-cal magnitudes are mentally represented. In Western societies, smaller numbers are typically located left from larger numbers.

MVPA – multi-voxel pattern analysis; multivariate analysis of imag-ing data that is based on supervised machine learning algorithms (e.g. support vector machines); parameter estimates from voxels serve as features

Numeral – number word or Arabic digit that refers to a number

Numerosity – number of items in a set

OTS – object tracking system (synonym: parallel individuation system); cognitive system that allows subitizing; also allows identi-fication, representation, and tracking of a small set of objects

Overall occupied area – area that is covered by items, usually summed up over all items in a set; important non-numerical fea-ture of dot sets

PFC – prefrontal cortex; part of the neocortex located in the frontal part of the brain

PR – percentile rank

RSA – representational similarity analysis; data analysis technique for imaging data in which the similarity of activation patterns across voxels is compared between two or more conditions; the underly-ing idea is that a given stimulus (e.g. a human face) always evokes the same activation pattern in FMRI that is distinguishable from other stimuli (e.g. a monkey face)

SD – standard deviation

Subitizing – fast and accurate enumeration of small sets of objects (typically up to 3 or 4)

VIP – ventral intraparietal cortex; region in the macaque brain which hosts neurons that are tuned to specific numerosities

INTRODUCTION

DEFINITION OF NUMERICAL COGNITION – A MULTIDISCIPLINARY ENDEAVOR

Checking your bank account, logging in on your smartphone, choosing the floor number in an elevator – numerical information is ubiquitous in our everyday lives. But what enables us to understand and use numerical information? Numerical cognition describes the neural and cognitive mechanisms underlying this ability. Numerical cognition covers various topics: How do we estimate the number of objects in a set? How do we understand and represent Arabic numbers and other magnitude information? How do we learn and memorize arithmetic facts and procedures? What factors determine the successful acquisition of numerical concepts during development? How can we explain specific, math-related learning disorders? These questions provide a guideline for the current book.

Like few other topics, numerical cognition benefits from contributions from a variety of complementary disciplines such as cognitive psychology, functional neuroimaging, electrophysiology, and computational modeling. I will describe the contributions of these disciplines to our understanding of numerical cognition. The description will not only cover the cognitive perspective. Rather, considering myself a cognitive neuroscientist, I will also include the neural and neuronal mechanisms that give rise to the numerical competencies we are endowed with. This also includes an evolutionary perspective when investigating numerical competencies across species – from newly hatched chicks to nonhuman primates and humans. The book will also describe the development of numerical competencies from newborn to adult age. Finally, I will demonstrate the origins and consequences of failed acquisition of numerical competencies and its remediation. I use the term numerical rather than mathematical cognition because I limit the scope of this book to basic core concepts and processes. This includes the understanding of numbers (e.g. Arabic digits), numerosities (i.e. the number of items in a set), and basic mental computations (e.g. addition, subtraction, multiplication, . . .). The book does not cover higher mathematical competencies such as algebra, logic, or geometry.

In the following, I will try to briefly introduce some of the central terms and the cognitive neuroscience perspective I took in writing this book. Since the introduction of these terms is not the main focus of this book, I will provide only a dramatically synthesized overview that cannot deliver the detailed knowledge provided by some of the textbooks I refer to at the end of this chapter. Providing the reader with the basic terms and concepts can nevertheless serve as an introduction to cognitive neuroscience and can help the readers' understanding without consulting additional literature. A definition of central terms and concepts can be found in the glossary.

The term cognitive neuroscience refers to disciplines that aim at clarifying the principles of the mind at two levels. First, it includes techniques and methods that have been developed within psychology and cognitive sciences. The key motivation of these disciplines is to decipher the functional principles of the mind that give rise to (more or less intelligent) behavior. In this context, behavior does not only refer to overt behavior that is visible to the naked eye. Quite the contrary, most of the phenomena that I will describe throughout the book require the precise measurement of behavioral parameters such as reaction times in the millisecond range, finger trajectories during pointing movements or the rate at which participants are providing a correct or incorrect response over hundreds of trials. Over and above these methodological considerations, the term *behavior* also refers to a variety of concepts that have been conceived in order to organize mental behavior and render it accessible to scientific investigation. These include, for example, visuo-spatial attention, memory, perception, or problem solving. We will see examples for each of these throughout the book.

Second, cognitive neuroscience embraces those disciplines that investigate the principles of brain function and their relation to mental life. This comes in different flavors. Originally, clinical observations of patients with circumscribed brain damage and their associations with behavioral deficits have paved the way for a rudimentary understanding of the functional scope of a given brain area. Following brain damage (e.g. stroke), neuropsychological patients often suffer from distinguishable and sometimes unique patterns of functional deficits. The profile of these deficits crucially depends on which site of the brain was damaged, supporting the idea that different brain areas are indeed tightly associated with different cognitive functions. More information about the relationship between putatively different cognitive processes can be inferred when comparing complementary deficit patterns across patients. Finding that patient X is able to perform function *a* but not *b* while patient Y presents the exact opposite functional pattern (spared function *b* but impaired function *a*) tells us that functions *a* and *b* are independently implemented in the brain. This pattern of results is referred to as a double dissociation. For example, a double dissociation in two patients (BOO and MAR; when reporting to the public, neuropsychologists identify their patients using their initials) allowed researchers to postulate that numerical meaning can be represented in different mental codes (Dehaene & Cohen, 1997). BOO was a 60-year-old retired teacher who suffered from a left-hemispheric lesion in language-related areas. BOO was particularly impaired in solving multiplication problems (e.g. $4 \times 7 = ?$), while she was still able to solve addition and subtraction problems. Patient MAR was a 68-year-old, left-handed painter who suffered from a right-hemispheric lesion of posterior occipito-parietal areas. MAR was able to solve most multiplication problems but failed at very simple subtraction problems such as $6 - 2 = ?$ (MAR responded "2"). From this pattern of results, Dehaene and Cohen (1997) concluded that numbers can be represented in a phonological code that is important for storing arithmetic facts, and an analogue code that gives access to numerical meaning and is of pivotal importance in subtraction problems. In Chapter 2, we will learn more about the different codes and the model proposed by Dehaene and Cohen.

NEUROIMAGING OF COGNITION

Recent technical developments allow us nowadays to record signatures of brain activity without intervening in mental activities or damaging the brain. Notably, the principles of functional magnetic resonance imaging (fMRI) that have been developed during the last 30 or so years allow analyzing brain processes that are associated with perception, memory or problem solving "online", that is, while participants engage in a given activity. This is a major achievement since cognitive neuroscientists are no longer dependent on "nature's experiments" resulting in more or less circumscribed brain lesions and their functional consequences to infer the association between different brain areas and their cognitive functions. Neither do they rely entirely on inferring cognitive processes from so-called "omnibus" measures such as reaction times. These measures are usually taken once all cognitive processes that contribute to a given function are terminated. That is, in a simple cognitive task (e.g. "What is 6×7?"), these measures include all subprocesses and routines such as the perception and encoding of the written input, retrieving a solution, and choosing an adequate response, for example. Neuroimaging provides an online window onto these processes while they unfold. It provides us with techniques to isolate different components of the mental activity that lead to the correct response and to study their characteristics. It is important to understand the outcome of functional neuroimaging studies. Most studies will project the statistically significant association of a given condition with changes in blood flow onto a brain template that has been created by averaging several hundred individual brain images. In the simplest of all analysis approaches, researchers contrast the brain activation from two conditions against each other (i.e. they subtract one from the other) in order to isolate those regions in the brain that are more active in one condition compared to the other. For example, researchers present participants with simple arithmetic problems (e.g. "$4 \times 5 = ?$") in one condition and meaningless letter strings in the other (e.g. "r k t # s"). When subtracting the latter from the former, researchers seek to isolate arithmetic problem-solving processes (i.e. activation of numerical number meaning; retrieval of the correct result from long-term memory) from more basic shared perceptual processes such as letter recognition. Comparing the activity between calculation and reading reveals areas that are more involved in mental arithmetic than letter reading, such as bilateral areas along the intraparietal sulcus (IPS) and dorsolateral prefrontal cortex (dlPFC), for instance. The fact that certain areas do not show up in the resulting statistical map (e.g. occipital cortex) does not imply that these areas are not involved in the task at hand. For example, we know that the occipital cortex hosts a variety of perceptual mechanisms without which we would not be able to read. It merely reflects the idea that the occipital cortex (and hence visual perception) equally contributes to both conditions (letter reading and arithmetic problem solving). Since two conditions are subtracted from each other, this is referred to as subtraction logic. In another approach, researchers parametrically vary the experimental variable of interest and seek brain areas where activation closely follows this variation. For example, when participants are asked to judge whether a given digit (e.g. 3) is smaller or larger than a given standard (e.g. 5), reaction times vary as a function of the distance between the digit and standard (here: 2). The smaller the distance, the longer the decision takes. We will see in Chapter 2 why this is the case. If we find brain areas in which the activation increases as numerical distance decreases, we can conclude that these areas are closely associated with the representation of numerical distance. This technique has a limited spatial resolution of approximately 8 mm³ to 64 mm³ and hence reflects the summed activity of millions of neurons. Other techniques in nonhuman primates allow recording the activity of single neurons at high spatial and temporal precision (e.g. 1000 Hz, meaning that 1 second delivers 1000 measurements). All of these approaches have yielded important building blocks to our understanding of how numerical cognition is implemented in the brain.

MENTAL REPRESENTATION – A KEY CONCEPT

One of the most important ideas in cognitive psychology is the concept of a mental representation. A mental representation is a

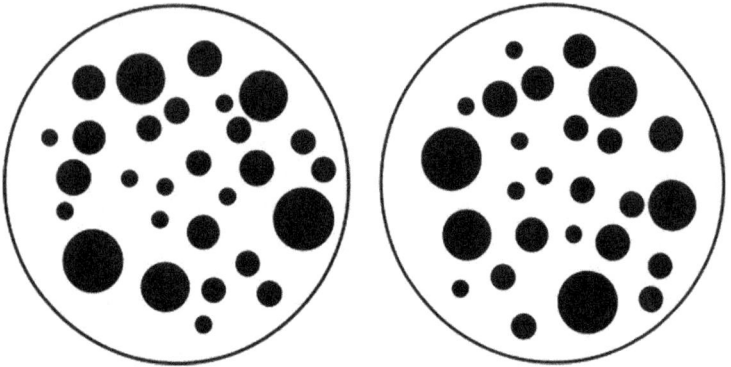

FIGURE 1.1 Two numerosities (i.e. sets of items). Guess where you see more dots – left or right?

psychological construct. It refers to the temporary or stable mental signature that reflects previously perceived (or remembered) content or a cognitive process. Similarly, a cortical representation is the neural state that is associated with the presence of a given external or internal event. The mental representation does not necessarily need to have the same characteristics or features as the original (e.g. external) content. It is not a veridical mirror image of the original input. For example, when quickly comparing the number of elements in two sets such as the dots in Figure 1.1, you may perceive them as identical. Hence, the initial mental representation of both sets is identical. Yet when taking a second look, you may see that the left set contains two dots more than the right one. This means that our mental system (i.e. the brain) constructs representations of the external world that we operate on even if they are not veridical (i.e. exact). To understand the functional principles of the cognitive system, it is of key importance to define the content of the mental representations, their functional properties, and their deviations from the external world. For example, I will describe in Chapter 2 the human ability to determine the numerical difference between two numerosities (i.e. the number of elements in a set) and what rules this ability follows.

MEMORY – HOW DO WE REMEMBER THINGS?

Humans are endowed with the ability to permanently represent information in memory. Different forms of memory can be distinguished according to either the duration of retention (sensory memory, short-term memory, and long-term memory) or to their content (procedural memory, declarative memory). Sensory memory provides a short-lived representation of sensory input (up to ~1 second), while short-term memory acts in the range of about 1 second to several minutes. Both are thought to be limited in capacity. Long-term memory, on the other hand, has a theoretically unlimited capacity and retains information for years. Declarative memory contains semantic (e.g. "6 times 4 equals 24.") and episodic information (e.g. "I learned arithmetic facts in elementary school and I remember exactly what the classroom looked like and what smell it had.") and requires conscious recall. Procedural knowledge is employed during the accomplishment of a task and can be retrieved without conscious control (also referred to as implicit memory). Riding a bicycle is a good example of procedural knowledge.

Much like our mental system constructs flawed representations of sensory events, the way semantic information is represented in and recalled from memory is often not a veridical snapshot of the original content. This can influence our behavior. Multiplication facts, for example, are thought to be represented in a so-called semantic network. Semantic networks consist of nodes that are interconnected with each other. Each node stands for a given piece of information. Inspired from the general network structure of neural systems, semantic networks are defined by a number of characteristics. Much like the neural system receives activating input from our senses (e.g. light falls on the retina and activates cone and rod photoreceptors), semantic networks represent information by activating certain nodes. Activation is projected along the weighted connections between nodes – much like action potentials travel between neurons. The connection between two nodes can be excitatory (i.e. activation from node 1 gradually increases activation state of node 2) or inhibitory (i.e. activation from node 1 lowers activation state of node 2). Connections vary in strength. Connection strength increases when nodes are repeatedly activated together. Another factor that determines the connection strength is the (semantical) distance between nodes. Nodes that do not share a direct connection but only an indirect one exert lower mutual influence on each other since spreading activation decreases with increasing distance.

Semantic networks can explain a number of empirical phenomena. For example, it was found that participants took more time to reject incorrect results of multiplication problems when they were part of the same multiplication table compared to unrelated responses. It takes more time to reject 28 as the response to the problem $4 \times 6 = ?$ compared to 27. Since arithmetic facts are represented in a network structure, activation will spread to all nodes connected to 4 and 6. In this situation, the node 28, which is connected to 4, will receive more activation than the node 27 that does not share any connection (or digits) with either 4 or 6. Due to this pre-activation of the node 28, it will be more difficult for the participant to inhibit the prepotent response "correct" compared to a situation where the response alternative is not pre-activated at all.

NUMERICAL COGNITION FROM AN EVOLUTIONARY PERSPECTIVE

Apart from the investigation of human behavior at various levels, numerical cognition has received important insights from research with non-human subjects. Surprisingly, numerical competencies have been discovered in a broad variety of species, not all of which possess a neocortex. For example, fish have been shown to swim towards the more numerous of two shoals when placed in the middle between them. Since shoals provide shelter against predators, larger shoals provide better shelter by lowering the probability of being eaten. Recognizing the larger of two shoals therefore has an evolutionary benefit. Yet a fish brain is radically different from a human brain – let alone the difference in weight (1.2–1.4 kg vs. ca. 0.000003 kg [=3 mg] in guppies; Kotrschal et al., 2013). Investigating numerical competencies in different species provides a fascinating window into evolution and has floated the idea that number is a primary visual concept that provides useful guidance for many species in their respective ecological niches. Chapter 3 describes numerical cognition from an evolutionary perspective.

SUMMARY

- Cognitive neuroscience comprises methods and research approaches from psychology, cognitive science, and neuroscience.
- Precise measurements of behavioral parameters (e.g. reaction times) characterize the scientific investigation of the mind and its relation to the brain.
- Mental representations are transient or stable states of the cognitive system that reflect (internal or external) stimuli.
- Associative semantic networks are a way by which semantic memory representations can be modeled.

FURTHER READINGS

Anderson, J. R. (2015). *Cognitive psychology and its implications* (8th ed.). New York: Worth Publishers.

Gazzaniga, M., Ivry, R. B., & Mangun, G. R. (2019). *Cognitive neuroscience – The biology of the mind* (5th ed.). New York: W. W. Norton & Company.

Poldrack, R. A., Mumford, J. A., & Nichols, T. E. (2011). *Handbook of functional MRI data analysis*. Cambridge: Cambridge University Press.

   This book provides an excellent and easy-to-understand overview of basic neuroimaging techniques, the nature and origin of the signal, and how to interpret the results. Also check the accompanying website, www.fmri-data-analysis.org/.

REFERENCES

Dehaene, S., & Cohen, L. (1997). Cerebral pathways for calculation: Double dissociation between rote verbal and quantitative knowledge of arithmetic. *Cortex*, *33*(2), 219–250.

Kotrschal, A., Rogell, B., Bundsen, A., Svensson, B., Zajitschek, S., Brannstrom, I., . . . Kolm, N. (2013). Artificial selection on relative brain size in the guppy reveals costs and benefits of evolving a larger brain. *Curr Biol*, *23*(2), 168–171. doi:10.1016/j.cub.2012.11.058

2

THE FORMS – WE ENCOUNTER AND REPRESENT NUMERICAL QUANTITIES IN MANIFOLD WAYS

Numerical information is ubiquitous in our everyday lives. Only typing in the correct PIN at the ATM or on your smartphone device will grant you access. In France, it is rather usual to have PINs to enter a given building. Numbers help us find the right platform in a train station and our seats in the right compartment. Numbers tell you about the price of your coffee on your way to university or the speed limit on your weekend trip to the mountains.

Although all these examples refer to situations in which we have to read and encode Arabic digits, the type of numerical information that is conveyed differs between situations. The digits in a PIN do not have an inherent numerical meaning. A given code 2554 is not any larger or smaller than the code 3554. Both numbers have a qualitative meaning that follows so-called nominal scaling. The scaling is defined – in part – by the operations that are meaningful for a given number. For the example given, one can neither order, compare, nor use PINs for any arithmetic procedures. It just does not make any sense to add up two PINs. They are nominally scaled and can be treated like proper names. Other examples include Levi's Jeans model 501; the term 9/11 to refer to the attacks on the World Trade Center in New York on September 9, 2001; the perfume Chanel No. 5; or your personal ID card or tax identification number.

When looking for the right platform in a train station, however, numbers can at least be used to infer the order of the platforms. That is, when looking for platform five while standing at platform one, for example, we know which direction we have to go (unless the architects of the train station you are at had a funny day). Platforms are aligned according to their position in the numerical sequence. Yet this does not necessarily imply that the distances between all platforms are equal, as is the case for the number sequence. For example, in Germany, it is quite common to find platforms ranging from one to – say – eight plus an additional number of platforms numbered 101 and 102. Even though these latter platforms are usually on the other side of the station building, they are not 100 times farther apart from the other platforms. Here, we speak of the ordinal information that numbers convey. It allows comparing numbers in terms of their relative positions to each other. Platform 5 comes right after platform 4 and before platform 6, regardless of their absolute distance to each other. Ordinal scaling does not allow us to apply any arithmetic operations (except for comparisons such as "5 is not equal to 6"). For example, it does not make sense to say "platform 8 is twice platform 4". Similarly, the ordinal property of numbers is used when referring to the outcome of a given race (Eliud Kipchoge came in first in the 2018 Berlin marathon) or competition (Bayern Munich were ranked first in the German football league in the season 2018/2019). But, again, it does not make sense to numerically relate two football clubs by saying, for example, that Bayern Munich is five times as good a team as Borussia Mönchengladbach, who ended up in fifth place that season.

All this changes when we refer to measures on a ratio scale. It does make sense to say, for example, that Germany has won the FIFA world cup twice as often (four times) as France (twice), even though one would have guessed otherwise watching the German team play at the 2018 tournament in Russia, where they showed a horrible performance. The distance between Berlin and Geneva is (approximately) twice as long (1141 km) as the distance between Berlin and Frankfurt (570 km). That does not change when using miles instead of kilometers and dividing the distances by 1.609. Beyond an arbitrary scale, ratio scales have a naturally defined zero or starting point (e.g. 0°C).

When referring to the number of elements in a set (e.g. the number of kilometers in a given distance), we speak of the cardinality of a set. The cardinal meaning of numbers is thus the quantity represented by its corresponding set.

Why is it important to distinguish between the different types of information that numbers can convey? First, it shows the rich spectrum of information that can be conveyed by numbers. The cardinal meaning of numbers is surely what comes to mind first and foremost. Yet understanding the ordinal relationships between numbers appears to be of substantial importance during development. It has been shown that a good mastery of the ordinal relationships between numbers is increasingly associated with good performance in arithmetic up to 5 years later (Lyons, Price, Vaessen, Blomert, & Ansari, 2014).

The distinction is not only important at a purely theoretical level. It is also reflected in the organization of knowledge at the neural level. For Arabic digits, Lyons and Beilock (2013) showed distinct, that is nonoverlapping, brain networks for processing ordinal information (e.g. judging whether a number triplet such as 2_5_4 was in ascending order) and cardinal information (e.g. judging which of two numbers is numerically larger). This suggests that these two properties are processed by distinguishable networks at the neural level.

Another convincing piece of evidence for the neural distinction of these two types of information comes from patient studies where a double dissociation (see Chapter 1) has been reported for ordinal and cardinal number understanding. Patient SE was massively impaired in performing mental arithmetic or numerical magnitude comparisons (Delazer & Butterworth, 1997). For example, he was unable to answer the question "which number is larger: 5 or 8?"). Yet not all numerical knowledge was lost in this patient. SE was perfectly able to recite the number sequence or decide which number comes next after a given number. Thus, while being impaired in treating cardinal content of numerical information, processing ordinal content was relatively spared. Another patient, CO, showed the complementary pattern of performance (Turconi & Seron, 2002). CO was able to compare numbers in terms of magnitude. Yet CO was unable to judge the ordinal relationship between numbers or days of the week. Hence, patient CO was impaired in processing the ordinal content of a number, while processing cardinal information did not pose any difficulties. From this we can infer that understanding the ordinal and cardinal information numbers convey is implemented in distinct brain areas. At the behavioral level, too, cardinality and ordinality give rise to distinct phenomena. When participants are asked to judge whether a given number comes before or after another number, reaction times increase (error rates decrease) as numerical distance increases (Franklin & Jonides, 2009; Turconi, Campbell, & Seron, 2006). Hence, the ordinal distance effect is the inverse of the cardinal distance effect (see subsequently).

THE TRIPLE CODE MODEL OF NUMBER PROCESSING

In the 1990s, a very prominent model in cognitive psychology hypothesized that all numerical quantity information would be transformed into a single and central representation before the cognitive system could make use of it. For example, to transcode the written number word "three" into the spoken number word /three/, the visual input needs to be transformed into a central semantic representation (McCloskey, 1992) before it can be transformed into a phonological code by the speech system. However, several findings in neuropsychological patients were hard to reconcile with this idea (see Chapter 6). Consequently, the triple-code model (TCM) of number processing (Dehaene & Cohen, 1995) has been derived from neuropsychological case studies and cognitive models. It has been remarkably successful in providing a theoretical framework for the subsequent functional neuroimaging upturn with the advent of functional magnetic resonance imaging, even if a number of updates have been proposed recently (Arsalidou & Taylor, 2011; Klein et al., 2016). According to the TCM, numerical information is internally represented by three separate but interacting codes: a verbal number code is activated in linguistically mediated operations like number naming, counting, and retrieval of arithmetic facts from long-term memory (e.g. addition results < 10, multiplication table facts). The verbal code recruits the general-purpose modules for language processing that are neurally associated with left perisylvian language areas and left angular gyrus (AGs). A visual number code allows for recognizing Arabic digits and multi-digit numbers. It is associated with bilateral fusiform and lingual regions of the ventral object recognition stream. The analogue magnitude code represents numerical quantity information and is part of a preverbal system for arithmetic reasoning. It allows for comparing numerosities and approximately estimating numerosity. Originally, it was also involved in subitizing, a capacity that it now assumed to be independent from the analog magnitude code (see subsequently). It is the source of numerical meaning, that is, the cardinal value a given number refers to. It is conceived as being approximate and analog. It is often referred to as the approximate number system (ANS, see subsequently). Visual and verbal number codes are asemantic. Based on neuropsychological case studies (Dehaene & Cohen, 1997), the TCM identified the bilateral intraparietal sulcus as the key cortical region in numerical magnitude processing, which received further support from early functional imaging studies (Dehaene, Spelke, Pinel, Stanescu, & Tsivkin, 1999;

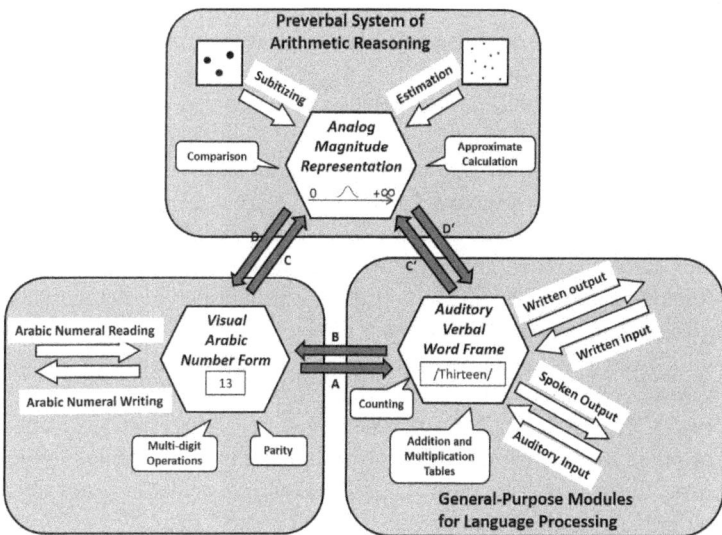

FIGURE 2.1 The triple code model of number processing (Dehaene & Cohen, 1995).

Source: Adapted from Dehaene (1992).

Eger, Pinel, Dehaene, & Kleinschmidt, 2015; Eger, Sterzer, Russ, Giraud, & Kleinschmidt, 2003; Naccache & Dehaene, 2001a; Pinel, Dehaene, Riviere, & LeBihan, 2001). Extending the TCM, Dehaene and colleagues (Dehaene, Piazza, Pinel, & Cohen, 2003) proposed that the semantic number system in the IPS is supported by the bilateral posterior-superior parietal lobe (PSPL). The PSPL is involved in orienting attention along the supposedly spatially oriented mental number line. This may become relevant in situations that require the combination (e.g. addition or subtraction) of several entries on the mental number line (MNL).

THE APPROXIMATE NUMBER SYSTEM

Most naturally, cardinal numerical information is conveyed by the number of elements in a given set. Imagine you have to choose between four lines in a supermarket. Following Murphy's law, you will most likely find that all the other lines move faster than yours. But before switching lines or freaking out, you may want to think about why you ended up there in the first place. You may have chosen the line with the fewest people waiting without even paying attention to the fact that you made that decision based on the approximate estimate of people waiting in the lines. That is, unless you deliberately engaged in counting the customers waiting in each line, you may have simply relied on what is sometimes referred to as the "sense of numbers". The number sense, also referred to as the approximate number system, describes a cognitive system that humans are endowed with. It allows us to approximately estimate the number of elements in a given set, approximately compare them to each other, or add them up. I insist on the approximate character of this estimation because this system is a preverbal system that is independent from any counting procedure. Instead, it follows the laws that characterize a number of other senses such as object weight, loudness of sounds, or brightness. These laws have been investigated and described in great detail by early psychologists in the nineteenth century (Ernst Weber, Gustav Fechner). In thousands of trials, Weber measured whether participants were able to distinguish two weights that differed by a certain number of grams, for example. He (and Fechner, who followed up on this work later) realized and formalized that the determining factor to distinguish between the weight of two objects is the difference in relation to the overall magnitude. For example, participants were able to distinguish between two cubes A and B weighing 100 g and 120 g, respectively. With two cubes C and D weighing 1000 g and 1020 g, the decision would be much more difficult, despite the fact that the absolute difference (20 g) is identical in both situations. Weber and Fechner established that the just noticeable difference (JND) is relative to the overall magnitude (in fact, it is expressed as a ratio). Hence, we would need to increase the weight of cube D from 1020 g to 1200 g in order to obtain the same accuracy in distinguishing between both cubes (1000:1200 = 100:120 = 1:1.2). The increase in magnitude difference (20% in our example) has to be proportional to the overall magnitude range in order to keep subjective distinguishability constant.

How is the internal impression of the weight or loudness of a sound associated with the physical unit? Is a sound with 50 decibels (50 dB) perceived as half as loud as a sound with 100 dB? The short answer is: no. The actual physical intensity of a stimulus relates to the subjectively perceived intensity via a logarithmic relationship. This has been formally expressed by Weber and Fechner and is referred to as the Weber-Fechner law. Why is this interesting in the current context? Because the Weber-Fechner law applies to various sensory dimensions such as brightness, weight, or loudness, including number perception. Two hallmark effects in numerical cognition have been described in line with the Weber-Fechner law. First, in numerical magnitude comparison tasks where participants have to decide which of two sets contains more elements, performance is inversely related to numerical distance: the larger the numerical distance between sets, the better the performance. For example, when deciding which of two sets contains more items, participants are faster and make fewer errors when distinguishing between two sets with 10 and 20 items, respectively, compared to two sets with 10 and 11 items, respectively. Hence, the cardinal *distance effect* describes increasing reaction times and error rates with decreasing numerical distance between the to-be-compared stimuli. Second, with increasing overall numerical magnitude of the stimulus pair, numerical distance must increase proportionally to guarantee constant performance in discrimination tasks – the *size effect*.

It may appear natural that performance in tasks where we have to estimate the number of elements in a given set is dominated by the same laws that govern perception of other natural dimensions such as brightness, loudness, or weight. Surprisingly, however, some of these laws have also been observed with *symbolic* numbers. The distance effect has been observed with Arabic digits (Moyer & Landauer, 1967), for instance. This is surprising since there is no obvious uncertainty when comparing one digit with another. Computer programs take an equal amount of time comparing 5 with 6 or 5 with 52. How do psychologists explain that humans take more time to decide with the former number pair compared to the latter? The most commonly used metaphor to characterize numerical magnitude representation is the *mental number line* (see Figure 2.2). According to this idea, numerical quantity is mentally represented along a spatially oriented line with smaller numbers left from larger numbers. The second concept that psychologists use to explain the cardinal distance effect is internal noise (see Box 2.1). Whenever we activate an entry on the MNL, 5, for example, we also co-activate neighboring sites such as 4 and 6. This is due to the fact that

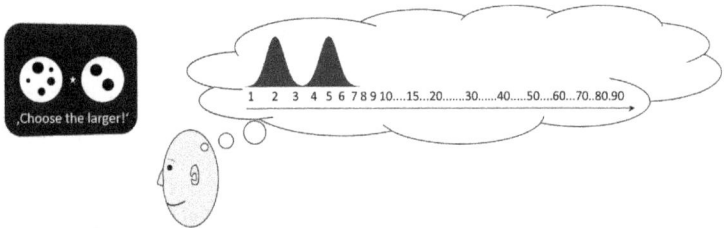

FIGURE 2.2 The mental representation of numerical magnitude is often described by the metaphor of the mental number line. On a left-to-right oriented line, smaller numbers are positioned left from larger numbers. As numerical magnitude increases, distance between neighboring entries decreases, giving rise to a logarithmic compression. The presentation of two numerosities (here: 2 and 5) activates the corresponding position on the mental number line, as well as surrounding entries. This noise is thought to take the form of a Gaussian distribution. The less these distributions overlap, the easier (faster and less error prone) it is to decide on the larger numerosity.

BOX 2.1

The concept of noise in a system has its origin in the middle of the twentieth century when radar technology was used to spot airplanes. When staring at the screen, the operators needed to distinguish between real objects and other signals that were generated by the system itself or by other items (e.g. flock of birds). The idea is that a signal is detected when its signal strength exceeds a given threshold. Yet most systems (e.g. neurons, radio transistors) generate some subthreshold activity that can sometimes add up to exceed the threshold even in the absence of a real signal. This is due to the stochastic nature of spreading activation in a system.

The nervous system contains noise. In 1952, Fatt and Katz (1952) described the subthreshold synaptic activity of muscle fibers that occurred spontaneously, without any external or internal stimulation. This spontaneous subthreshold activity has been observed in most parts of the nervous system. Subthreshold activity can have functional consequences. For example, when a motor neuron exhibits an elevated amount of subthreshold activity, any incoming signal only needs to add a smaller amount of energy to make the neuron "tip over" the threshold and transmit a motor command. Hence, the smaller amount of required energy affords faster response latencies as compared to neurons with smaller amounts of subthreshold activity.

Psychologists have transferred these concepts to the internal structure of semantic knowledge, such as cardinal magnitude knowledge. Much like neurons represent information by firing in response to an incoming signal, in semantic networks, so-called nodes become activated to represent a given semantic concept. For example, a given number of nodes along the MNL may be tuned to a certain range of numbers – each node representing one number. Once a given number node becomes activated after accumulating supra-threshold input, the numerical information has been encoded by the system. Inspired by the actual interconnected organization of the nervous system where the firing of a neuron excites other neurons that are synaptically connected, nodes are thought to be connected with each other, too. When a given number node becomes activated, neighboring nodes will accumulate a weaker amount of input and will generally reach a lower level of overall activation. The connection strength between nodes is not fixed, however, but contains a certain level of random activation – noise. The same is true for the connection to the sensory signals that activate the nodes. Due to this random process of activation, sometimes a neighboring node receives more activation and may erroneously be taken as the system's response. The closer the neighboring node, the more frequently such errors occur. This renders the differentiation between two neighboring nodes more difficult compared to the differentiation between two nodes that are far apart.

activating the position on the MNL is associated with some internal noise. When thinking of the numerical magnitude representation as a mental number line, the noise may take the form of a Gaussian distribution of activation centered on the to-be-activated number. When presented with the numbers 2 and 5, for example, surrounding entries on the MNL will be activated, leading to an overlap of activations that renders it more difficult to distinguish between both and determine the larger number compared to a presentation of the numbers 2 and 9, for example. See Figure 2.2 for a depiction of a numerosity comparison.

How does the cognitive system extract the numerical quantity information from a visual scene? Put differently, how do we estimate the number of people in a crowd? There exist a number of theoretical models of numerosity perception. In an early model, a hierarchy of number-sensitive and number-selective processing steps (Dehaene & Changeux, 1993; Verguts & Fias, 2004) has been assumed (see Figure 2.3).

The raw visual input is normalized and represented in a topologically organized map of the scene with activation peaks indicating the position of the elements in the scene. Dedicated units sum the activation peaks from this map, leading to a monotonic increase of activity in this number-sensitive instance activity with increasing number of objects (Dehaene & Changeux, 1993; Verguts & Fias, 2004). The summed activation is then fed into the next instance that contains number-selective units. Here, units are tuned to specific numerosities and activity decreases monotonically as numerical distance between preferred and actual numerosity increases.

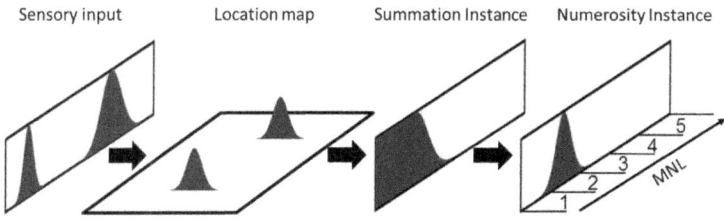

FIGURE 2.3 Computational numerosity processing model by Dehaene and Changeux (1993). The first processing instance provides the system with discretized, individuated information about the objects in a given scene. In the second step, the objects' locations are topographically represented in a location map, which is not number specific but serves domain-general purposes such as visual short-term memory and can be used to guide hand or eye movements. Activity in the location map is normalized for size and location. For example, larger objects do not take up more representational space than smaller objects. In the next instance, the activity in the location map is summed up (summation code); hence, more objects lead to higher activation in this instance. In the final instance, number-specific detectors combine the excitatory and inhibitory information from the active and inactive summation levels, respectively. As a consequence, the units at this level exhibit a number tuning function (place coding). These units are maximally activated when a specific preferred numerosity or number is presented to them. Activation decreases proportionally with increasing numerical distance between preferred and actual number, yielding an inversely U-shaped tuning function when plotting the activation level against the presented number.

Source: Adapted from Dehaene and Changeux (1993).

This dovetails with the idea of a MNL and has been found to be reflected at the neural level in occipital and parietal areas (Cavdaroglu & Knops, 2018). In an fMRI study, Roggeman and colleagues tested how these hierarchical instances of numerosity perception map onto the neural system (Roggeman, Santens, Fias, & Verguts, 2011). Participants were adapted to visually presented dot arrays. After adapting to a given numerosity (e.g. 3), deviants were presented that varied either in location of the dots or in terms of numerosity. By categorizing numerosity deviants into the category smaller-larger (e.g. 1 and 2 vs. 4 and 5) or close-far (e.g. 2 and 4 vs. 1 and 5), this design allowed the mapping of neural circuits that either followed a summation coding or a number-selective scheme. The former would show increased activity for larger compared to smaller deviants. The latter would show increased activity for far compared to close deviants. The authors found a hierarchical organization along an occipital-to-parietal pathway (Roggeman et al., 2011). While occipital regions exhibited the strongest activation recovery for location deviants, areas in the superior occipital cortex and the adjacent transition region between the occipital and parietal cortex were most sensitive to deviants from the smaller-larger category, indicating a summation coding scheme. Areas in the PSPL and IPS exhibited a recovery profile that implied number selectivity. This means that activity in these areas increased as the numerical distance between adapted numerosity and deviant increased – a neural instantiation of the distance effect. Together, this suggests that numerosity is extracted from visual input in areas along an occipital-to-parietal pathway. As the activity travels out from the occipital cortex into the parietal cortex, it first passes through number-sensitive neural circuits in the middle occipital and PSPL exhibiting a summation coding schema, before reaching number-selective circuits in the IPS. Cavdaroglu and Knops (2018) extended these findings to a larger numerical range but found – in essence – a similar gradient of increasing numerosity specificity as one travels from occipital to parietal cortex. Interestingly, as number specificity increases, the importance of non-numerical features of the scene decreased. For example, increasing the number of dots in a given set while keeping constant the individual dot size will inevitably lead to increasing area that is covered by all dots together. Hence, overall occupied area and numerosity are confounded in this situation. To control for this confounding, a second set of stimuli can be created where overall occupied area is kept constant, for example, while numerosity changes. In that situation, individual dot size will be negatively correlated with numerosity (i.e. dots become smaller as their number increases). In the context of numerosity perception, non-numerical stimulus features usually include the individual dot size, the overall area occupied by all dots (akin to the summed number of pixels covered by the dots), the smallest contour that can be drawn around the set (convex hull), and the density (or its inverse, sparsity). Cavda-roglu and Knops (2018) found that the neural representation of these non-numerical features becomes increasingly fuzzy as one travels from early visual cortex toward parietal cortex.

Currently, there is a lively debate concerning the extent to which the estimation of a numerosity depends on these non-numerical features. On the one hand, there is mounting evidence suggesting that numerical estimates are actually independent from these visual characteristics. In an early fMRI study, Piazza and colleagues repeatedly presented dot displays with either 20 or 50 dots to participants in the scanner (Piazza, Pinel, Le Bihan, & Dehaene, 2007). They observed two effects in bilateral areas around the IPS. First, activity decreased as one numerosity was repeated over and over again (in fact, they changed all non-numerical parameters of the dot sets except the number of dots), reflecting the adaptation of the neural system. Second, when they changed numerosity (e.g. from 50 to 20 dots), activity increased and reached pre-adaptation level. Hence, bilateral areas around the IPS were sensitive to changes in numerosity. The organization of parietal cortex may even bear more resemblance to the metaphor of the MNL. At the macroscopic neural level, a study recently found a topographic organization of numerosity-tuned voxels in fMRI. That is, in the human parietal cortex, a spatially organized gradient of numerosity specificity was observed (Harvey, Klein, Petridou, & Dumoulin, 2013). Harvey and colleagues, too, presented participants with sets of dots in various changing layouts while recording brain activity with a high-field (7 Tesla) scanner. They found that specific voxels at one end of the topographically organized parietal area were tuned to numerosity one, while adjacent voxels were tuned to two. This spatial organization continued until numerosity 7, located at the other extreme of the area. The cortical area devoted to these numerosities decreased as numerosity increased. The most area was devoted to numerosity one, while numerosity seven showed minimal cortical extent. In a nutshell, these results can be described as a cortical instantiation of the number line, including logarithmic compression and independence from non-numerical features.

In another striking example, Burr and Ross (2008) demonstrated that numerosity is subject to behavioral adaptation – comparable to other visual dimensions – and can hence be likened to these as a perceptual primitive. To better understand this phenomenon, have a look at the fixation cross in the middle of Figure 2.4 and keep fixating on it for 30 seconds. Then, turn the page and quickly estimate the side where you see more dots – left or right?

Chances are you estimated a larger number of dots on the left side of Figure 2.5. Yet when taking a closer look, you will realize that both sets contain an equal number of dots. In fact, they are identical. In their study, Burr and Ross measured the size of this adaptation effect. After adapting participants to 400 dots, numerosities at the adapted site need to be 2 to 2.5 times larger to be perceived as equally numerous. For example, after adaptation, seeing 40 to 50 dots leads to the impression of seeing 20 dots only. Subsequent experiments helped exclude alternative interpretations that were based on texture or density perception, or adaptation at the retinal level (Franconeri, Bemis, & Alvarez, 2009; He, Zhang, Zhou, & Chen, 2009; Ross & Burr, 2010). In line with the idea that numerosity perception is a visual primitive, estimation performance shows limited influence to variations of non-numerical parameters (Kramer, Di Bono, & Zorzi, 2011), and humans are more sensitive to changes in numerosity compared to changes in other dimensions such as density or area (Cicchini, Anobile, & Burr, 2016).

On the other hand, it has been argued that numerosity is indirectly derived by weighing up the quantity information from different dimensions, including the ratio of energy in different spatial frequency bands (Dakin, Tibber, Greenwood, Kingdom, & Morgan, 2011), or all available sensory information such as overall occupied area, density, size, and other dimensions together (Gebuis, Cohen Kadosh, & Gevers, 2016). Supporting evidence for this idea comes from studies that find numerosity discrimination to be influenced by the variation of non-numerical stimulus parameters, both in behavioral (Smets, Sasanguie, Szücs, & Reynvoet, 2015; Tokita & Ishiguchi, 2010, 2012) and in electroencephalographic (Gebuis & Reynvoet, 2014) measures. Other studies did not converge on these findings, however (Guillaume, Mejias, Rossion, Dzhelyova, & Schiltz, 2018; Pinheiro-Chagas et al., 2014). Neural overlap of activations in response to quantity changes along various dimensions such as physical size (Pinel, Piazza, Le Bihan, & Dehaene, 2004) have been taken as evidence for a holistic processing of numerosities (Leibovich, Katzin, Harel, & Henik,

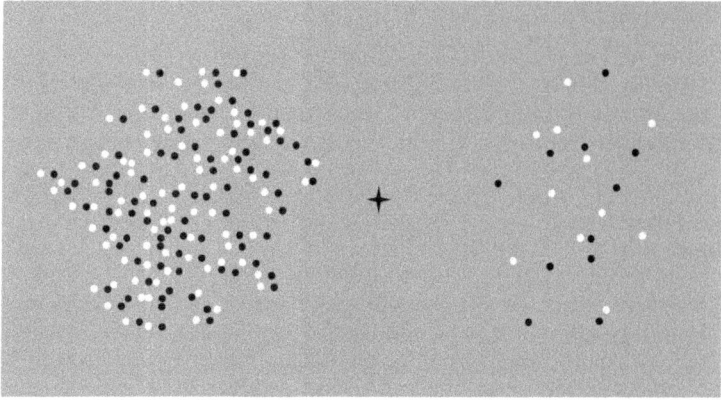

FIGURE 2.4 Fixate on the star in the center for ca. 30 seconds without moving your eyes. Then turn the page and quickly tell on which side there are more dots.

2016). In fact, a theory of magnitude has been proposed that assumes that space, time, and number share common cortical circuits in the parietal cortex (Bueti & Walsh, 2009).

While the jury is still out on the debate, the alternative proposals (e.g. sense of magnitude, theory of magnitude, sensory integration theory) lack a level of detail in predicting performance and the underlying neurocognitive mechanisms that the approximate number system approach has provided. Moreover, several biologically plausible computational models successfully simulated the evolution and performance of a numerosity system that shares central features with the assumption of an approximate number system (Stoianov & Zorzi, 2012, 2017; Verguts & Fias, 2004). Additionally, functional neuroimaging studies converge on the notion that the IPS hosts cortical circuits that process the numerosity of spatially distributed items in line with the predictions from these models (Cavdaroglu & Knops, 2018; Roggeman et al., 2011; Santens, Roggeman, Fias, & Verguts, 2010). Finally, converging evidence from single-unit recordings in non-human primates and behavioral studies in other species jointly point to the idea that humans share an innate system for processing numbers with various species, underlining the idea that numerosity is indeed an important visual dimension that has co-evolved in diverging species (see Chapter 3). Notwithstanding the intertwined relation between numerical and non-numerical features, disentangling the exact neural and cognitive mechanisms that enable us to extract the numerosity from a scene will be an exciting scientific endeavor.

SUBITIZING

An important limit to the ANS is the number range. While discrimination performance for numerosities remains constant over a large numerical range and can readily be described by the Weber-Fechner law, very low numerosities diverge systematically from this behavior. Humans are extremely precise in enumerating sets that comprise between one and three or four objects only. In this numerical range, accuracy is close to 100% and reaction times (RTs) do not vary as a function of number of items. This capacity to arrive at rapid and exact numerical judgments for sets with few items (usually ≤4) is referred to as *subitizing* (Kaufman, Lord, Reese, & Volkmann, 1949). Subitizing was initially thought to invoke the same mechanisms as numerosity estimation (Ross, 2003) or be based on a pre-attentive mechanism that assigns a Finger of INSTantiation (FINST; i.e. a sort of index or pointer) to individual (or grouped) items until the limited capacity of FINSTs is depleted (Trick & Pylyshyn, 1994). Recent evidence, however, suggests that subitizing does not rely on the same mechanisms as estimation but rather is associated with a flexible, attention-based individuation mechanism. Revkin and colleagues (Revkin, Piazza, Izard, Cohen, & Dehaene, 2008) tested naming performance for all numerosities between 1 and 8 on the one hand and for decade numerosities between 10 and 80 (10, 20, 30, etc.) on the other. Results showed that the variation of naming performance (reaction times, error rates, variation coefficient) differed dramatically between these number ranges, despite comparable discrimination difficulty within sets (i.e. the ratio between items 1 through 8 is equal to the ratio between items between 10 and 80). This speaks against the idea that a single set of cognitive mechanisms guides performance in both number ranges. A second line of research shows that subitizing and estimation are differentially influenced by the modulation of available processing resources. While

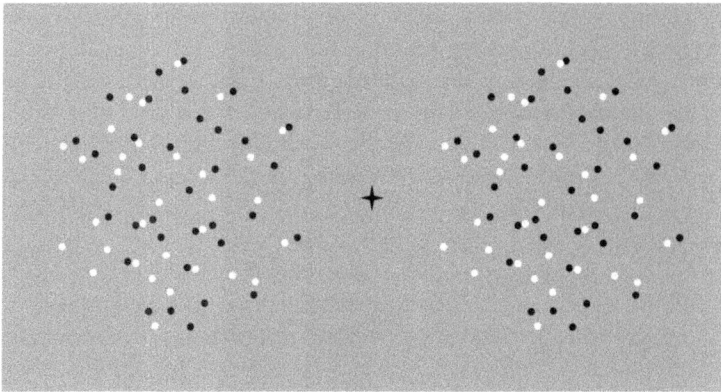

FIGURE 2.5 On which side do you see more dots?

subitizing was largely unaffected by a rivaling concurrent task, estimation performance declined under dual-task conditions (Anobile, Turi, Cicchini, & Burr, 2012; Burr, Turi, & Anobile, 2010). A series of recent studies suggests that subitizing capacity (i.e. the number of items that can be immediately and effortlessly enumerated) is functionally associated with working memory limits (Melcher & Piazza, 2011; Piazza, Fumarola, Chinello, & Melcher, 2011). In contrast to the FINST approach that assumes a fixed limit of available pointers (Trick & Pylyshyn, 1994), Melcher and Piazza assume that the visual system can flexibly assign a variable amount of limited resources to individual items – depending on task demands and the saliency of the items (Franconeri, Alvarez, & Cavanagh, 2013; Todd & Marois, 2004). In line with this assumption, individual visuo-spatial working memory capacity was positively correlated with subitizing range (Piazza et al., 2011). By manipulating task demands, Melcher and Piazza were able to influence the amount of resources that were assigned to individual items. In tasks that required a precise and rich representation, items were assigned more resources compared to situations in which coding the mere presence or absence of items sufficed. Subitizing was reduced when few resources were left compared to situations where task demands were low, hence leaving more resources for subitizing. Using fMRI, we were able to demonstrate that the posterior superior parietal cortex contains topographic information of individuated objects that the visual system can flexibly exploit for the current goals (Knops, Piazza, Sengupta, Eger, & Melcher, 2014). This attention-grabbing mechanism provides relevant information for visual short-term memory, object tracking, grasping, or the enumeration of sets of objects. Depending on the level of detail needed for the current task, the amount of attentional resources dedicated to individual items varies and gives rise to different neural response profiles with varying numerosity. Results from electrophysiological studies converge on the idea that subitizing crucially depends on "an attention-based individuation mechanism that binds specific features to locations and provides a stable representation of a limited set of relevant objects" (Mazza & Caramazza, 2015).

In sum, subitizing needs to be separated from estimation because it is characterized by different behavioral performance profiles and invokes different cognitive mechanisms.

SYMBOLIC NUMBERS

One of the most striking capacities of humans is their ability to represent numerical quantities in an exact fashion that goes beyond the precision of the ANS, as introduced previously. Symbolic numbers can be noted using number words or Arabic digits. The most important characteristic of the number system we use nowadays is that digits change their value according to their spatial position within a number. Our number system is a base 10 system. We have to correctly attribute the respective power of 10 to a particular digit depending on its spatial position in the two-digit string (e.g. in 23, the value of the 2 is $2 \times 10^1 = 20$, while in 32, the value of the 2 is $2 \times 10^0 = 2$). For this reason, our number system is called a place-value system with the base 10. Several hints in our language suggest that the base-10 system has not been the only number system that had been used. For example, the fact that we have proper number words for numbers up to 12 ("twelve" in English, "zwölf" in German, "douze" in French, to name a few only) represents a remainder of a base-12 system. The English term "dozen" ("Dutzend" in German) to refer to 12 items is further proof of this idea. The French number word system also shows traces of a base-20 system. For example, there is no proper decade break after

69 ("soixante-neuf"). Instead of introducing a proper composite term for 70 like in English ("seventy" or "siebzig" in German), the French expression for 70 is "soixante-dix" (literally: "sixty-ten"), followed by "soixante-et-onze" (literally: "sixty-and-eleven") and so on until "soixante-dix-neuf" ("sixty-nineteen"). Although it appears natural to us, having a dedicated symbol for zero is of crucial importance to this system. In essence, the 0 in 403 simply translates into 4 hundreds, no tens and 3 units. Denoting the absence of a given power of ten in a number is important and cannot easily and unambiguously be replaced by, for example, leaving a blank at that position, a technique that Babylonians would have used some 1800 years before common era. Our number notation was initially developed by the Indian civilization and is referred to as "Arabic" digits merely because it became known to Western culture via Persian mathematicians.

Provided the fragmented notational system we use to express and denote numerical values, what does the internal magnitude representation look like? As introduced previously, the TCM assumes a unitary semantic representation of numerical value, most often described by the metaphor of a mental number line. According to this view, a two-digit number such as 56, for example, would activate a given position on this continuum, with co-activation spilling over to neighboring sites. However, in a series of experiments, Nürk and Willmes were able to demonstrate that the mental magnitude representation of multi-digit numbers is more complex than assumed in the TCM (Nuerk, Weger, & Willmes, 2001). They presented participants with two two-digit numbers (e.g. 47 vs. 62) and asked them to indicate which of them was numerically larger (62). In the given example, the overall distance between the numbers is 15. According to the TCM, all number pairs with a distance of 15 (and in the same overall numerical range) would consequently lead to comparable response latencies since the representational overlap on the MNL is comparable. In striking contrast to this prediction, Nürk and colleagues found that number pairs such as 47_62 would take systematically longer to respond to when compared to pairs such as 42_57 despite comparable overall distance. They explained this by assuming that units and decades of the two-digit numbers were represented and compared separately. Hence, we would not be endowed with a unitary numerical magnitude representation but rather with a decomposed representation, reflecting the place-value code of our number notation (Knops, 2006). In the previous examples, the comparison of units, decades, and overall magnitude all point to the same number for the pairs 42_57 because 4 < 5, 2 < 7, and 42 < 57. For the pair 47_62, however, this is not the case. There is an incompatibility of the units and decades comparison because 4 < 6 but 7 > 2. That is, the smaller number has the larger unit. This incompatibility needs to be resolved by taking into account (assigning a higher weight to) the place-value information according to which the decade value is crucial here and should guide decision. In later studies, Nürk and colleagues found that overall magnitude was a significant predictor over and above unit and decade value, which led them to propose a hybrid model of multi-digit number representation that consists of a combination of parallel and sequential processing of the constituting digits and leads to a hybrid mental magnitude representation comprising not only the overall numerical magnitude (akin to the TCM) but also the decomposed representations of the digits according to their position in the number (Meyerhoff, Moeller, Debus, & Nuerk, 2012).

AUTOMATIC PROCESSING OF NUMBERS

At this point, one may wonder why participants would actually engage in all these comparisons of units when all they would actually need to do is to focus on the decades to get the comparison task right. The unit-decade compatibility effect implies that the semantic processing of numerical magnitude is automatic and cannot be suppressed. In line with this assumption, masked priming studies found that congruent primes would speed up responses, while incongruent primes would slow responses down. In masked priming studies, participants are presented with a target digit for which they would need to indicate whether it is numerically larger or smaller than a predefined standard (e.g. 5). The target is preceded by the presentation of a prime digit. To prevent participants from consciously perceiving the prime, it is temporally embedded in a random letter string. That is, immediately before the prime comes on screen, a letter string (forward mask; e.g. XTKLW) is presented for 70 ms. The prime stays on screen for only a brief period (e.g. 30 ms) before it is replaced by another letter string, the backward mask. This procedure prevents the participant from consciously perceiving the prime digit. Interestingly, when both prime and target are smaller or larger than the standard, reaction times are faster compared to trials in which prime and target are associated with diverging responses (e.g. prime: 2 target: 6) (Naccache & Dehaene, 2001b). This priming was observed across notations (e.g. prime: number word target: Arabic digits) and extended to primes that were not consciously seen throughout the entire experiment (Naccache & Dehaene, 2001b). Together, this corroborates the idea that numerical magnitude is automatically processed – even when not being consciously perceived (see also Huckauf, Knops, Nuerk, & Willmes, 2008, but see Kunde, Kiesel, & Hoffmann, 2003 for an alternative explanation). Currently, there is a debate about whether non-conscious semantic processing would extend beyond symbolic numbers and hold true for non-symbolic numerosities, too. While some authors reported such priming (Bahrami et al., 2010), we recently demonstrated that the reported effect was due to a flawed statistical analysis (Hesselmann & Knops, 2014). When tested properly, no conclusive evidence for non-conscious priming from non-symbolic numerosities was observed (Hesselmann, Darcy, Sterzer, & Knops, 2015).

SPATIAL-NUMERICAL ASSOCIATIONS

The assumption of a MNL also implies an association of numerical magnitudes with space. Since larger numbers are located to the right of smaller numbers on the MNL, this spatial relation may have an impact on performance. Many researchers understand the spatial numerical association of response codes (SNARC) as evidence supporting a spatially organized mental magnitude representation. The SNARC effect describes the finding that in various tasks (e.g. magnitude judgment or parity [odd-even] judgment), smaller numbers are associated with faster left-sided responses compared with right-sided responses. A corresponding advantage exists for right-sided responses and larger numbers (Dehaene, Bossini, & Giraux, 1993). In a typical SNARC experiment, participants have to judge the parity of numbers (i.e. decide whether it is an odd or even number) by pressing a right button for even numbers and a left button for odd numbers. In the middle of the experiment, this button assignment is reversed. Now participants have to push the right button for odd and the left button for even numbers. Thanks to this counterbalancing, for every number, the experiment yields responses from both hands. When subtracting left from right responses per number, the difference is positive for smaller numbers, indicating that participants take longer when responding with the right hand compared to the left hand. For larger numbers, however, the difference is negative, indicating that participants are faster with the right hand compared to the left hand. When regressing numbers against the reaction time difference (i.e. calculating a linear regression), the regression line has a negative slope, starting with positive differences for smaller numbers and ending with negative differences for larger numbers. Hence, the spatial response is associated with the numerical magnitude of the numbers. According to the most commonly held interpretation, this association is due to the correspondence between a given number's position on the MNL and the response side. Because larger numbers are represented right from smaller numbers, they are associated with right-sided responses. A similar congruency effect has been observed in the evaluation of numerical distances between adjacent numbers in a triplet (Koten, Lonnemann, Willmes, & Knops, 2011). Participants are faster when judging the side with the smaller numerical interval in a triplet such as 53__62_____98 compared with a triplet of the form 53_____62__98 because of the (task-irrelevant) congruency between numerical and spatial distances that separate the numbers. Using functional magnetic resonance imaging, we also demonstrated that this interference is due to a central semantic processing stage rather than reflecting mere response conflicts. Finally, Nicholls and colleagues (Nicholls, Loftus, & Gevers, 2008) observed that numbers influence the perception of luminance, presumably via deflection of visual attention in accordance with the position of the number in space (i.e. on the MNL). They superimposed numbers on two grayscale gradients. Participants were asked to choose the more luminous of the two gradients that were shown on top of each other. Each display contained one bar with a change from white on the left to black on the right and another bar with black on the left to white on the right. They found that participants' judgments were influenced by the superimposed numbers. For example, a bar that gradually changed from white on the left to black on the right was perceived as brighter when a superimposed small number (e.g. 1) oriented attention to the left (white) portion of the bar. These results suggest that the spatial position of a number on the MNL systematically affect perception and responses. Numbers might affect perception by deflecting visual attention to the left or right for smaller and larger numbers, respectively. Responses may be affected by the congruency between position on the MNL and response side.

The assumption of a direct mapping between the position of a number on the MNL and response side has been challenged by the dual-route model (Gevers et al., 2010; Gevers, Verguts, Reynvoet, Caessens, & Fias, 2006) and the working memory (WM) account (Ginsburg, van Dijck, Previtali, Fias, & Gevers, 2014; van Dijck & Fias, 2011).

The dual-route model introduces an intermediate level of processing (between the MNL and the response stage) that codes numbers into binary categories such as magnitude (i.e. small vs. large), parity (i.e. odd vs. even), or other dichotomous features of the stimulus. As the name suggests, this model includes two routes of parallel information processing. The unconditional route codes numbers based on their magnitude and is automatically activated regardless of the task requirements. This route activates the long-term pre-existing links between magnitude and space coordinates, that is, the associations small–left and large–right. The conditional route codes numbers into a binary category based on task-specific requirements. It activates short-term links between numbers and an arbitrary mapping based on task requirements, such as small–right and large–left (for magnitude) or odd–right and even–left (for parity). The SNARC effect emerges from the congruence, or lack of it, between the response sides activated by the two routes. On the one hand, the conditional route activates a response side based on task-specific mapping. On the other hand, the unconditional route can cooperate or compete to activate the same or the opposite response side, respectively. If the task-related mapping is consistent with the long-term number-space links, the two routes cooperate; otherwise, they converge on opposite spatial response codes. The response selection process takes longer and response latency is slower when the routes diverge, and this generates the SNARC effect. Since both routes are always simultaneously activated independently of the task, the level of semantic processing required by the task should not influence the SNARC effect.

In a recent experiment (Didino, Breil, & Knops, 2019), we tested the MNL hypothesis against the dual-route model by systematically varying the depth of semantic processing of the digits. Participants engaged in two tasks with little semantic elaboration demands (color discrimination, phoneme detection) and in two tasks that required a little (parity judgment) or in-depth semantic elaboration (magnitude comparison). According to the MNL account, one would expect that deeper semantic processing of a number leads to a stronger activation of the MNL, and in turn more interference (i.e. a stronger SNARC effect) is expected. According to the dual-route model, however, the strength of the SNARC effect is influenced by the duration of the number processing.

In line with the dual-route model, the strength of the SNARC effect was proportional to the overall RTs (the slower the RT, the larger the effect), suggesting that response latency is the main factor that affects the strength of the SNARC effect.

Both the MNL account and the dual-route model assume that the association between numbers and space coordinates is an intrinsic property of the long-term memory representation of numbers. The working memory account instead assumes that no spatial information is co-represented together with numbers and that the long-term representation only includes serial order information. The number-space association would emerge from a temporary binding of numbers to a spatially oriented template in working memory.

In sum, it seems that numbers are associated with space. Whether this reflects a congruency between response and MNL, a temporary congruency in working memory, or is the result of information processing along a dual-route architecture remains debated.

DOES THE INTRAPARIETAL SULCUS HOST AN ABSTRACT NUMBER SYSTEM?

The TCM stipulates that the quantity system in IPS is abstract. This means that all numerical information activates the same system, whether is it perceived visually or auditorially, whether the information is symbolic (e.g. Arabic digits) or non-symbolic (e.g. sets of dots).

The previously mentioned study by Piazza and colleagues suggests that the IPS hosts a system that responds to both symbolic and non-symbolic number information. Besides dot sets, Piazza and colleagues repeatedly presented Arabic digits (50 or 20). Interestingly, the recovery upon change of the presented number was observed for deviants from both formats, that is, sets of dots and Arabic digits, implying an abstract magnitude coding in the IPS. Partial format independence of IPS activation was also observed using multivariate pattern analysis (MVPA). In MVPA, a classifier is trained to distinguish between two or more stimulus categories (e.g. numbers) by identifying the characteristic spatial pattern of activation that is associated with each stimulus category. The classifier is then tested with a stimulus pair that was not part of the training set. Eger and colleagues (Eger et al., 2009) found distinguishable activation patterns for numbers between two and eight in the parietal cortex. The numerical content of the stimulus partially generalized across formats. When trained with Arabic digits, the classifier successfully predicted the numerosity of dots in a set. However, the classifier that was initially trained with non-symbolic numerosities did not generalize to Arabic digits. The asymmetric generalization might be due to the less precise tuning function for non-symbolic format compared with symbolic numerals, which in turn leads to less precise generalization across formats (Verguts & Fias, 2004). These results support the idea of an abstract number representation in the IPS.

However, recent fMRI evidence suggests that the spatial organization of number-specific activation in the IPS does not reflect a purely abstract number representation. In particular, two recent studies demonstrated format-dependent coding of non-symbolic (dot patterns) and symbolic (Arabic digits) numerals. Applying multivariate decoding, Bulthé and colleagues (Bulthe, De Smedt, & Op de Beeck, 2014) failed to generalize classifiers across formats. Whether a classifier was trained with non-symbolic dot patterns or Arabic digits, the distinctive pattern allowing for within-format classification of numerals was format specific and did not allow classifying numerals in a different format. In a similar vein, Lyons and colleagues (Lyons, Ansari, & Beilock, 2015) used representational similarity analysis (RSA) to assess the overlap between different number tuning functions. RSA provides a within-subject similarity measure for the spatial activation patterns associated with pairs of experimental conditions. Based on the notion of number-selective neural circuits in the parietal cortex, Lyons and colleagues reasoned that a larger amount of representational overlap between adjacent numbers would be reflected by greater similarity measures at the neural level. If symbolic and non-symbolic number information is represented in an abstract form, similarity would also be preserved across notations. Participants indicated via button press whether a numeral (Arabic digits or set of dots) would match the preceding numeral. For non-symbolic notation, similarity between adjacent numerosities increased as numerical magnitude increased. In contrast, the spatial patterns associated with Arabic digits neither correlated with each other nor did similarity change as a function of numerical distance. Hence, while the neural correlates of the mental magnitude representation of non-symbolic numerosities adhere to the proposed spatial organization along a MNL with increasing overlap between neighboring magnitudes as number increases, the mental representation of Arabic digits and their neural correlates differs qualitatively from the non-symbolic representation. Possibly due to extensive experience with Arabic digits, number symbols may be represented with infinite precision or categorically.

In sum, the question whether the IPS hosts an abstract number system remains debated.

FRACTIONS

When children learn fractions, one frequently observes a so-called whole number bias (Mack, 1995). For example, they often assume that ¼ is larger than ⅓, applying what they learned for whole numbers, where 4 is larger than 3. This bias is not limited to students but can also be found in adults (DeWolf & Vosniadou, 2015), and even mathematical experts tend to show this natural (or whole) number bias when the to-be-compared fractions contain a common nominator or denominator (Obersteiner, Van Dooren, Van Hoof, & Verschaffel, 2013). What is the reason for this? There are currently two classes of theories that try to explain this phenomenon: first, the learning account argues that we commit this error because fractions are perceived in a decomposed fashion (Gelman & Williams, 1998; Vosniadou, Vamvakoussi, & Skopeliti, 2008). As introduced earlier, multi-digit numbers are represented in a hybrid fashion. All constitutive parts of the number (e.g. units and decades for two-digit numbers) are represented alongside the overall numerical meaning of the number. The natural number bias makes it very likely that a decomposed processing of fractions that is based on our previously acquired knowledge about natural numbers prevails – even in educated adults. If participants would actually represent the overall numerical meaning of a fraction, no natural number bias would be expected. The fact that participants independently compare only sub-parts of the fractions suggests that fractions – like multi-digit numbers – are subject to a decomposed processing. In the previous example, the natural number 4 is larger than the natural number 3. Hence, the perception of fractions would be guided by knowledge that we acquired for natural numbers (positive integers: 1, 2, 3, . . .), and applying this knowledge to fractions leads to incorrect conclusions. Learning fractions would therefore require a conceptual change.

Alternatively, the integrated theory of numerical development (Siegler, Thompson, & Schneider, 2011) relies on two crucial assumptions. First, fractions, much like natural numbers, can be represented by assigning a position on a spatial magnitude scale – the MNL. Second, learning about fractions requires one to accept that many properties of natural numbers (e.g. each number has a unique successor, each interval consists of a finite number of elements) may not hold for fractions. According to the integrated theory of numerical development, the latter would be of major importance for the acquisition of mathematical concepts and should hence lead to a strong association between fraction understanding and mathematical skills. In support of this idea, Siegler and colleagues observed that fraction magnitude knowledge highly correlated with mathematics achievement and that different measures of fraction knowledge highly intercorrelate with one another (Siegler et al., 2011). The integrated theory stipulates that children become increasingly proficient in representing the holistic magnitude of a fraction rather than its composing terms. In partial support of this, Ischebeck, Schocke, and Delazer (2009) found no evidence for a neural correlate of the decomposed processing of fractions. Rather, the only variable that determined activity in the IPS during a fraction magnitude comparison task was the overall numerical distance between two to-be-compared fractions. This implies holistic processing of fractions. At odds with this result from the neural data, the distances between the denominators and nominators were significant predictors of behavioral performance in the same participants (see also Bonato, Fabbri, Umiltà, & Zorzi, 2007 for decomposed processing of fractions). Hence, the lack of a neural correlate of decomposed fraction processing may have been due to insufficient sensitivity of the functional brain data analysis. The question of whether fractions are represented holistically or in a decomposed fashion may reflect an oversimplification of the various strategies and approaches participants use when being engaged in fraction magnitude comparisons. That is, the strategy appears to be determined by a number of factors, including experience with fractions, task demands, and overall number knowledge (Alibali & Sidney, 2015). A more important question would be what actually fosters the understanding of fractions – beyond fraction comparison skills? The conceptual change theory assumes that previously acquired knowledge induces a "change resistance" that impedes learning and hence necessitates a conceptual change. In stark contrast to the conceptual change theory, whole number understanding has been found to directly support the acquisition of fraction comparison strategies (Bailey, Siegler, & Geary, 2014; Rinne, Ye, & Jordan, 2017) rather than impeding its acquisition.

> Nonverbal reasoning, verbal ability, and attentive behavior, are related both to children's initial strategy . . . and to their probabilities of transitioning to more advanced strategies. . . . Whole number line estimation ability predicted transitions to normative strategy use across the first two time points – even while controlling for the effects of other cognitive factors and general mathematics achievement.
>
> (Rinne et al., 2017, pp. 725–726)

Beyond concept-specific understanding of the numerator-denominator relation and fraction procedures, central executive functions have been identified as a domain-general (i.e. applying not only to numerical cognition but also to other cognitive domains such as language, reasoning, etc.) predictor of fraction magnitude knowledge in eighth and ninth grades (Mou et al., 2016). Other factors include classroom attention, multiplication fluency, and (whole) number line estimation accuracy (Resnick et al., 2016).

Taken together, knowledge about the structure of the place-value system we acquired during the first years of schooling influences the way we represent and operate with fractions later on. However, contrary to the conceptual change theory, this may not explain why students often struggle with the understanding of fractions. Rather, it may represent a stepping-stone for a mastery of fraction understanding.

Yet a third proposal puts the idea of a core component at the center of understanding fractions. Matthews and Hubbard (2017; Matthews, Lewis, & Hubbard, 2016) propose that humans possess a dedicated ratio processing system (RPS) that enables humans to intuitively access the holistic magnitude of proportions and fractions. They demonstrate that "individual differences in RPS acuity predict performance on four measures of mathematical competence, including a university algebra entrance exam" (Matthews et al., 2016, p. 191). This idea is based on the observation that both infants and monkeys are sensitive to ratios. McCrink and Wynn (2007) habituated 6-month-old infants to a graphical representation of a 2:1 ratio (e.g. 20 Pac-Men and 10 pellets). Non-numerical properties of the stimuli were carefully counterbalanced and hence did not induce adaptation to non-numerical properties of the stimuli. Upon the presentation of a numerical deviant with a 4:1 ratio, infants' looking time was significantly longer compared to a control condition of numerically non-deviant ratios (2:1). These results suggest that preverbal infants can detect differences between two ratios when one is twice as large as the other. Similarly, a recent training study with macaques revealed that monkeys were sensitive to ratio changes (Drucker, Rossa, & Brannon, 2016). By proposing a core system that operates largely independently from the ANS, Matthews and colleagues converge with the integrative theory of numerical development on the notion that fractions may represent an important enrichment of numerical abilities. Training children to locate fractions on a number line, finally, has proven a useful tool for improving fraction understanding (Hamdan & Gunderson, 2017).

It remains an empirical question whether the ANS and the RPS actually represent independent core capacities (Matthews & Hubbard, 2017; Matthews et al., 2016). This implies that they are not necessarily correlated with each other. Results showing that whole number knowledge (which correlates with ANS) predicts fraction understanding imply non-independence. Further support for the independence of fraction understanding from the ANS comes from a recent training study. Adult participants were trained over a long time (a minimum of 22 sessions corresponding to 8448 trials; maximum: 15,744 trials) on a numerosity discrimination task. While ANS acuity improved over the entire training period and generalized over visual quadrants, this improvement did not generalize to ratio comparison, arithmetic, or multiple object tracking (Cochrane, Cui, Hubbard, & Green, 2019). The exact neural cascade of processes that allow an understanding of fractions remains largely elusive (Jacob & Nieder, 2009; Jacob, Vallentin, & Nieder, 2012). What remains puzzling, though, is the observation that humans' intuitive capacity to appreciate proportional information fails to translate into a proficient mastery of fractions. Put differently, why are humans able to appreciate the golden section in objects, paintings, and photographs but show striking deficits in dealing with fractions?

SUMMARY

In this chapter, I described the different forms through which we encounter numerical magnitude information and their different properties.

- Numbers can be represented in three different codes: the visual number code, the phonological code, and the analog magnitude code.
- The ANS is a cognitive system that allows the rapid and approximate estimation of the number of objects in a set.
- There is evidence for the assumption that numerosity represents a perceptual primitive and is sensed directly via dedicated mechanisms that are hosted along the dorsal pathway and terminate in the intraparietal sulcus.
- The most common metaphor for describing the mental magnitude representation is the mental number line.
- Convergent evidence suggests a hybrid representation of numerical magnitude that reflects both a holistic and a decomposed representation of numerical magnitude.

- Numbers (but not numerosities) are automatically and non-consciously processed.
- Numbers are associated with space, as indexed by the SNARC effect, for example, which is most parsimoniously explained by a dual route model.
- Fractions build upon the knowledge we acquired during early schooling.
- A good mastery of natural numbers appears beneficial for fraction understanding and can help reduce cognitive fallacies.

FURTHER READINGS

Several reviews exist that provide an excellent entry to the bodies of literature on the questions whether there is an ANS (Burr, Anobile, & Arrighi, 2017; Leibovich et al., 2016; Nieder & Dehaene, 2009), how space and number are associated (Knops, 2018; van Dijck, Ginsburg, Girelli, & Gevers, 2015), and the neurocognitive mechanisms of subitizing (Franconeri et al., 2013; Mazza & Caramazza, 2015; Melcher & Piazza, 2011).

REFERENCES

Alibali, M. W., & Sidney, P. G. (2015). Variability in the natural number bias: Who, when, how, and why. *Learn Instr, 37*, 56–61. doi:10.1016/j. learninstruc.2015.01.003

Anobile, G., Turi, M., Cicchini, G. M., & Burr, D. C. (2012). The effects of cross-sensory attentional demand on subitizing and on mapping number onto space. *Vision Res, 74*, 102–109. doi:10.1016/j.visres.2012.06.005

Arsalidou, M., & Taylor, M. J. (2011). Is $2 + 2 = 4$? Meta-analyses of brain areas needed for numbers and calculations. *Neuroimage, 54*(3), 2382–2393. doi:10.1016/j.neuroimage.2010.10.009

Bahrami, B., Vetter, P., Spolaore, E., Pagano, S., Butterworth, B., & Rees, G. (2010). Unconscious numerical priming despite interocular suppression. *Psychol Sci, 21*(2), 224–233. doi:10.1177/0956797609360664

Bailey, D. H., Siegler, R. S., & Geary, D. C. (2014). Early predictors of middle school fraction knowledge. *Dev Sci, 17*(5), 775–785. doi:10.1111/desc.12155

Bonato, M., Fabbri, S., Umiltà, C., & Zorzi, M. (2007). The mental representation of numerical fractions: Real or integer? *J Exp Psychol Hum Percept Perform, 33*(6), 1410–1419. doi:10.1037/0096-1523.33.6.1410

Bueti, D., & Walsh, V. (2009). The parietal cortex and the representation of time, space, number and other magnitudes. *Philos Trans R Soc Lond B Biol Sci, 364*(1525), 1831–1840. doi:10.1098/rstb.2009.0028

Bulthe, J., De Smedt, B., & Op de Beeck, H. P. (2014). Format-dependent representations of symbolic and non-symbolic numbers in the human cortex as revealed by multi-voxel pattern analyses. *Neuroimage, 87*, 311–322. doi:10.1016/j.neuroimage.2013.10.049

Burr, D. C., Anobile, G., & Arrighi, R. (2017). Psychophysical evidence for the number sense. *Philos Trans R Soc Lond B Biol Sci, 373*(1740). doi:10.1098/rstb.2017.0045

Burr, D., & Ross, J. (2008). A visual sense of number. *Curr Biol, 18*(6), 425–428. doi:10.1016/j.cub.2008.02.052

Burr, D. C., Turi, M., & Anobile, G. (2010). Subitizing but not estimation of numerosity requires attentional resources. *JVis, 10*(6), 20. doi:10.1167/10.6.20

Cavdaroglu, S., & Knops, A. (2018). Evidence for a posterior parietal cortex contribution to spatial but not temporal numerosity perception. *Cereb Cortex.* doi:10.1093/cercor/bhy163

Cicchini, G. M., Anobile, G., & Burr, D. C. (2016). Spontaneous perception of numerosity in humans. *Nat Commun, 7*, 12536. doi:10.1038/ncomms12536

Cochrane, A., Cui, L., Hubbard, E. M., & Green, C. S. (2019). "Approximate number system" training: A perceptual learning approach. *Atten, Percept Psychophys, 81*(3), 621–636. doi:10.3758/s13414-018-01636-w

Dakin, S. C., Tibber, M. S., Greenwood, J. A., Kingdom, F. A., & Morgan, M. J. (2011). A common visual metric for approximate number and density. *Proc Natl Acad Sci U S A, 108*(49), 19552–19557. doi:10.1073/pnas.1113195108

Dehaene, S. (1992). Varieties of numerical abilities. *Cognition, 44*(1–2), 1–42.

Dehaene, S., Bossini, S., & Giraux, P. (1993). The mental representation of parity and number magnitude. *J Exp Psychol Gen, 122*(3), 371–396. doi:10.1037/0096-3445.122.3.371

Dehaene, S., & Changeux, J. P. (1993). Development of elementary numerical abilities: A neuronal model. *J Cogn Neurosci, 5*(4), 390–407. doi:10.1162/jocn.1993.5.4.390

Dehaene, S., & Cohen, L. (1995). Towards an anatomical and functional model of number processing. *Math Cogn, 1*, 83–120.

Dehaene, S., & Cohen, L. (1997). Cerebral pathways for calculation: Double dissociation between rote verbal and quantitative knowledge of arithmetic. *Cortex, 33*(2), 219–250.

Dehaene, S., Piazza, M., Pinel, P., & Cohen, L. (2003). Three parietal circuits for number processing. *Cogn Neuropsychol, 20*(3), 487–506. doi:10.1080/02643290244000239

Dehaene, S., Spelke, E., Pinel, P., Stanescu, R., & Tsivkin, S. (1999). Sources of mathematical thinking: Behavioral and brain-imaging evidence. *Science, 284*(5416), 970–974. doi:10.1126/science.284.5416.970

Delazer, M., & Butterworth, B. (1997). A dissociation of number meanings. *Cogn Neuropsychol, 14*(4), 613–636.

DeWolf, M., & Vosniadou, S. (2015). The representation of fraction magnitudes and the whole number bias reconsidered. *Learn Instruct, 37*, 39–49. doi:10.1016/j.learninstruc.2014.07.002

Didino, D., Breil, C., & Knops, A. (2019). The influence of semantic processing and response latency on the SNARC effect. *Acta Psychol (Amst), 196*, 75–86. doi:10.1016/j.actpsy.2019.04.008

Drucker, C. B., Rossa, M. A., & Brannon, E. M. (2016). Comparison of discrete ratios by rhesus macaques (*Macaca mulatta*). *Anim Cogn, 19*(1), 75–89. doi:10.1007/s10071-015-0914-9

Eger, E., Michel, V., Thirion, B., Amadon, A., Dehaene, S., & Kleinschmidt, A. (2009). Deciphering cortical number coding from human brain activity patterns. *Curr Biol, 19*(19), 1608–1615. doi:10.1016/j.cub.2009.08.047

Eger, E., Pinel, P., Dehaene, S., & Kleinschmidt, A. (2015). Spatially invariant coding of numerical information in functionally defined subregions of human parietal cortex. *Cereb Cortex, 25*(5), 1319–1329. doi:10.1093/cercor/bht323

Eger, E., Sterzer, P., Russ, M. O., Giraud, A. L., & Kleinschmidt, A. (2003). A supramodal number representation in human intraparietal cortex. *Neuron, 37*(4), 719–725.

Fatt, P., & Katz, B. (1952). Spontaneous subthreshold activity at motor nerve endings. *J Physiol, 117*(1), 109–128.

Franconeri, S. L., Alvarez, G. A., & Cavanagh, P. (2013). Flexible cognitive resources: Competitive content maps for attention and memory. *Trends Cogn Sci, 17*(3), 134–141. doi:10.1016/j.tics.2013.01.010

Franconeri, S. L., Bemis, D. K., & Alvarez, G. A. (2009). Number estimation relies on a set of segmented objects. *Cognition, 113*(1), 1–13. doi:10.1016/j.cognition.2009.07.002

Franklin, M. S., & Jonides, J. (2009). Order and magnitude share a common representation in parietal cortex. *J Cogn Neurosci, 21*(11), 2114–2120. doi:10.1162/jocn.2008.21181

Gebuis, T., Cohen Kadosh, R., & Gevers, W. (2016). Sensory-integration system rather than approximate number system underlies numerosity processing: A critical review. *Acta Psychol (Amst), 171*, 17–35. doi:10.1016/j.actpsy.2016.09.003

Gebuis, T., & Reynvoet, B. (2014). The neural mechanism underlying ordinal numerosity processing. *J Cogn Neurosci, 26*(5), 1013–1020. doi:10.1162/jocn_a_00541

Gelman, R., & Williams, E. M. (1998). Enabling constraints for cognitive development and learning: Domain specificity and epigenesis. In *Handbook of child psychology: Volume 2: Cognition, perception, and language* (pp. 575–630). Hoboken, NJ: John Wiley & Sons Inc.

Gevers, W., Santens, S., Dhooge, E., Chen, Q., Van den Bossche, L., Fias, W., & Verguts, T. (2010). Verbal-spatial and visuospatial coding of number-space interactions. *J Exp Psychol Gen*, *139*(1), 180–190. doi:10.1037/a0017688

Gevers, W., Verguts, T., Reynvoet, B., Caessens, B., & Fias, W. (2006). Numbers and space: A computational model of the SNARC effect. *J Exp Psychol Hum Percept Perform*, *32*(1), 32–44. doi:10.1037/0096-1523.32.1.32

Ginsburg, V., van Dijck, J. P., Previtali, P., Fias, W., & Gevers, W. (2014). The impact of verbal working memory on number-space associations. *J Exp Psychol Learn Mem Cogn*, *40*(4), 976–986. doi:10.1037/a0036378

Guillaume, M., Mejias, S., Rossion, B., Dzhelyova, M., & Schiltz, C. (2018). A rapid, objective and implicit measure of visual quantity discrimination. *Neuropsychologia*, *111*, 180–189. doi:10.1016/j.neuropsychologia.2018.01.044

Hamdan, N., & Gunderson, E. A. (2017). The number line is a critical spatial-numerical representation: Evidence from a fraction intervention. *Dev Psychol*, *53*(3), 587–596. doi:10.1037/dev0000252

Harvey, B. M., Klein, B. P., Petridou, N., & Dumoulin, S. O. (2013). Topographic representation of numerosity in the human parietal cortex. *Science*, *341*(6150), 1123–1126. doi:10.1126/science.1239052

He, L., Zhang, J., Zhou, T., & Chen, L. (2009). Connectedness affects dot numerosity judgment: Implications for configural processing. *Psychon Bull Rev*, *16*(3), 509–517. doi:10.3758/PBR.16.3.509

Hesselmann, G., Darcy, N., Sterzer, P., & Knops, A. (2015). Exploring the boundary conditions of unconscious numerical priming effects with continuous flash suppression. *Conscious Cogn*, *31*, 60–72. doi:10.1016/j.concog.2014.10.009

Hesselmann, G., & Knops, A. (2014). No conclusive evidence for numerical priming under interocular suppression. *Psychol Sci*, *25*(11), 2116–2119. doi:10.1177/0956797614548876

Huckauf, A., Knops, A., Nuerk, H. C., & Willmes, K. (2008). Semantic processing of crowded stimuli? *Psychol Res*, *72*(6), 648–656. doi:10.1007/s00426-008-0171-5

Ischebeck, A., Schocke, M., & Delazer, M. (2009). The processing and representation of fractions within the brain: An fMRI investigation. *Neuroimage*, *47*(1), 403–413. doi:10.1016/j.neuroimage.2009.03.041

Jacob, S. N., & Nieder, A. (2009). Notation-independent representation of fractions in the human parietal cortex. *J Neurosci*, *29*(14), 4652–4657. doi:10.1523/JNEUROSCI.0651-09.2009

Jacob, S. N., Vallentin, D., & Nieder, A. (2012). Relating magnitudes: The brain's code for proportions. *Trends Cogn Sci*, *16*(3), 157–166. doi:10.1016/j.tics.2012.02.002

Kaufman, E. L., Lord, M. W., Reese, T. W., & Volkmann, J. (1949). The discrimination of visual number. *Am Psychol*, *62*(4), 498–525. doi:10.2307/1418556

Klein, E., Suchan, J., Moeller, K., Karnath, H. O., Knops, A., Wood, G., . . . Willmes, K. (2016). Considering structural connectivity in the triple code model of numerical cognition: Differential connectivity for magnitude processing and arithmetic facts. *Brain Struct Funct, 221*(2), 979–995. doi:10.1007/s00429-014-0951-1

Knops, A. (2006). *On the structure and neural correlates of the numerical magnitude representation and its influence in the assessment of verbal working memory* (Dissertation/PhD thesis). Publikationsserver der RWTH Aachen University, Aachen. Retrieved from http://publications.rwth-aachen.de/record/52100

Knops, A. (2018). Neurocognitive Evidence for Spatial Contributions to Numerical Cognition. In A. Henik & W. Fias (Eds.), *Heterogeneity of function in numerical cognition* (pp. 211–232). Academic Press, London, UK

Knops, A., Piazza, M., Sengupta, R., Eger, E., & Melcher, D. (2014). A shared, flexible neural map architecture reflects capacity limits in both visual short-term memory and enumeration. *J Neurosci, 34*(30), 9857–9866. doi:10.1523/JNEUROSCI.2758-13.2014

Koten, J. W., Jr., Lonnemann, J., Willmes, K., & Knops, A. (2011). Micro and macro pattern analyses of FMRI data support both early and late interaction of numerical and spatial information. *Front Hum Neurosci, 5*, 115. doi:10.3389/fnhum.2011.00115

Kramer, P., Di Bono, M. G., & Zorzi, M. (2011). Numerosity estimation in visual stimuli in the absence of luminance-based cues. *PLOS ONE, 6*(2), e17378. doi:10.1371/journal.pone.0017378

Kunde, W., Kiesel, A., & Hoffmann, J. (2003). Conscious control over the content of unconscious cognition. *Cognition, 88*(2), 223–242.

Leibovich, T., Katzin, N., Harel, M., & Henik, A. (2016). From "sense of number" to "sense of magnitude": The role of continuous magnitudes in numerical cognition. *Behav Brain Sci, 40*, e164. doi:10.1017/S0140525X16000960

Lyons, I. M., Ansari, D., & Beilock, S. L. (2015). Qualitatively different coding of symbolic and nonsymbolic numbers in the human brain. *Hum Brain Mapp, 36*(2), 475–488. doi:10.1002/hbm.22641

Lyons, I. M., & Beilock, S. L. (2013). Ordinality and the nature of symbolic numbers. *J Neurosci, 33*(43), 17052–17061. doi:10.1523/JNEUROSCI.1775-13.2013

Lyons, I. M., Price, G. R., Vaessen, A., Blomert, L., & Ansari, D. (2014). Numerical predictors of arithmetic success in grades 1–6. *Dev Sci, 17*(5), 714–726. doi:10.1111/desc.12152

Mack, N. K. (1995). Confounding whole-number and fraction concepts when building on informal knowledge. *J Res Math Educ, 26*(5), 422–441. doi:10.2307/749431

Matthews, P. G., & Hubbard, E. M. (2017). Making space for spatial proportions. *J Learn Disabil, 50*(6), 644–647. doi:10.1177/0022219416679133

Matthews, P. G., Lewis, M. R., & Hubbard, E. M. (2016). Individual differences in nonsymbolic ratio processing predict symbolic math performance. *Psychol Sci*, *27*(2), 191–202. doi:10.1177/0956797615617799

Mazza, V., & Caramazza, A. (2015). Multiple object individuation and subitizing in enumeration: A view from electrophysiology. *Front Hum Neurosci*, *9*(162). doi:10.3389/fnhum.2015.00162

McCloskey, M. (1992). Cognitive mechanisms in numerical processing: Evidence from acquired dyscalculia. *Cognition*, *44*(1–2), 107–157.

McCrink, K., & Wynn, K. (2007). Ratio abstraction by 6-month-old infants. *Psychol Sci*, *18*(8), 740–745. doi:10.1111/j.1467-9280.2007.01969.x

Melcher, D., & Piazza, M. (2011). The role of attentional priority and saliency in determining capacity limits in enumeration and visual working memory. *PLOS ONE*, *6*(12), e29296. doi:10.1371/journal.pone.0029296

Meyerhoff, H. S., Moeller, K., Debus, K., & Nuerk, H. C. (2012). Multi-digit number processing beyond the two-digit number range: A combination of sequential and parallel processes. *Acta Psychol (Amst)*, *140*(1), 81–90. doi:10.1016/j.actpsy.2011.11.005

Mou, Y., Li, Y., Hoard, M. K., Nugent, L. D., Chu, F. W., Rouder, J. N., & Geary, D. C. (2016). Developmental foundations of children's fraction magnitude knowledge. *Cogn Dev*, *39*, 141–153. doi:10.1016/j.cogdev.2016.05.002

Moyer, R. S., & Landauer, T. K. (1967). Time required for judgments of numerical quantity. *Nature*, *215*, 1519–1520.

Naccache, L., & Dehaene, S. (2001a). The priming method: Imaging unconscious repetition priming reveals an abstract representation of number in the parietal lobes. *Cereb Cortex*, *11*(10), 966–974. doi:10.1093/cercor/11.10.966

Naccache, L., & Dehaene, S. (2001b). Unconscious semantic priming extends to novel unseen stimuli. *Cognition*, *80*(3), 215–229.

Nicholls, M. E., Loftus, A. M., & Gevers, W. (2008). Look, no hands: A perceptual task shows that number magnitude induces shifts of attention. *Psychon Bull Rev*, *15*(2), 413–418.

Nieder, A., & Dehaene, S. (2009). Representation of number in the brain. *Annu Rev Neurosci*, *32*, 185–208. doi:10.1146/annurev.neuro.051508.135550

Nuerk, H. C., Weger, U., & Willmes, K. (2001). Decade breaks in the mental number line? Putting the tens and units back in different bins. *Cognition*, *82*(1), B25–B33.

Obersteiner, A., Van Dooren, W., Van Hoof, J., & Verschaffel, L. (2013). The natural number bias and magnitude representation in fraction comparison by expert mathematicians. *Learn Instruct*, *28*, 64–72. doi:10.1016/j.learninstruc.2013.05.003

Piazza, M., Fumarola, A., Chinello, A., & Melcher, D. (2011). Subitizing reflects visuo-spatial object individuation capacity. *Cognition*, *121*(1), 147–153. doi:10.1016/j.cognition.2011.05.007

Piazza, M., Pinel, P., Le Bihan, D., & Dehaene, S. (2007). A magnitude code common to numerosities and number symbols in human intraparietal cortex. *Neuron, 53*(2), 293–305. doi:10.1016/j.neuron.2006.11.022

Pinel, P., Dehaene, S., Riviere, D., & LeBihan, D. (2001). Modulation of parietal activation by semantic distance in a number comparison task. *Neuroimage, 14*(5), 1013–1026. doi:10.1006/nimg.2001.0913

Pinel, P., Piazza, M., Le Bihan, D., & Dehaene, S. (2004). Distributed and overlapping cerebral representations of number, size, and luminance during comparative judgments. *Neuron, 41*(6), 983–993.

Pinheiro-Chagas, P., Wood, G., Knops, A., Krinzinger, H., Lonnemann, J., Starling-Alves, I., . . . Haase, V. G. (2014). In how many ways is the approximate number system associated with exact calculation? *PLOS ONE, 9*(11), e111155. doi:10.1371/journal.pone.0111155

Resnick, I., Jordan, N. C., Hansen, N., Rajan, V., Rodrigues, J., Siegler, R. S., & Fuchs, L. S. (2016). Developmental growth trajectories in understanding of fraction magnitude from fourth through sixth grade. *Dev Psychol, 52*(5), 746–757. doi:10.1037/dev0000102

Revkin, S. K., Piazza, M., Izard, V., Cohen, L., & Dehaene, S. (2008). Does subitizing reflect numerical estimation? *Psychol Sci, 19*(6), 607–614. doi:10.1111/j.1467-9280.2008.02130.x

Rinne, L. F., Ye, A., & Jordan, N. C. (2017). Development of fraction comparison strategies: A latent transition analysis. *Dev Psychol, 53*(4), 713–730. doi:10.1037/dev0000275

Roggeman, C., Santens, S., Fias, W., & Verguts, T. (2011). Stages of nonsymbolic number processing in occipitoparietal cortex disentangled by fMRI adaptation. *J Neurosci, 31*(19), 7168–7173. doi:10.1523/JNEUROSCI.4503-10.2011

Ross, J. (2003). Visual discrimination of number without counting. *Perception, 32*(7), 867–870. doi:10.1068/p5029

Ross, J., & Burr, D. C. (2010). Vision senses number directly. *J Vis, 10*(2), 10.11–10.18. doi:10.1167/10.2.10

Santens, S., Roggeman, C., Fias, W., & Verguts, T. (2010). Number processing pathways in human parietal cortex. *Cereb Cortex, 20*(1), 77–88. doi:10.1093/cercor/bhp080

Siegler, R. S., Thompson, C. A., & Schneider, M. (2011). An integrated theory of whole number and fractions development. *Cogn Psychol, 62*(4), 273–296. https://doi.org/10.1016/j.cogpsych.2011.03.001

Smets, K., Sasanguie, D., Szücs, D., & Reynvoet, B. (2015). The effect of different methods to construct non-symbolic stimuli in numerosity estimation and comparison. *J Cogn Psychol, 27*(3), 310–325. doi:10.1080/20445911.2014.996568

Stoianov, I. P., & Zorzi, M. (2012). Emergence of a "visual number sense" in hierarchical generative models. *Nat Neurosci, 15*(2), 194–196. doi:10.1038/nn.2996

Stoianov, I. P., & Zorzi, M. (2017). Computational foundations of the visual number sense. *Behav Brain Sci, 40*, e191. doi:10.1017/S0140525X16002326

Todd, J. J., & Marois, R. (2004). Capacity limit of visual short-term memory in human posterior parietal cortex. *Nature, 428*(6984), 751–754. doi:10.1038/nature02466

Tokita, M., & Ishiguchi, A. (2010). How might the discrepancy in the effects of perceptual variables on numerosity judgment be reconciled? *Atten Percept Psychophys, 72*(7), 1839–1853. doi:10.3758/APP.72.7.1839

Tokita, M., & Ishiguchi, A. (2012). Behavioral evidence for format-dependent processes in approximate numerosity representation. *Psychon Bull Rev, 19*(2), 285–293. doi:10.3758/s13423-011-0206-6

Trick, L. M., & Pylyshyn, Z. W. (1994). Why are small and large numbers enumerated differently? A limited-capacity preattentive stage in vision. *Psychol Rev, 101*(1), 80–102.

Turconi, E., Campbell, J. I. D., & Seron, X. (2006). Numerical order and quantity processing in number comparison. *Cognition, 98*(3), 273–285. doi:10.1016/j.cognition.2004.12.002

Turconi, E., & Seron, X. (2002). Dissociation between order and quantity meanings in a patient with Gerstmann syndrome. *Cortex, 38*, 911–914.

van Dijck, J. P., & Fias, W. (2011). A working memory account for spatial-numerical associations. *Cognition, 119*(1), 114–119. doi:10.1016/j.cognition.2010.12.013

van Dijck, J. P., Ginsburg, V., Girelli, L., & Gevers, W. (2015). Linking numbers to space. In R. Cohen Kadosh & A. Dowker (Eds.), *The Oxford handbook of numerical cognition* (pp. 89–105). Oxford, UK: Oxford University Press.

Verguts, T., & Fias, W. (2004). Representation of number in animals and humans: A neural model. *J Cogn Neurosci, 16*(9), 1493–1504. doi:10.1162/0898929042568497

Vosniadou, S., Vamvakoussi, X., & Skopeliti, I. (2008). The framework theory approach to conceptual change. In S. Vosniadou (Ed.), *International handbook of research on conceptual change* (pp. 3–34). Mahwah, NJ: Erlbaum.

3

THE ORIGINS – NUMERICAL COMPETENCIES IN EVOLUTION

As we saw in Chapter 2, humans are endowed with the ability to approximately perceive and process numerical information. However, this does not make us special. We share this ability with a number of species, including other mammals (e.g. mice, rats, dolphins, or monkeys), fish, reptiles (e.g. tortoises), birds (e.g. pigeons and crows), and even insects (e.g. bees). The parallel co-evolution of numerosity sensitivity in these species underlines the idea that numerosity represents an important natural category to adapt behavior to environmental factors.

While different species might use different mechanisms to detect and process numerosity, investigating the neural and behavioral characteristics in other species may nevertheless reveal interesting parallels to human numerosity perception. This is in particular true for species with which humans share a large amount of their genetic material – monkeys and apes. The investigation of cognitive capacities in non-human primates poses a number of methodological challenges, though, that are absent when working with human participants. Monkeys do not report back their impressions and need training to understand their task in a given paradigm. For example, one may well ask human participants to sit down in front of a computer screen and decide which of two numerosities is larger whenever two sets are displayed on screen. This will not work with monkeys. Non-human participants will need to be trained on a particular task before we can meaningfully record their performance changes as a function of varying stimulus or task features. One problem that arises with this approach is the question of whether the actual behavior we observe is spontaneous and to what extent it may actually merely reflect the training procedure. We will see later the procedures researchers use to disentangle spontaneous from trained numerosity sensitivity.

I will first delineate behavioral evidence for number sensitivity in other species before describing a number of recent findings concerning the neural correlates of numerosity processing in non-human primates.

BEHAVIORAL EVIDENCE FOR NUMEROSITY SENSITIVITY

Anecdotal hints for numerosity processing abilities in animals can be found in fairy tales and anecdotes. In his famous book *The Number Sense*, Stanislas Dehaene (2011) reports an anecdote according to which a crow had built its nest on top of a tower in a nobleman's domain. Whenever the nobleman entered the tower with a gun to shoot the crow, it would fly out of gun reach and wait until the nobleman had left. Asking his neighbor for help, the nobleman wanted to trick the crow. Now two men entered the tower but only one came out again. However, the crow simply waited until all hunters had left the tower before returning. The trick would not even work when increasing the number of men to three, four, or five. The crow always waited until all (!) hunters had left the tower before returning. However, when six hunters entered the tower but only five of them came out again, the crow would come back to its nest – only to be shot by the remaining hunter. Hence, the crow had observed whether the number of hunters that had entered the tower would be smaller than the number of hunters that exited. The crow would not come back until all hunters had left the building in order not to get shot. This strategy worked out up to a total of five men entering and leaving the tower. This requires several amazingly complex skills. First, the crow needed to remain focused on the tower over a long period of time. Second, it needed to keep track of the number of hunters in the tower and update it regularly. Third, updating requires applying arithmetic procedures to the current estimate: addition for entering hunter/s or subtraction for exiting hunter/s. Hence, this behavior would require cognitive abilities that include long-term attention (sometimes referred to as sustained attention), maintenance of information in working memory, and deriving rather precise numerical estimates. But do we have sound empirical evidence that allows assuming such numerical abilities in animals?

Indeed, early studies by animal psychologists demonstrated amazing numerical performance but were not free from criticisms concerning confounding variables and were not widely received. In the middle of the twentieth century, the German psychologist Otto Koehler successfully trained a raven named Jacob to recognize numerosity, for example. The raven was presented with a number of boxes that contained food items and could be opened by lifting a lid that bore a specific number of spots. Jacob was trained to open the box whose lid bore the same number of spots as the sample lid lying on the ground in front of the boxes. If he failed, he was shooed away. Jacob reliably succeeded in this task. Earlier reports of numerical abilities in animals had been shown to entirely rest on the animals' capacity to adaptively respond to faint bodily signals from the trainer, the most famous example being a horse named "clever Hans". Hans was allegedly able to count up to a number that was uttered by his trainer by tapping his hoof on the ground the required number of times. However, careful examination of this performance revealed that Hans merely kept tapping his hoof until the trainer would make a small bodily signal (a faint shrug, for example) which Hans interpreted as a stop signal. Hence, Koehler paid enormous attention to ruling out confounding factors that could have been exploited by Jacob. He changed the position of the boxes in an unpredictable fashion before each trial. He changed the configuration of the spots on the lids of the food boxes and the sample lid. He changed the numerosity of the sample before each trial. Nevertheless, both Jacob and another parrot succeeded in the task. Koehler went even further and demonstrated that Jacob was able to add up the number of baits he took from several boxes that were lined up and contained zero, one, or two baits each until he reached a predefined target number. Unfortunately, his results did not reverberate in the scientific community, partly due to the fact that they were published in German. Remarkably, however, Koehler's experiments already contained a systematic attempt to eliminate alternative explanations for Jacob's performance. Later scholars criticized a lack of odor control, however, which Koehler implemented in only a very small fraction of his trials (37 out of 55,000 according to Wesley, 1961).

More widely acknowledged were the studies conducted by the American researcher Francis Mechner. With clever experimental setups, he was able to resolve some inherent problems that animal psychologists encountered when using so-called fixed ratio (FR) reinforcement procedures. The FR reinforcement procedure had been established by Skinner and describes a schedule where a response is reinforced (i.e. a reward is provided to the animal) only after a specified number of responses. For example, a rat would be reinforced with a food pellet after pressing a lever n times. The problem with this procedure is that lever pressing was abolished as soon as the reinforcement stimulus was delivered. So in theory, an animal could have simply pressed the lever until the reinforcement would be delivered – irrespective and unaware of the number of responses. Mechner (1958) introduced a clever change to this procedure. Rats were reinforced only when they pushed a lever B after n presses of lever A. Hence, the animal signals task completion by a response on lever B. For example, an animal would be reinforced after 8 lever presses. In this case, the animal would have to press the lever (at least) 8 times before switching to lever B. Over time and with repeated trials, the animals' estimates of n would become more and more precise. Whatever n was (4, 8, 12, or 16), the animals were able to press lever A about n times. However, the estimates were not exact counts of n, but the number of responses varied. On some trials, the animal would press only 7 times, on other trials 9 or 10 times when n was 8, for example. The variability increased proportionally with the target number – the higher the target number, the higher the variability – thus conforming to Weber's law. However, the distributions of responses were not symmetrically centered on n. Often the animals would press only n − x times before switching to lever B. To overcome this, a time penalty was introduced when animals prematurely ended counting responses. That is, whenever an animal responded prior to the required n responses, a 10-second time-out was started during which the animal was not able to press any lever, and the counter was set to zero. Using this procedure, the distributions of lever presses were not only characterized by a peak that was centered on the required number of lever presses but also was more symmetrical compared to paradigms without penalty (Davis & Memmott, 1982). On the flip side, when required to execute 4 lever presses, for example, the animals would rather err on the side of caution and press 5 or 6 times than fall short of 4 responses. It appears that counting behavior can be adapted to the situational requirements.

What cognitive mechanism allowed for this performance? Clearly, the animals did not count in the sense that humans would do, "for they lack words" (Koehler cited after Davis & Memmott, 1982). Gibbon and Church proposed an accumulator model to explain this performance. Initially, this model had been proposed to explain time estimation. However, with only slight changes, it could also account for counting-like behavior.

In essence, the model was composed of a pacemaker, a switch, and an accumulator instance. The pacemaker would continuously generate pulses at a constant temporal rate. The detection of a stimulus would open a switch unit that passed the incoming pulses to the next instance – the accumulator. The accumulator would integrate over (i.e. sum up over time) the incoming pulses in a mode that depended on the task requirements. In their mode-control model, Meck and Church (1983) proposed that the accumulator could operate in different modes, a "run" mode, a "stop" mode, and a "counter" mode. The run mode would take the first incoming pulse and start integrating continuously until the end of the last event – hence providing an estimate of duration. In stop mode, the accumulator would only accumulate over the periods a stimulus was actually present, hence taking into account their individual duration and the non-stimulus intervals that separated the individual events. The counter mode, finally, would integrate over the number of items by adding a fixed and limited amount of signal upon each new event onset. The counter mode is therefore insensitive to variations in individual event duration or the intervals between stimuli, unlike run or stop modes.

In the case of the previously mentioned tasks where the animals had to match the number of responses to a predefined number n, the internal signal in the accumulator is compared with an internally generated estimate of the reference numerosity n after each response. Only if the comparison instance detects a match between these estimates does the animal abandon pressing lever A and move to lever B.

With the mode-control model, Meck and Church (1983) can explain performance in different tasks such as duration and counting using a single architecture. One might wonder, however, if animals were actually counting the number of items or relied on a temporal estimate as a proxy for the number of stimuli instead. Duration and numerosity are indeed perfectly confounded when all individual stimuli have the same length and are separated by the same inter-stimulus interval. In fact, clockworks use exactly this property when measuring time by the number of ticks. To establish that animals were indeed able to estimate the numerosity of a sequence of stimuli, Meck and Church varied the temporal properties of the stimuli. Rats were trained to push lever 1 for a sequence that lasted 2 seconds and contained two stimuli and lever 2 for sequences with eight stimuli that lasted 8 seconds. Upon testing, Meck and Church presented the animals with two conditions. In condition A, the number of stimuli was fixed to four, while duration varied between 2 and 8 seconds. In condition B, however, the overall duration of the sequences was kept constant (4 seconds), while the number of stimuli was varied. As a consequence, individual stimuli became shorter in condition B as numerosity increased. Number of stimuli varied from two to eight. Since the animals had been trained before, in condition A where the number was fixed, the animals would press lever 1 when the stimulus train lasted 2 seconds and lever 2 when the train lasted 8 seconds. In condition B, where the overall duration was constant, the animals would press the lever 1 for two and lever 2 for eight stimuli. Now let's think about what happens in the intermediate durations and numerosities the animals had not encountered before. How would a rat respond to three stimuli? Which button would they press for six, for example? Without further training (during the test, animals were rewarded for all responses), the animals spontaneously categorized numerosity three as being closer to two and hence pressed lever 1 – albeit an increased percentage of lever 2 presses. Conversely, five, six, and seven were gradually and increasingly categorized as more similar to eight, and the percentage of lever 2 presses increased as the distance from eight decreased. Four stimuli were perceived as the subjective midpoint between two and eight since the rats pressed lever 1 and lever 2 in half of the trials, respectively. A similar pattern of performance was observed for hitherto unknown intermediate durations. In sum, rats were able to use both types of information in a very similar fashion: numerosity and duration.

The examples of animals that spontaneously recognize and use numerosity information are legion and extend beyond mammals, including insects, fish, and birds. Ants use an integrator mechanism that measures the distance traveled in terms of number of steps. Consequently, when researchers elongated the ants' leg length by attaching pig bristles to the legs (as if they put the ants on stilts), the ants misgauged travel distance, overshooting the to-be-traveled distance due to the elongated stride length (Wittlinger, Wehner, & Wolf, 2006). Fish seek shelter in shoals. A shoal with more animals provides better shelter. Hence, fish that can choose the larger of two shoals benefit from an evolutionary advantage. In line with this reasoning, Agrillo and colleagues investigated the behavior of mosquitofish in laboratory settings. They found that mosquitofish would spontaneously use cumulative surface area and overall space occupied by the stimuli to distinguish between sets of objects (Agrillo, Dadda, Serena, & Bisazza, 2009). However, in subsequent experiments, the researchers carefully controlled for those non-numerical stimulus features during training and found that mosquitofish possess enumeration capacities that they would readily apply to sets of abstract objects (geometrical shapes; Agrillo, Dadda, Serena, & Bisazza, 2008; Agrillo, Piffer, & Bisazza, 2011). Similar abilities have been demonstrated in angelfish, too. Their shoaling behavior (preference for the larger shoal) can readily be described by Weber's law (Gómez-Laplaza & Gerlai, 2011). More recently, Ditz and Nieder re-established that carrion crows can discriminate numerosities in small (1–5) and large (up to 30) number ranges (Ditz & Nieder, 2015, 2016). Birds were trained on numerosity discrimination in a delayed match-to-sample task. Because this paradigm has been used in a large number of experiments, I will describe it in more detail here. In a typical trial, the animal is presented with a sample numerosity (e.g. seven dots) for 800 ms. This is followed by a delay period during which no numerosity is presented for 1000 ms. Then, a test numerosity is displayed that requires a decision based on numerosity discrimination. In half of the trials, the test numerosity (e.g. seven dots) matches the sample numerosity. In this case, the animal needs to show a predefined response. The crows, for example, were required to peck on the screen if they deemed that the test numerosity matched the sample. If correct, the animal is rewarded. In the other half of the trials, the test numerosity does not match the sample numerosity (e.g. four dots). In this case, the animal needs to withhold the response. After 800 ms with no response, a second test numerosity is presented that matches the sample and the animal is rewarded. This procedure guarantees that animals are rewarded for both types of correct responses: recognizing a match between sample and test numerosity by showing a response and recognizing a divergence between test and sample numerosity by withholding responses. For each sample numerosity (e.g. seven items), the percentage of "match" responses is analyzed as a function of the test numerosity (e.g. 1, 4, 7, 12, 20, and 30). What Ditz and Nieder found was a systematic relationship of performance with the numerical distance between test and sample numerosity that was similar for all sample numerosities. The largest percentage of "match" responses was observed when the test numerosity matched the sample. As numerical distance between test and sample increased, the percentage of trials in which the animals considered that the test matched the sample decreased. By analyzing the shape of the performance functions, Ditz and Nieder were even able to test which underlying scaling scheme would best fit the data: logarithmically compressed or linear scaling. Data were best described by a logarithmically compressed scale with constant variability, suggesting that the internal number representation follows a logarithmic scale. Together, these experiments demonstrate that various different species are sensitive to numerical information from the environment. Mammals – including humans – are no exception to this finding.

NEURONAL MECHANISMS OF NUMEROSITY PERCEPTION

To understand the neural mechanisms of numerosity perception, similar delayed match-to-sample experiments have been conducted with non-human primates (i.e. macaques) who are similarly endowed with the ability to discriminate between numerosities (Nieder, 2016). Moreover, just like the crows' performance, the macaques' performance nicely followed Weber's law. But Nieder and collaborators went one step further and also recorded the activity from single units while the monkeys were performing the task. To this end, electrodes were placed inside the parietal and frontal lobes of the monkeys' brains. In the parietal cortex, a specific part on the ventral aspect of the intraparietal sulcus was targeted, the ventral intraparietal area, or VIP. The electrodes record the electrical discharges of a few neurons in close vicinity to the electrode and hence allow analyzing the change of firing rate over time. Typically, neurons increase their firing rate (spikes per second) when the stimulus matches the neurons' preference. In a circumscribed region of the visual cortex, for example, neurons are tuned to a given orientation of a line-like stimulus in the real world. A given neuron would show maximal activity when presented with a line at 45° orientation, for instance. Whenever the light reflection of a line with such an orientation hits the retina and is passed on, that particular neuron reacts with a burst of activity. Interestingly, the amount of activity scales with the extent to which the external stimulus matches the neuron's preference. A little less activity would be caused by a line with 40° or 50° orientation (i.e. a 5° angular disparity). Even less would follow the presentation of a line with 35° or 55° orientation (i.e. a 10° angular disparity). In fact, to the extent that the angular disparity between the neuron's preference and the external stimulus increases, activity will decrease. When plotting the neuron's firing rate as a function of angular disparity, a bell-shaped curve will emerge, closely resembling a normal distribution.

The question that motivated Nieder was whether there exist neurons in the macaque brain that are tuned to particular numerosities. Earlier studies had revealed that neurons in the cat's association cortex were indeed tuned to specific numerosities, regardless of modality (auditory, visual, tactile) or mode of presentation (sequential or simultaneous) and even consciousness since the cats were anesthetized (Thompson, Mayers, Robertson, & Patterson, 1970). Nieder's results strongly suggest that this is the case in monkeys, too. Initially, Nieder and colleagues observed a notable proportion of neurons

in the prefrontal cortex (PFC) that responded selectively to a specific numerosity (Nieder, Freedman, & Miller, 2002). For example,
a given neuron would show maximal activity when the monkey
was presented with three dots. The same neuron would still respond
when two or four dots were presented to the animal – but to a lesser
degree. Note that neither the actual shape of the objects (dots, tri-
angles, squares) nor their spatial arrangement or their density would
explain the changes in firing rate. In addition to number-neurons
in the PFC, Nieder and colleagues later showed that neurons in
the parietal cortex (PC) area VIP showed the same response profile
(Nieder & Miller, 2004). While the animals were initially presented
with very small numbers of items only (one to five), later studies
reported neurons that were tuned to larger numerosities (e.g. up to
30) in a comparable fashion (Nieder & Merten, 2007). Interestingly,
the response in parietal cortex temporally preceded the PFC activity, suggesting differential roles of the PC and PFC in the coding
of numerical information. While the PFC appears to be involved
in selecting goal-directed number processing behavior, parietal
cortex activity appears to be crucial in encoding and maintaining
numerical information in working memory (Jacob & Nieder, 2014).
Neurons in the parietal cortex do not only code the number of items
in a set (i.e. spatially separated items) but also the number of items
that are separated in time, presented sequentially (Nieder, Diester, &
Tudusciuc, 2006). The latter had previously been observed when
the animals were required to execute a precise number of identical hand movements (Sawamura, Shima, & Tanji, 2002). Since the
animals in this type of experiments need to be trained to perform
the task, one might argue that the tuning property of these neurons emerges only during training and may hence be only artificial.
To counter this hypothesis, Nieder and colleagues (Viswanathan &
Nieder, 2013) trained two monkeys on a color discrimination task
using colored sets of items. Monkeys were trained to release a lever
if the color of a set of dots matched that of a previously presented
set. Note that in this context, the number of items was completely
task irrelevant. Nevertheless, Viswanathan and Nieder observed the
very same type of numerosity-tuned neurons in the parietal cortex
with the hitherto observed and well-known response profile (Viswanathan & Nieder, 2013). This underlines the idea that number is a

primary signal from the environment that animals spontaneously and flexibly use for various purposes and that this capability offers important evolutionary advantages. Together, the experiments by Nieder and colleagues revealed that the mammalian brain possesses dedicated neuronal architecture for encoding cardinal information. Akin to other basic visual dimensions, specific neurons in the PC and PFC appear to be tuned to numerosity. The firing rate of these neurons is maximal when presented with the preferred numerosity and decreases as the numerical distance between the presented and the preferred numerosity increases.

Roitman and colleagues (Roitman, Brannon, & Platt, 2007) observed a second type of neurons in lateral intraparietal area LIP, an area of the parietal cortex that is located posterior and lateral to the aforementioned area VIP. Monkeys were presented with sets of dots that contained between 2 and 32 dots. Irrespective of the change in non-numerical features (density, occupied area, individual dot size), neurons in the LIP monotonically increased or decreased their firing rate as numerosity increased. The type of response (increase or decrease) varied between neurons, but within each type of neurons, the relationship between numerosity and firing rate was monotonic. This type of coding is called summation coding and has been implemented in the computational model by Dehaene and Changeux (1993) that I described in Chapter 2.

In sum, these studies demonstrate that the brain possesses a dedicated network that encodes and maintains numerical information that can be used to guide and adapt behavior. By extracting the abstract number property from the sensory input, the brain saves computational resources since it is no longer necessary to maintain a separate working memory trace for each individual item in a set. This allows it to quickly and efficiently compare two sets with each other, for example, without detouring via establishing a one-to-one mapping until the number of items in one set exceeds the number in the other. Hence, extracting number as an abstract category is a highly beneficial capability. In line with the computational model of Dehaene and Changeux (1993) that I presented in Chapter 2, coding of numerosity involves two types of neurons: one type that is tuned to specific numerosities and decreases firing rate as the shown numerosity deviates from the preferred numerosity (place coding), and a second type that changes firing rate proportionally with numerosity (summation coding; see Figure 2.3).

EVOLUTIONARY ORIGIN OF NUMBER-SPACE ASSOCIATIONS

In Chapter 2, I introduced the idea that the mental representation of numerical magnitude may take the form of a mental number line that is oriented in space with smaller numbers left from larger numbers. The series of experiments described previously established that a similar labeled line coding may be found in non-human primates. The parallels go even deeper. In Chapter 2, I argued that the MNL was logarithmically compressed and variability of the activation functions of individual numbers were of a constant width. The same properties have been shown for non-human primates at both the behavioral and neural level. And even at the macroscopic level, a recent study found a topographic organization of numerosity-tuned voxels in fMRI. That is, in the human parietal cortex, a spatially organized gradient of numerosity specificity was observed (Harvey, Klein, Petridou, & Dumoulin, 2013). Specific voxels at one end of the topographically organized area were tuned to numerosity one, while adjacent voxels were tuned to two. In a nutshell, these results can be described as a cortical instantiation of the number line, including logarithmic compression. Does this mean that animals, too, exhibit a spatial-numerical association that facilitates left-sided responses to smaller numbers and right-sided responses to larger numbers? A recent study in newly hatched chicks suggests that this is indeed the case (Rugani, Vallortigara, Priftis, & Regolin, 2015). Three-day-old domestic chicks were taught to go around an obstructing panel to obtain a food reward that was hidden behind it. During training, a set with five objects was displayed on the panel. At test, the chicks were presented with two panels that were in the left and right corners of a triangular born in which the chicks were positioned in the central corner, midway between both panels. Both panels showed the same number of items. In consecutive trials, the panels showed a smaller (i.e. 2) or a larger number (i.e. 8) compared to the training. The question was whether the chicks showed any spatial preference and whether this preference was modulated by the displayed number. Preference was inferred by the initial side inspected by the chick. The results were surprisingly clear cut. When tested with two small numbers (2–2), the chicks preferred the left over the right target (70.67% vs. 29.33% for left and right side, respectively). When tested with large numbers (8–8), chicks showed the opposite preference for the right target (29% vs. 71% for left vs. right side, respectively). As clear as these results seem, what makes a number a small number? Is 8 a small or a large number? Of course, the answer depends on the context. This is also true for chicks. In a second experiment, the procedure was identical except for the number displayed during training. Rather than showing 5, the panel showed 20 items. As a consequence, the number 8 now appeared a small number and led to a left-sided preference in the subsequent test trials (70% vs. 30% for left and right side, respectively). A panel with 32 dots served as a large test numerosity and induced a right-sided preference in chicks (22.5% vs. 77.5%). These results suggest that the mapping of smaller and larger numbers to the left and right side of space, respectively, reflects a universal cognitive strategy that may be innate (or at least available very soon after birth). Recent failures to observe a comparable spatial-numerical association in rhesus monkeys and capuchin monkeys raises a note of caution concerning the universality of this mapping, however (Beran, French, Smith, & Parrish, 2019).

Given that we see number sensitivity in so many species and from early on in life, how would such a system emerge during development? A recent computational model simulates the emergence of a visual sense of numbers (Stoianov & Zorzi, 2012, 2017). The model uses deep networks with two hidden layers that were trained to reproduce visual input numerosities (Stoianov & Zorzi, 2012). Stoianov and Zorzi trained the model by presenting it with sets of dots (up to 32) in various spatial configurations. The model's task was to reproduce the input – no explicit numerosity training was applied. After training, most units in hidden layer one (HL1) were center-surround detectors, covering the entire space of the input images. That means that these units were activated whenever a visual item was present in the center of a specific area. It also inhibited surrounding units in close vicinity. Other units in HL1 decreased activity as cumulative surface area (i.e. the number of pixels covered by the dots) increased. Hidden layer two (HL2) was characterized by two types of units. The first type exhibited a positive correlation between activity and cumulative surface area. In contrast, the second type of neurons can be classified as numerosity detectors and was characterized by a negative correlation between population activity and numerosity. That is, the more dots presented, the less overall activity observed in these neurons (a type of summation coding). The response profile of numerosity detectors in HL2 mirrors electrophysiological data recorded from the lateral intraparietal area in monkey (Roitman et al., 2007). The response of units in HL2 was unaffected by non-numerical features of the stimuli such as size or density of the input images, thereby providing a computational instantiation of a visual sense of numbers (Anobile, Turi, Cicchini, & Burr, 2012) that emerged spontaneously during unsupervised learning. This suggests that the visual system spontaneously develops the necessary architecture for perceiving numerosity.

APPROXIMATE ARITHMETICS IN ANIMALS

Based upon the tale at the beginning of this chapter, I questioned whether animals do indeed show signs of numerical competencies in controlled experimental settings that allow them to exclude a number of confounds. I then delineated that a vast amount of empirical studies indeed do support the idea that this is the case. I also questioned whether animals do actually have the cognitive skills to maintain numerical information in working memory and combine them in an additive or subtractive fashion. In the following, I will briefly describe some of the findings that support this idea. Beran and colleagues tested capuchin monkeys that were presented with two sets of food items, one at a time (Beran, Evans, Leighty, Harris, & Rice, 2008). The number of food items varied between one and six. Performance was determined by the ratio of sets. The larger the ratio, the more consistently the monkeys correctly chose the larger of two sets. But the monkeys even succeeded in this task when covered food items were combined with additional food items. This means that the monkeys did indeed keep track of the number of items under each cover and were able to mentally combine this working memory representation with the estimated number of added food items. Some monkeys even succeeded in this task when the items were added one food item at a time, that is, in a sequential fashion. These results from a controlled laboratory setting underline the idea that non-human primates can use their numerical abilities in a flexible way and even possess the cognitive potential to perform approximate additions. However, can monkeys apply these abstract procedures to concrete situations only? That is, are monkeys limited to applying approximate combination of quantities only when the quantity refers to a concrete set of items such as food items, for example? The answer is no. Monkeys were shown to be equally able to combine digital representations of objects, even when the non-numerical properties were carefully controlled for. Cantlon and Brannon sequentially presented macaques with two sets of dots on screen (Cantlon & Brannon, 2007). Each numerosity was presented for 500 ms only. Then, after the presentation of the second set, the monkeys were presented with two response alternatives and were rewarded for choosing the alternative that represented the sum of the two initially presented sets. The arithmetic problems included tie problems with operands 1, 2, and 4, yielding sums of 2, 4, and 8, respectively. The percentage of correct responses of the tested monkeys was modulated by the ratio between the correct and the incorrect response alternative. Non-human primates are hence able to mentally combine numerosity representations in an additive fashion. Interestingly, the performance was by and large comparable to the performance that university students showed when presented with the same task.

This type of mental ability was not restricted to the combination of two numerosities. It also applies to approximate subtractions. For example, New Zealand robins spent more time inspecting a box that contained an unexpected number of mealworms (Garland & Low, 2014). In this experiment, free-ranging New Zealand robins were presented with congruent and incongruent trials. They observed an experimenter placing a number of mealworms into a container box that they were allowed to inspect subsequently (and take out the worms). In congruent trials, the number of worms corresponded to what the robins had observed (e.g. $1 + 1 \rightarrow 2$ or $2 - 1 \rightarrow 1$). In incongruent trials, the final number did not correspond to what they expected (e.g. $1 + 1 \rightarrow 1$ or $3 - 1 \rightarrow 1$). While they inspected the box for 23.34 seconds and pecked 1.25 times on average in congruent trials, in incongruent trials, they spent 42.96 seconds and pecked 6.82 times on average. Pigeons, too, were shown to be capable of subtracting one numerosity from another (Brannon, Wusthoff, Gallistel, & Gibbon, 2001), but see Dehaene (2001) for an alternative interpretation. Together, this implies that animals are capable of combining and subtracting sets of elements in an approximate fashion (although empirical evidence is still somewhat scarce for subtraction).

As we will see in Chapter 4, arithmetic performance in humans is characterized by a number of hallmark effects. These include the problem-size effect and the tie effect. The problem-size effect refers to the observation that reaction times increase and accuracy decreases as arithmetic problems become numerically larger. For example, it is more difficult to provide a response to the problem $3 + 2 = ?$ compared to the problem $43 + 62 = ?$. The tie effect describes the fact that problems with repeated operands (e.g. $2 + 2; 3 + 3, 4 + 4$, etc.) are easier to solve. Several explanations exist for these effects that will be discussed in more detail in Chapter 4. One explanation assumes that these effects reflect the increasing fuzziness of the mental magnitude representation. Adding two values should indeed become increasingly blurred as the inherent variability of the operands increases. This follows from the logarithmic compression of the mental magnitude representation. As concerns the tie effect, one may assume that the repeated presentation of a single operand may represent a certain kind of priming which then reduces variability and leads to a facilitated solution. Given that non-human primates and humans share basic properties of the approximate number system, any effect that has its origin here should pertain to both species. Put differently, one may wonder whether non-human primates, too, show similar performance patterns as humans when it comes to mental arithmetic. Cantlon and colleagues (Cantlon, Merritt, & Brannon, 2016) recently investigated this question by analyzing the performance of two macaque monkeys while solving non-symbolic addition and subtraction problems. Monkeys were presented with sets of dots that were occluded by a rectangle that moved in front of them. During addition trials, a second set of dots would appear and move behind the screen, while in subtraction trials a subsample of the initially hidden dots would move out from behind the screen and disappear from sight. After the presentation of the problem, two sets were shown and the monkeys' task was to indicate which of both represented the correct solution. The initial training comprised arithmetic problems with the solutions 2, 4, and 8. The test problems, however, included new problems with the outcomes 3, 6, and 12. Monkeys transferred from well-known training problems to unfamiliar test problems and reached a comparable level of accuracy. The acquired arithmetic knowledge allowed the monkeys to flexibly adapt to the new problems. More importantly, however, both monkeys showed both a problem-size effect and a tie effect. This allows the speculation that the observed problem-size and tie effects may in fact represent "vestigial effects from the primitive ability to perform arithmetic without symbols rather than a consequence of mathematics instruction in school" (Cantlon et al., 2016, pp. 413–414).

NATURE OR NURTURE – NUMERICAL COMPETENCIES IN THE ABSENCE OF FORMAL MATHEMATICAL EDUCATION

One crucial aspect of the numerical capacities described so far is their spontaneous emergence. Many species are capable of exploiting numerical information from their environment without having experienced any sort of training. How can we test the idea that humans, too, show this spontaneous capability? Two major strands can be distinguished in this endeavor. First, we may investigate the numerical competencies of infants and newborns who have not yet experienced any formal numerical education. The results of these studies will be described in more detail in Chapter 5. Second, we may look for populations that do not receive formal numerical education in school and/or do not have a fully developed numerical lexicon (i.e. number words). In the following, I will briefly describe some of the seminal findings from this latter strand.

In the Amazonian rain forest live the Mundurukú, an indigenous population of an estimated 13,755 people. What is the most striking characteristic of their language for the current purposes is that the

Mundurukú have a very limited number word lexicon that has fixed expressions from 1 to 5 only (Pica, Lemer, Izard, & Dehaene, 2004). Members of the Mundurukú (9 adults and 9 children without second language skills) were shown sets of dots and were asked to name how many dots they saw. Only for a single dot and a set of two dots, all participants consistently used the same expression *(pũg/pũg ma* = 1; *xep xep* = 2). Three dots, however, were sometimes referred to with a proper expression *(eba pũg)* and sometimes by using the word that was most often used for four items *(eba dip dip)*. Even more variance was observed with sets of four dots that were referred to as *eba dip dip* in roughly 68% of the trials only. A term that also means "one hand" *(pũg pogbi)* was used for 5 dots, but in 28% of trials only. For sets beyond 5, linguistic quantifiers such as "some" *(adesũ)*, "many" *(ade)*, or "a small quantity" *(bũrũmaku)* were used. "The Mundurukú did not use their numerals in a counting sequence, nor to refer to precise quantities. They usually uttered a numeral without count-ing, although (if asked to do so) some of them could count very slowly and nonverbally by matching their fingers and toes to the set of dots" (Pica et al., 2004). Hence, the Mundurukú do not use exact number words to refer to the cardinality of sets as do cultures with a fully fledged number word lexicon. Rather, they labeled the numerosity of sets with approximate terms. The absence of precise number words allowed Pica and colleagues to test the hypothesis that numerical concepts emerge as an abstraction from language, "pre-serving the mechanisms of discrete infinity and eliminating the other special features of language" (Chomsky, 1988). In an approximate numerosity comparison and addition task, the Mundurukú showed exactly the same performance pattern as French control subjects. In exact non-symbolic subtraction, however, French controls were more accurate compared to the Mundurukú. In the exact task, the results of non-symbolic addition and subtraction problems were always in the range of 0 to 2. The first operand ranged up to 8. Mundurukú partic-ipants' performance decreased rapidly as the first operand increased. This decrease was much less pronounced in French controls. This performance difference can be understood as a consequence of the approximate encoding of both the initial quantities and the response alternatives that were much more variable and approximate in the Mundurukú. Together, these results support the idea that approximate numerical competencies are independent from language. I will come back to the relation between language and numerical competencies in Chapter 4.

In a second set of experiments, Pica, Dehaene, and Izard demonstrated that Mundurukú participants mapped numerosities to a line in a way that suggests a very imprecise understanding of numerosities larger than 4 (Dehaene, Izard, Spelke, & Pica, 2008). Participants in this study were presented with sets of dots or sequences of tones (1 to 10) and a labeled line with one dot at the left end and 10 dots at the right end of the line. The task was to indicate where a given numerosity would be positioned on this line. Ideally, the mapping would resemble a standard ruler with equidistant spacing between adjacent numbers across the entire number range (i.e. linear mapping). In Western cultures, however, children before the age of ~6 years dedicate way too much space to small numbers. For example, they would place the number 4 at the position where the number 8 would actually have to go. In contrast, larger numbers would all fall in a relatively circumscribed area at the right end of the labeled line. This non-linear mapping has been interpreted as reflecting the internal compression of the mental number line. Due to schooling, children successively shift from the initially non-linear mapping to a linear mapping. In adulthood, participants no longer show any non-linear mapping but evenly spread the numbers across the entire spatial range. Mundurukú adults, however, showed a non-linear mapping that implies that logarithmic thinking persists into adulthood due to the absence of a fully fledged number word lexicon. It should be mentioned, however, that the idea whether the mapping of numerals onto a labeled line reflects the internal spatial layout of the mental number line remains under scrutiny (Cohen & Quinlan, 2018). It has been argued, for example, that participants place the numerals with respect to spatial landmarks such as the center or the endpoints of the line (Ashcraft & Moore, 2012). Hence, the task would assess the development of measurement skills rather than the underlying mental number representation (Cohen & Sarnecka, 2014).

Similar results were obtained with Indigenous Australian children who live in the Northern territory and only spoke the Australian languages Warlpiri or Anindilyakwa. Crucially, these languages – like

Mundurukú – have a very limited number word lexicon only, operating basically with linguistic quantifiers (many, much, few, . . .). Anindilyakwa-speaking children were tested on a non-symbolic addition task and a number of other cognitive tasks, including a test of spatial working memory, a magnitude comparison task, and a non-verbal intelligence task (Raven's Matrices [Reeve, Reynolds, Paul, & Butterworth, 2018]). A group of age-matched children from a major Australian city was tested on the same tasks but solved symbolic addition problems instead of the non-symbolic problems. Both groups of children were well above chance when solving the addition tasks (non-symbolic or symbolic). Crucially, performance was predicted by the same variables in both groups: visuo-spatial working memory was the most important predictor of arithmetic performance. Hence, the very same visuo-spatial processes support calculation abilities – irrespective of the format of the numerical information the calculation was carried out in. This highlights the importance of visuo-spatial processes for mental arithmetic. We will see in more detail that the transformation and maintenance of spatial information share resources and procedures with mental arithmetic at the cognitive and neural level in Chapter 4.

To sum up, education and language do not seem to be major prerequisites to spontaneously and skillfully exploit numerical information from the environment. Even in the absence of a fully-fledged number lexicon, proto-mathematical operations such as additions can be carried out on non-symbolic quantities. The limits of the ANS determine the upper boundary of the performance that participants show on these tasks.

SUMMARY

In this chapter, I described the numerical competencies that can be found in other species or in humans that did not receive formal schooling.

- Not only humans can recognize and classify numerical information.
- This ability is present in many species.
- Animals are even able to combine numerical information in an additive fashion, resembling approximate addition.

- These numerical competencies are not a product of intense training but can be found in spontaneous behavior.
- On the neuronal level, neurons in the monkey's prefrontal and parietal cortex have been found that show summation coding (activity change is proportional to change in numerosity) and place coding (neurons are tuned to a specific number of items).
- Basic, approximate numerical skills do not depend on language but rather form a separate domain of information processing in our mind.

How we operate on exact symbolic representations of number and retrieve the result of a given arithmetic operation will be described in the next chapter.

FURTHER READINGS

A recent review by Andreas Nieder (2016) nicely summarizes the rich body of evidence coming from his lab.

REFERENCES

Agrillo, C., Dadda, M., Serena, G., & Bisazza, A. (2008). Do fish count? Spontaneous discrimination of quantity in female mosquitofish. *Anim Cogn, 11*(3), 495–503. doi:10.1007/s10071-008-0140-9

Agrillo, C., Dadda, M., Serena, G., & Bisazza, A. (2009). Use of number by fish. *PLOS ONE, 4*(3), e4786. doi:10.1371/journal.pone.0004786

Agrillo, C., Piffer, L., & Bisazza, A. (2011). Number versus continuous quantity in numerosity judgments by fish. *Cognition, 119*(2), 281–287. doi:10.1016/j.cognition.2010.10.022

Anobile, G., Turi, M., Cicchini, G. M., & Burr, D. C. (2012). The effects of cross-sensory attentional demand on subitizing and on mapping number onto space. *Vision Res, 74*, 102–109. doi:10.1016/j.visres.2012.06.005

Ashcraft, M. H., & Moore, A. M. (2012). Cognitive processes of numerical estimation in children. *J Exp Child Psychol, 111*(2), 246–267. doi:10.1016/j.jecp.2011.08.005

Beran, M. J., Evans, T. A., Leighty, K. A., Harris, E. H., & Rice, D. (2008). Summation and quantity judgments of sequentially presented sets by capuchin monkeys (*Cebus apella*). *Am J Primatol, 70*(2), 191–194. doi:10.1002/ajp.20474

Beran, M. J., French, K., Smith, T. R., & Parrish, A. E. (2019). Limited evidence of number-space mapping in rhesus monkeys (*Macaca mulatta*) and capuchin monkeys (*Sapajus apella*). *J Comp Psychol*. doi:10.1037/com0000177

Brannon, E. M., Wusthoff, C. J., Gallistel, C. R., & Gibbon, J. (2001). Numerical subtraction in the pigeon: Evidence for a linear subjective number scale. *Psychol Sci*, *12*(3), 238–243. doi:10.1111/1467-9280.00342

Cantlon, J. F., & Brannon, E. M. (2007). Basic math in monkeys and college students. *PLoS Biol*, *5*(12), e328. doi:10.1371/journal.pbio.0050328

Cantlon, J. F., Merritt, D. J., & Brannon, E. M. (2016). Monkeys display classic signatures of human symbolic arithmetic. *Anim Cogn*, *19*(2), 405–415. doi:10.1007/s10071-015-0942-5

Chomsky, N. (1988). *Language and problems of knowledge* (Vol. 16). Cambridge, MA: MIT Press.

Cohen, D. J., & Quinlan, P. T. (2018). The log-linear response function of the bounded number-line task is unrelated to the psychological representation of quantity. *Psychon Bull Rev*, *25*(1), 447–454. doi:10.3758/s13423-017-1290-z

Cohen, D. J., & Sarnecka, B. W. (2014). Children's number-line estimation shows development of measurement skills (not number representations). *Dev Psychol*, *50*(6), 1640–1652. doi:10.1037/a0035901

Davis, H., & Memmott, J. (1982). Counting behavior in animals: A critical evaluation. *Psychol Bull*, *92*(3), 547–571. doi:10.1037/0033-2909.92.3.547

Dehaene, S. (2001). Subtracting pigeons: Logarithmic or linear? *Psychol Sci*, *12*(3), 244–246; discussion 247. doi:10.1111/1467-9280.00343

Dehaene, S. (2011). *The number sense – How the mind creates mathematics* (2nd ed.). New York, NY: Oxford University Press.

Dehaene, S., & Changeux, J. P. (1993). Development of elementary numerical abilities: A neuronal model. *J Cogn Neurosci*, *5*(4), 390–407. doi:10.1162/jocn.1993.5.4.390

Dehaene, S., Izard, V., Spelke, E., & Pica, P. (2008). Log or linear? Distinct intuitions of the number scale in Western and Amazonian indigene cultures. *Science*, *320*(5880), 1217–1220. doi:10.1126/science.1156540

Ditz, H. M., & Nieder, A. (2015). Neurons selective to the number of visual items in the corvid songbird endbrain. *Proc Natl Acad Sci USA*, *112*(25), 7827–7832. doi:10.1073/pnas.1504245112

Ditz, H. M., & Nieder, A. (2016). Numerosity representations in crows obey the Weber–Fechner law. *Proc Biol Sci*, *283*(1827), 20160083. doi:10.1098/rspb.2016.0083

Garland, A., & Low, J. (2014). Addition and subtraction in wild New Zealand robins. *Behav Processes*, *109*(Pt B), 103–110. doi:10.1016/j.beproc.2014.08.022

Gómez-Laplaza, L. M., & Gerlai, R. (2011). Can angelfish (*Pterophyllum scalare*) count? Discrimination between different shoal sizes follows Weber's law. *Anim Cogn*, *14*(1), 1–9. doi:10.1007/s10071-010-0337-6

Harvey, B. M., Klein, B. P., Petridou, N., & Dumoulin, S. O. (2013). Topographic representation of numerosity in the human parietal cortex. *Science*, *341*(6150), 1123–1126. doi:10.1126/science.1239052

Jacob, S. N., & Nieder, A. (2014). Complementary roles for primate frontal and parietal cortex in guarding working memory from distractor stimuli. *Neuron*, *83*(1), 226–237. doi:10.1016/j.neuron.2014.05.009

Mechner, F. (1958). Probability relations within response sequences under ratio reinforcement. *J Exp Anal Behav*, *1*(2), 109–121.

Meck, W. H., & Church, R. M. (1983). A mode control model of counting and timing processes. *J Exp Psychol Anim Behav Process*, *9*(3), 320–334.

Nieder, A. (2016). The neuronal code for number. *Nat Rev Neurosci*, *17*(6), 366–382. doi:10.1038/nrn.2016.40

Nieder, A., Diester, I., & Tudusciuc, O. (2006). Temporal and spatial enumeration processes in the primate parietal cortex. *Science*, *313*(5792), 1431–1435. doi:10.1126/science.1130308

Nieder, A., Freedman, D. J., & Miller, E. K. (2002). Representation of the quantity of visual items in the primate prefrontal cortex. *Science*, *297*(5587), 1708–1711. doi:10.1126/science.1072493

Nieder, A., & Merten, K. (2007). A labeled-line code for small and large numerosities in the monkey prefrontal cortex. *J Neurosci*, *27*(22), 5986–5993. doi:10.1523/JNEUROSCI.1056-07.2007

Nieder, A., & Miller, E. K. (2004). A parieto-frontal network for visual numerical information in the monkey. *Proc Natl Acad Sci U S A*, *101*(19), 7457–7462. doi:10.1073/pnas.0402239101

Pica, P., Lemer, C., Izard, V., & Dehaene, S. (2004). Exact and approximate arithmetic in an Amazonian indigene group. *Science*, *306*(5695), 499–503. doi:10.1126/science.1102085

Reeve, R. A., Reynolds, F., Paul, J., & Butterworth, B. L. (2018). Culture-independent prerequisites for early arithmetic. *Psychol Sci*, *29*(9), 1383–1392. doi:10.1177/0956797618769893

Roitman, J. D., Brannon, E. M., & Platt, M. L. (2007). Monotonic coding of numerosity in macaque lateral intraparietal area. *PLoS Biol*, *5*(8), e208. doi:10.1371/journal.pbio.0050208

Rugani, R., Vallortigara, G., Priftis, K., & Regolin, L. (2015). Number-space mapping in the newborn chick resembles humans' mental number line. *Science*, *347*(6221), 534. doi:10.1126/science.aaa1379

Sawamura, H., Shima, K., & Tanji, J. (2002). Numerical representation for action in the parietal cortex of the monkey. *Nature*, *415*(6874), 918–922. doi:10.1038/415918a

Stoianov, I. P., & Zorzi, M. (2012). Emergence of a "visual number sense" in hierarchical generative models. *Nat Neurosci*, *15*(2), 194–196. doi:10.1038/nn.2996

Stoianov, I. P., & Zorzi, M. (2017). Computational foundations of the visual number sense. *Behav Brain Sci*, *40*, e191. doi:10.1017/S0140525X16002326

Thompson, R. F., Mayers, K. S., Robertson, R. T., & Patterson, C. J. (1970). Number coding in association cortex of the cat. *Science*, *168*(3928), 271–273.

Viswanathan, P., & Nieder, A. (2013). Neuronal correlates of a visual "sense of number" in primate parietal and prefrontal cortices. *Proc Natl Acad Sci U S A*, *110*(27), 11187–11192. doi:10.1073/pnas.1308141110

Wesley, F. (1961). The number concept: A phylogenetic review. *Psychol Bull*, *58*, 420–428.

Wittlinger, M., Wehner, R., & Wolf, H. (2006). The ant odometer: Stepping on stilts and stumps. *Science*, *312*(5782), 1965–1967. doi:10.1126/science.1126912

MENTAL ARITHMETIC – HOW WE SOLVE ARITHMETIC PROBLEMS

When thinking about mathematical abilities, mental arithmetic is among the most prominent skills that come to mind. We all spend years in school to acquire the most basic mathematical competencies for solving simple addition, subtraction, multiplication, and division problems. Later in school, we move further and further away from manipulating concrete numerical quantities to learning more abstract mathematical skills such as solving equations with one or more unknowns $(2x + 3y = 23)$. Of course, this is only where "real" mathematics starts. In this chapter, I will mainly focus on the basic mathematical concepts of arithmetic for two reasons. First, these are the essential skills every child in Western societies needs to acquire and hence we all can refer to that. Second, most psychological and neurocognitive research has focused on these basic skills since they represent the foundations for any skills acquired later on.

HOW DO WE RETRIEVE THE SOLUTION OF A GIVEN ARITHMETIC PROBLEM?

One of the most prominent conceptual distinctions in the realm of basic arithmetic skills concerns the question of how we solve a given problem. Most researchers distinguish between procedural strategies and direct retrieval from long-term memory. Think of, for example, how you retrieve the answer to the problem "32 − 21 = ?" Chances are you can solve this in a short time. But what were the cognitive steps you engaged in? Broadly speaking, we can divide this procedure into *decomposing* and *retrieving* operations. You will have most likely engaged in one of the following sequences of mental operations. (a) You subtracted 20 from 30 and 1 from 2 before summing the respective outcomes. (b) You added 9 to 21 and 2 to 9 to arrive at 11. That is, you decomposed the problem into smaller units (e.g. tens and units) and subsequently solved those units while keeping in working memory their respective solutions. The solving of this problem hence comprised both a procedural aspect (e.g. decomposing) and a retrieval of facts from memory. Although there exist more idiosyncratic strategies for solving this type of problems, most of you did not engage in counting up or down but retrieved the solutions to the decomposed problems from long-term memory. In second and third graders, however, incrementing (counting up) and decrementing (counting down) are the two major strategies that children choose. They take into account the estimated time and effort in order to choose the most beneficial strategy (Woods, Resnick, & Groen, 1975). Hence, counting (up or down) is the most important strategy during childhood, while retrieval from long-term memory becomes more and more prominent as we grow older. Researchers have identified the shift from counting strategies to retrieval strategies as one of the cornerstones of arithmetic development in children. This shift is reflected at the neural level by a change of activation patterns. In adults, training of arithmetic facts has been used to mimic this development. These studies show a decrease of prefrontal cortex activity and an increase of activity in the parietal cortex and notably in the angular gyrus (Zamarian, Ischebeck, & Delazer, 2009). In children, the semantically elaborated arithmetic reasoning (e.g. subtraction) activated a fronto–parietal network. However, retrieval of acquired arithmetic facts recruited hippocampal areas to a larger extent than previously observed in adults (De Smedt, Holloway, & Ansari, 2011). Subsequent studies suggest that hippocampal areas are mainly important for establishing arithmetic facts and recalling them from long-term memory. This demonstrates that the strategy is important and determines the flexible use of various brain networks. It should be noted, however, that even in adults, a mix of procedural and retrieval strategies persists and is flexibly applied to the problem at hand.

ARITHMETIC AND LANGUAGE

Counting is a genuinely linguistic procedure. Therefore, we might expect a tight link between language skills and mental arithmetic performance. In particular, so-called phonological awareness appears to be a crucial predictor of the development of arithmetic skills from second to fifth graders (Hecht, Torgesen, Wagner, & Rashotte, 2001). Children who showed better proficiency in accessing sound structures of language also showed a stronger improvement of math computation skills over this period. To test phonological awareness, children were asked, for example, "to say a word, then say what the word would be if a specified phoneme in the word were deleted (e.g. "what would the word 'cup' sound like without the sound /k/?"; Hecht et al., 2001, p. 201) or to tell "each sound you hear in the word in the order that you hear it" (Hecht et al., 2001, p. 202). This impact was independent from (a) previous math performance and (b) general intelligence. When measuring the impact of phonological awareness on math computation skills, Hecht and colleagues were able to "explain" about 10% of the variance. This means that by knowing the level of phonological awareness, our prediction of math computation skills is roughly 10% more accurate compared to a prediction without this knowledge. Lexical access (read aloud a number of digits as fast as possible) and phonological memory (recite a series of nine digits as accurately as possible) were shown to play a less important role. Later research found this association being mainly driven by the role of phonological processes in fact retrieval. Hence, the idea that arithmetic facts may be stored in a phonological code (Dehaene & Cohen, 1995) would favor a strong role of phonological awareness in arithmetic fact retrieval. Subsequently, I will come back to the question of how arithmetic facts are stored in long-term memory in more detail.

WORD PROBLEMS

Another factor that may explain the association between language and arithmetic is the use of word problems rather than pure mathematical notations. In word problems, mathematical problems are embedded in a narrative. An example:

> Kate had 80 cents. She returned 8 cans to the recycling center. Kate receives 5 cents for each can she recycles. How much money does Kate have?

Before we can engage in solving this problem, we first have to understand the relational structure of the information and "translate" this into adequate mathematical operations. Hence, beyond the mere mathematical complexity, additional layers of complexity add to the overall difficulty of a given word problem. According to Daroczy and colleagues (Daroczy, Wolska, Meurers, & Nuerk, 2015), this includes linguistic factors (structural and semantic factors) and more general factors (e.g. world knowledge, stereotypes, etc.). Structural factors on a linguistic level refer to questions like whether the word problem uses active or passive voice; common or less commonly used words; or even the presence of complex clause structures, using relative clauses, for example. A very prominent semantic factor is the question of whether the word problem contains verbal cues that (sometimes misleadingly) trigger an expectation toward which arithmetic operation has to be carried out. For example, in a problem like "Anna has 5 books. She has 2 books less than Pedro. How many books does Pedro have?", the term "less" triggers a subtraction that is inconsistent with the addition that is required (Pedro has $5 + 2 = 7$ books). Here, the incorrect extraction of the problem structure may trigger a mathematical operation that is correct in and by itself ($5–2 = 3$). Yet, due to the incorrect problem structure, this mathematical operation does not lead to the correct answer.

The mathematical structure itself is also subject to several factors that determine the word problem's difficulty. The number of digits in the numbers, as well as the presence or absence of carry/borrowing in addition/subtraction problems, play a role. In problems that rely on multiplication or division, the presence of related distractors can be detrimental to performance. For reasons that will be explained in more detail subsequently, it is more difficult to reject incorrect solutions if they are from the same table. For example, it is more difficult to reject the expression $4 \times 6 = 28$ as incorrect compared to the expression $4 \times 6 = 22$. This may render the solution of word problems with related distractors particularly difficult.

Example: "Drew found comic books on sale for €4. The regular price of the comic books is €6. He bought 3 of the comic books that were on sale from the €18 he had in his pockets. How much did he spend?"

Relatedly, the different series (4-series, 5-series, etc.) do not have comparable difficulties (5-series is easier than 7-series). Finally, the order in which information is provided may have an impact on task difficulty. Some argued that $4 + 2$ is faster to solve than $2 + 4$ (Butterworth, Zorzi, Girelli, & Jonckheere, 2001). This would be due to the idea that children (and sometimes even adults) use serial counting to solve the problem. Before counting up to the correct outcome in a problem like $2 + 4$, it is assumed that children at the age of 6 to 7 years start to compare the two numbers and choose the larger one as a starting value to minimize time needed to count up. This strategy, sometimes referred to as the min-counting strategy (Chen, Loehr, & Campbell, 2019), produces surprising predictions that contradict certain empirical phenomena. For instance, it is well known that reaction times increase as the difficulty of the arithmetic problem increases (Stazyk, Ashcraft, & Hamann, 1982). This problem-size effect predicts that the time (RT, for reaction time) to solve a given problem is a function of the outcome ($RT = f[outcome] = f[sum(o1 + o2)]$). However, the min-counting strategy predicts that reaction times depend on the number of counting steps associated with the second operand plus the time it takes to decide on the larger of the two addends plus the time to reorder them. Thus, for commutative addition problems, reaction times would vary between problems that need to be reordered and those that do not need to be reordered. Moreover, and again in contrast with the problem-size effect, problems with different outcomes may yield identical reaction times provided they involve the same minimal addend (e.g. $RT[9 + 3] = RT[4 + 3]$). Several studies tested whether this model provides a valid explanation of adults' performance in simple addition problems. Yet no evidence for a comparison of numerical magnitude was observed (Chen et al., 2019). This implies that (a) adults do not automatically compare the numerical magnitude of numbers in an addition problem (Blankenberger, 2005) and (b) that adults do not use a counting strategy to retrieve the solutions of simple addition problems.

Taken together, word problems that provide information in a transparent way will be easier to solve compared to those that provide information in a manner that has to be mentally restructured before applying the adequate mathematical operation. Word problems do not only measure the pure mathematical competencies of correctly carrying out a given mathematical procedure, they also test the children's capacity of correctly extracting the problem structure. Part of the difficulty of word problems is associated with different linguistic factors. Hence, when observing a close association between language and arithmetical skills, this may be – in part – driven by the use of word problems.

NEUROCOGNITIVE PERSPECTIVE

If arithmetic relies on linguistic processes, both should recruit over-lapping cortical circuits in the brain. However, the empirical evidence remains mixed on this issue. On the one hand, some researchers argue that mathematics forms a distinct brain network (Amalric & Dehaene, 2016, 2017). On the other hand, numerous functional neuroimaging studies have shown overlapping networks for language and arithmetic: Beyond obvious overlap in occipital areas that are associated with visual input, overlap was observed in regions like the inferior frontal, angular, and supramarginal gyrus and surrounding regions (Prado et al., 2011; Simon, Mangin, Cohen, Le Bihan, & Dehaene, 2002). These regions are particularly involved in phono-logical decoding. In the context of arithmetic problem solving, their (de)activation is modulated by the familiarity of arithmetic prob-lems. For example, Ischebeck and colleagues (Ischebeck, Zamarian, Egger, Schocke, & Delazer, 2007; Zamarian et al., 2009) found that already during the course of a single experiment, an increasing deac-tivation of the angular gyrus was observed for problems that were repeatedly presented compared to those that appeared only twice. However, since this modulation of activation was also observed for non-mathematical content, the angular gyrus appears to be involved in associative learning and memory-guided behavior in general rather than being specifically devoted to mathematical content (Grabner,

Ansari, et al., 2009; Grabner, Ischebeck, et al., 2009; Ranganath & Ritchey, 2012; Ritchey, Libby, & Ranganath, 2015). When looking in more depth at the patterns of the activated sites, Prado and colleagues (2011) observed qualitatively different patterns for multiplication and phonological processing (Do two presented words rhyme or not?) in middle temporal gyrus and inferior frontal gyrus. In this type of multivariate analysis, researchers not only look at which brain regions would show joint activation in two contrasts (e.g. letter rhyming > rest ∩ multiplication > rest) but rather correlate across a common set of voxels to measure to what degree the patterns of activation resemble each other. This type of analysis treats activation patterns like "fingerprints" and assumes that each cognitive state is associated with a specific pattern of activity across voxels. The fact that two contrasts jointly activate a common set of voxels does not in and of itself tell us anything about the content of the neural activity. It is comparable to judging the nature of two music shows on the basis of their overall loudness over time as compared to also taking into account different frequency bands. The absence of similarity in activation patterns between rhyme judgments and multiplication retrieval suggests qualitative differences between tasks. This, however, does not necessarily negate the idea that multiplication facts are stored in a phonological (i.e. verbal) code. Rather, the two tasks may simply have been different in too many respects (physical stimulus attributes, temporal structure of task, dependence on retrieval from long-term memory, . . .).

Amalric and colleagues (Amalric & Dehaene, 2016, 2017) argue that mathematical thinking is associated with a dedicated network of brain regions that is distinct from regions that are active when engaging in non-mathematical thinking. These researchers selected two groups of participants: a group of high-level professional mathematicians working at universities and a control group of academics who had a comparable level of education outside the mathematical domain. Both groups were presented with mathematical and non-mathematical statements that they were requested to confirm (or reject). The mathematical statements sampled a broad range of mathematical fields such as algebra (e.g. "Up to conjugacy, there only exist 5 crystallographic groups of the plane"), geometry (e.g. "In an ellipse, the ratio of the distance from the center to the directrix equals half the major axe over the eccentricity"), topology (e.g. "Any continuous bijection between two Hausdorff spaces is a homeomorphism"), and analysis (e.g. "An inequality between two functions remains valid for their primitives"). Non-mathematical statements covered knowledge about the French tax system ("The VAT is a French invention and is a direct consumption tax"), Esperanto community characteristics ("The flag of the Esperanto community is predominantly green"), or geographic knowledge ("Apart from the Vatican, Gibraltar is the world's smallest country"). Only in mathematicians, the mathematical statements (but not the non-mathematical statements) led to an amplification of brain activity in areas that are typically associated with numerical knowledge, such as the intraparietal sulcus, bilateral frontal, and ventrolateral temporal regions. Crucially, areas that were associated with language and general semantical knowledge did not show this type of amplified activity in response to mathematical statements. Based on these findings, the authors argue that mathematics is based on an integration of numerical, ordinal, logical, and spatial concepts that is independent of human language and syntax capacity. As intriguing as these findings may seem, it remains to be seen whether they are not only a mere artifact of comparing a highly homogeneous group of experts in a specific domain with a very heterogeneous control group. While for the experts, the presented statements may have evoked rich associations and even action implications ("Prove that . . ."), the associative richness of the non-mathematical statements was not comparable in the heterogeneous control group. Also, it remains open to what degree the network for mathematical thinking resembles other functional networks in the brain, for example, for spatial processing (see subsequently).

The role of language in arithmetic remains poorly understood at the moment. Given the vast variety of strategies and procedures that humans use to solve arithmetic problems, it seems unlikely that language and arithmetic are either completely independent or indistinguishable. A more fruitful approach to understand the brain mechanisms that underlie arithmetic thinking will require the definition of detailed cognitive models that allow us to subsequently identify how the involved processes map onto the neural level.

HOW IS ARITHMETIC FACT KNOWLEDGE STORED IN LONG-TERM MEMORY?

As introduced previously, direct retrieval from long-term memory characterizes some arithmetic problems, notably those of small additions and multiplications. It is very likely that you learned arithmetic facts by heart during your early years of schooling. Typically, the results for multiplications and additions with operands ≤10 are learned by rote at the age of 6–7 years. Several proposals have been made concerning the question of how simple arithmetic facts (e.g. $4 \times 7 = 28$ or $4 + 9 = 13$) are stored in long-term memory. The memory structure that stores multiplication problems will be referred to as multiplication fact memory (MFM).

Early hypotheses for children assumed that addition outcomes are retrieved by a counting strategy (see previously). Groen and Parkman (1972) assumed that the time to solve a given problem that takes the form of $O = A + xB$ (with O referring to the outcome and A and B to the time it takes to start the incrementation process [e.g. encoding, setting the start value, etc.] and the duration of incrementing, respectively) is proportional to the number of incrementation steps. For example, assume that each incrementation step takes 50 ms (most likely it takes longer than that) and it takes 450 ms to start the process. For a problem like $5 + 4 = ?$, this means that the time to solve the problem equals 450 ms + $(4 \times 50$ ms$)$ = 450 ms + 200 ms = 650 ms. Indeed, this model was tested and fit the data quite well (Groen & Parkman, 1972). The model has difficulties, though, in explaining certain empirical phenomena: first, it cannot explain why tie problems (problems with repeated operands; e.g. $5 + 5 = 10$) were solved much more quickly than predicted. Second, the model did not quite fit the behavior observed in adult participants where an estimated increment of 20 ms appeared to be utterly unrealistic (remember that it takes around 200 ms to blink your eyes). Finally, the model incorrectly predicts equal solution times for problems with equal minimal operands [e.g. solution time $(3 + 2)$ = solution time $(9 + 2)$].

NETWORK-RETRIEVAL MODEL

A different architecture has been proposed by Ashcraft (Ashcraft, 1987), who assume that arithmetic facts are stored in a semantic network. Semantic networks consist of nodes (or vertices) that are interconnected via arcs (or edges). Nodes represent concepts (e.g. tree, bicycle, etc.) and are characterized by a given level of activation. Within a given network, a selection mechanism chooses those nodes that show the highest activation level. Since nodes are connected with one another, activation travels across nodes. The further an activation travels, the more strongly it decays. With this idea, it is possible to explain why semantically closely related concepts are more strongly co-activated (e.g. tree–bird) compared to concepts that are only remotely associated concepts (tree–vacuum cleaner). Ashcraft applied this idea to the representation of arithmetic fact knowledge. In his network–retrieval model, the arithmetic fact network comprises nodes that represent operands or results. Result nodes and operand nodes are interconnected. Each operand (e.g. 8) is connected with all the entries of the given series (e.g. 8, 16, 24, 32, etc.). Likewise, all result entries of a given series are interconnected (see Figure 4.1, right). Let's imagine what happens when we encounter an arithmetic problem such as 8 × 4: the presentation of a given arithmetic problem (e.g. hearing the teacher asking for the solution) activates the operand nodes. Activation then travels along the connections to associated result entries. In the given problem 8 × 4, the node 32 receives activation from two series (8 series and 4 series), while all other entries only receive input from maximally one series. As a result, the entry 32 is activated maximally within the entire semantic network. Since a dedicated selection mechanism reads out the most active result node that also exceeds a given threshold, this information is provided as the solution to the arithmetic problem and transferred to the output system (e.g. oral response). An important question is what actually determines the strength of the edges between operands and results. Ashcraft assumes that smaller problems are encountered more frequently and hence their associations are stronger compared to those of larger problems. This would explain the problem-size effect in multiplication. Beyond the mere frequency of a given problem, idiosyncratic effects may further influence the association strengths within the network. For example, the 5-series is frequently associated with faster solution times and fewer errors compared to other series. While this can easily be implemented in the model, this also means that the model does not make strong assumptions concerning the association strengths. With a suited set of association strengths, any response pattern can be generated. From a methodological point of view, this is problematic since it means that the model cannot actually be proven wrong and hence is not testable. Furthermore, the tie effect (e.g. 4 × 4) was initially explained by the frequency account by Ashcraft and colleagues. However, tie problems (especially larger tie problems, which show the strongest advantage) do not occur more frequently in textbooks, invalidating the model's explanation (Verguts & Fias, 2005a).

NETWORK-INTERFERENCE MODEL

A similar model has been proposed by Campbell and colleagues (Campbell, 1995; Campbell & Graham, 1985). In contrast to Ashcraft, Campbell and colleagues incorporate the idea that during the acquisition of arithmetic facts, correct and incorrect solutions receive activations. That is, we have known for a long time that repeatedly presenting two objects in conjunction creates an association between those objects. Pavlov was among the first to systematically investigate this type of associative learning in dogs, for example. Similarly, learning arithmetic facts often entails the production of incorrect solutions that become in turn associated with the problem at hand. In Campbell's network-interference model, operands are connected with their respective solutions as well as with incorrect solutions. Furthermore, Campbell assumes that some problems are represented as a whole in the semantic network. Subsequently, Campbell augmented his model by assuming an additional level of subcategories that codes whether a given problem is considered "small", "medium", or "large". This resembles a rough approximate estimation on a MNL and therefore connects the MFM to the MNL. Responses within a given subcategory can create more interference compared to responses from another subcategory, and interference is stronger between large problems compared to small problems due to increased overlap on the MNL. This idea helps explain the problem-size effect. Figure 4.1 schematically depicts both models, the network-interference model (Figure 4.1, left) and the network-retrieval model (Figure 4.1, right). The tie effect and the five effect (better performance for the 5-series) are explained by assuming a separate representation of these problems

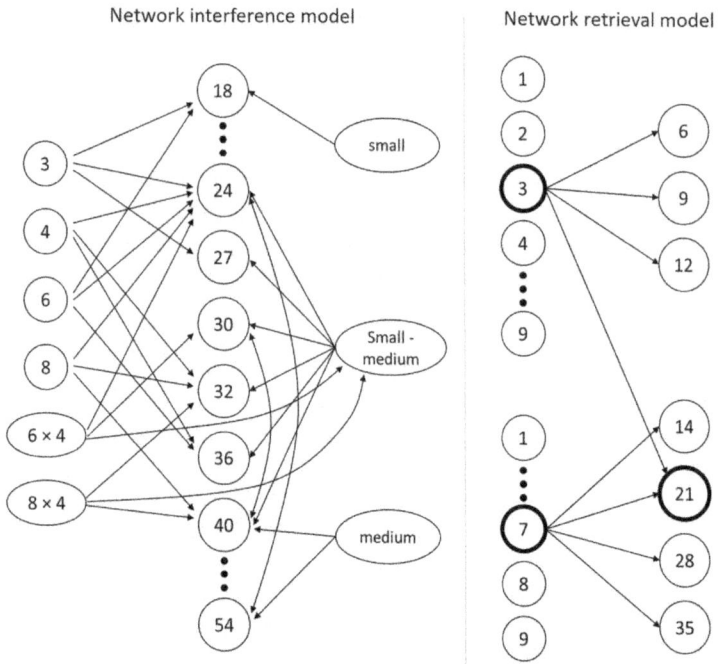

FIGURE 4.1 Schematic depiction of the network interference model by Campbell (left) and the network retrieval model by Ashcraft (right).

Source: Adapted from McCloskey and colleagues (McCloskey, Harley, & Sokol, 1991).

that is hence subject to less interference. However, it has been argued that this assumption has been added to the model post-hoc rather than being motivated by theoretical considerations. Furthermore, a separate representation of tie problems should lead to confusion with other tie problems when participants commit an error. However, "of all the errors to tie problems, only 16% were answers to other tie problems. Hence, the hypothesis that ties are stored separately is not supported" (Verguts & Fias, 2005a, p. 4).

Campbell assumes that the problem-size effect would persist even after extensive practice because it "reflects structural properties of the representation mediating number-fact retrieval (i.e. the psychophysical scale for magnitude representation is compressed as magnitude increases)" (Campbell, 1995, p. 159). This idea has been tested recently (Didino, Knops, Vespignani, & Kornpetpanee, 2015): participants were asked to evaluate the correctness of multiplication problems (e.g. $8 \times 4 = 32$). The proposed incorrect result could either be a below multiple (i.e. smaller entry in one of the operands' tables; e.g. $8 \times 4 = 24$), an above multiple (e.g. larger entry in one of the operands' tables; e.g. $8 \times 4 = 40$), a below neutral ($8 \times 4 = 25$), or an above neutral ($8 \times 4 = 39$). Above multiples were rejected significantly more slowly than below multiples, while neutral results did not show this effect. For example, participants were slower when rejecting $8 \times 4 = 40$ (above) compared with rejecting $8 \times 4 = 24$ (below). This asymmetric interference effect increased with problem size and is indicative of a functional connection between the mental magnitude representation (i.e. the mental number line; see Chapter 2) and the associative memory network for arithmetic facts. It suggests that the compressed metric of the MNL influences the activation spreading in the associative memory network for arithmetic facts: the MFM. In fact, the asymmetric interference effect can be explained by assuming that the magnitude similarity and thus representational overlap of a result and its neighbors are asymmetric. In other words, a result is more overlapped with its successor on the multiplication table (i.e. above neighbor) than with its predecessor (i.e. below neighbor; see Figure 4.2). This asymmetry in the representational overlap determines an equivalent asymmetry in activation spreading. Given a pair of operands, the above neighbor is more activated and thus generates more interference compared to the below neighbor. In a result verification task, therefore, rejecting an above neighbor is more difficult (i.e. delayed responses) because from a representational point of view it is more similar to the correct product. This indicates an association between MFM and ANS and hence provides evidence against the idea of a strict distinction between language and mathematics.

Hence, the network interference model can actually account for a number of empirical phenomena, but it has difficulties explaining the tie effect and the five effect.

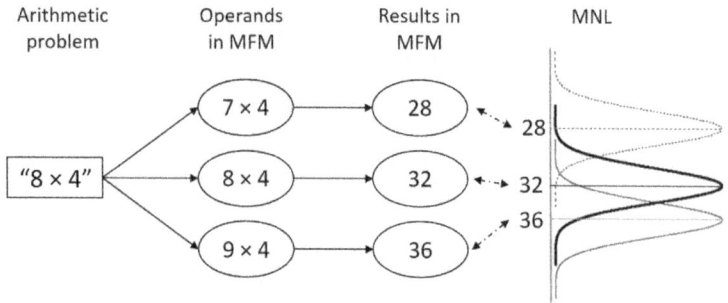

FIGURE 4.2 Depiction of the interaction between arithmetic facts that are stored in long-term memory and the mental number line during the verification of the arithmetic problem 8 × 4. Due to the compressed nature of the MNL, neighbors above overlap more with the correct result compared to neighbors below, given equal linear distance (here: 4).

Source: Adapted from Didino and colleagues (Didino et al., 2015).

INTERFERENCE FROM FEATURE OVERLAP

To explain performance in multiplication, recent work focuses on the role that overlapping features of the problems play during learning. The idea is that each item can be decomposed into features. Words, for example, can be decomposed into phonemes. The word "drum" can be decomposed into the phonemes /d/, /r/, /u/, and /m/ and the word "pub" into /p/, /u/, and /b/. When participants have to learn a word list containing the words drum and pub, they will build working memory representations of these words that contain the features. Since pub shares with the word drum the phoneme /u/, this phoneme can cause "proactive overwriting"; that is, it stays with the first item in the sequence and hence is missing in the representations of subsequent items (Oberauer & Lange, 2009). This overwriting was initially conceptualized to occur in working memory. Since long-term memory representations are thought to be built from working memory entries, degraded working memory entries lead to degraded entries in long-term memory. Recently, De Visscher and Noël (2014) argued that multiplication problems can be regarded in a similar manner, namely as containing features at the digit level. The problem $8 \times 4 = 32$ is composed of the features 2, 3, 4, and 8. The problem $6 \times 3 = 18$ contains the features 1, 3, 6, and 8. De Visscher and Noël further assumed that proactive overwriting (the authors use the term interference) occurs during acquisition of multiplication facts in school. The amount of interference is thought to accumulate over learning, and De Visscher and Noël assumed that the times tables are learned in ascending order, starting with the one times table, followed by the two times table, and so on. Features of problems that are learned earlier interfere with problems that are learned later on. Hence, the problem $8 \times 4 = 32$ will suffer from proactive interference from previously learned problems. For each of the 36 multiplication problems, De Visscher and Noël computed the accumulated level of interference from previous problems. Table 4.1 shows the example provided by De Visscher and Noël (2014). According to the authors, the problem $3 \times 9 = 27$ is associated with an interference level of 9. When testing the importance of the interference parameter against the importance of the problem size, authors found interference to be more influential across a wide age range from third grade to undergraduate students. The higher the interference parameter (and the problem size), the longer the response latencies. The authors conclude that, "Highly interfering problems are not stored, and more time is needed to solve them as a computing strategy is being used. This result supports the hypothesis that feature overlap provokes interference that disturbs storage in the memory" (De Visscher & Noël, 2014, p. 2392). Lower interference sensitivity is associated with better performance. Interestingly, at the neural level, interference sensitivity and problem-size effect are dissociated (De Visscher, Berens, Keidel, Noël, & Bird, 2015; De Visscher & Noël, 2014; Tiberghien, Sahan, De Smedt, Fias, & Lyons, 2019).

However, it should be noted that the interference parameter by De Visscher and Noël mainly explains response latencies but does not account for error rates. Also, there is no systematic and empirical evidence for the assumption that the times tables are acquired in the presumed ascending order. Also, the interference model is based on only one out of several interference mechanisms that have been proposed for storage in working memory. That is, Oberauer and Lange (2008) additionally assumed an overwriting mechanism according to

TABLE 4.1 Example for computing the interference parameter for the arithmetic problem 3 × 9 = 27 according to De Visscher & Noël (2014). For each of the 6 digit combinations (2_3, etc.) that occur both in the arithmetic problem and in previous problems, the interference score is incremented by 1. The total sum yields an interference score of 9.

Arithmetic problem	Previous problem	Combination of digits from problem					
3 × 9 = 27		2_3	2_7	2_9	3_7	3_9	7_9
	3 × 2 = 6	1					
	2 × 7 = 14		1				
	9 × 2 = 18			1			
	3 × 3 = 9					1	
	4 × 3 = 12	1				1	
	3 × 7 = 21	1	1				
	8 × 3 = 24	1					

Level of interference: 9

which in the previous example the phoneme /u/ would shift to the second item and would hence be lost for earlier items. Finally, a third mechanism called feature migration has been proposed by Oberauer and Lange according to which features shift between items and hence change their meaning. For example, the feature /iː/ from the word "reel" could accidently replace the feature /u/ in "drum", changing it into the word "dream" (/driːm/). This mechanism is particularly interesting since it explains why certain errors are more frequent than others. No reason is provided by De Visscher and Noël for not incorporating these mechanisms from the feature overlap model.

INTERACTING NEIGHBORS MODEL

A different idea of feature interaction has been proposed by Verguts and Fias (2005a). Starting from evidence suggesting that the decade and the unit values of two-digit numbers are represented separately (Nuerk, Weger, & Willmes, 2001), the interacting neighbors model (Verguts & Fias, 2005a) assumes that, in the MFM, results are represented in a componential fashion in two different structures, following the syntax of the base-10 system (e.g. the number 21 means $2 \times 10^1 + 1 \times 10^0$). For example, given the operand pair 3×7, the result (21) is represented by the co-activation of the node 2 in the decade representation and the node 1 in the unit representation. Therefore, during the retrieval process, activation spreads to both decade and unit candidates. A second core feature of this model is the consistency principle of decades and units among the candidate results. When activation spreads to the result nodes, decade and unit representations can cooperate or compete with the neighbor nodes. Neighbors are defined as the subset of problems co-activated during the retrieval process and within a distance of ± 2 from the considered problem. Namely, given the problem $N \times M$, the eight co-activated neighbors are $(N \pm 1) \times M$, $(N \pm 2) \times M$, $N \times (M \pm 1)$, and $N \times (M \pm 2)$. This limitation to direct adjacent neighbors was inspired by several findings: Niedeggen, Rösler, and Jost (1999) observed a differential modulation of brain potentials (i.e. N400 component) elicited by the presentation of direct neighbors compared with table-related results further from the correct results. The latter elicited brain potentials that were comparable to those of unrelated numbers (e.g. $3 \times 8 = 34$, with 34 being part of no times table). Hence, table-related neighbors that are further away do not receive co-activation that would allow differentiation from unrelated numbers. Put differently, only direct neighbors were measurably differently activated. It has also been shown that merely presenting two digits (e.g. 7 and 4) not only activates their product (28) but also their neighbors' products (e.g. 21 as 7×3 and 32 as 8×4; Galfano, Rusconi, & Umiltà, 2003). Cooperation occurs when consistent neighbors activate the same decade or unit, whereas competition occurs when inconsistent neighbors activate a different decade or unit. The retrieval of the product is facilitated by the cooperation and compromised by the competition with the neighbors. For example, given the problem $3 \times 7 = 21$, the neighbor $4 \times 7 = 28$ cooperates in (i.e. facilitates) the activation of the correct decade. The neighbor $2 \times 7 = 14$ competes with the correct result because the two decades (1×10 and 2×10) are inconsistent. This delays the activation of the correct decade 2×10. Verguts and Fias (2005b) computed a neighborhood consistency index by calculating "the number of neighbors of each problem that had the same digit in the decades position as the correct solution for that problem minus the number of neighbors that had a different digit as a decade. The same measure was calculated for the unit position, and the two measures (decades and units consistency) were added" (p. 134). The problem-size effect results from the structure of the multiplication table. Small problems have more consistent and less inconsistent neighbors compared to large problems. Verguts and Fias implemented their idea in a connectionist model that consists of a semantic field reflecting the previous considerations, a decomposed (i.e. separate) representation of units and decades, and a response field that contains the holistic (i.e. overall) magnitude of the response. With their model, Verguts and Fias were able to reproduce a large number of empirical effects, including the problem-size effect (which is due to more inconsistent neighbors for larger problems), an advantage for tie problems (e.g. $3 \times 3 = 9$) that was explained by the fact that tie problems have higher consistency on average and the empirical observation that during child development, reaction times become faster and error rate drops. Further evidence for the consistency effect is provided by Domahs and colleagues (Domahs, Delazer, & Nuerk, 2006), who found that, in a result production task, decade-consistent errors were significantly more likely than decade-inconsistent errors. Moreover, a regression analysis on error rates showed that after the number of consistent neighbors was introduced in the model, the problem-size factor was no longer significant. Domahs and colleagues reasoned that these results cannot be interpreted within the network interference model, which cannot explain why the problem-size effect disappears when neighbor consistency is taken into account. However, an important limitation of this study is that they analyzed only 13 out of 55 problems (i.e. $2 \times 6, 3 \times 6, 3 \times 7, 4 \times 4, 4 \times 5, 4 \times 7, 4 \times 8, 5 \times 6, 5 \times 7, 5 \times 8, 6 \times 7, 6 \times 8, 7 \times 7$).

Obviously, the model by Verguts and Fias is inconsistent with the idea of proactive interference put forward by De Visscher and Noël. While shared features/unit or decade digits are supposed to lead to interference with subsequent problems according to De Visscher and Noël, Verguts and Fias assume that this situation leads to cooperation and hence facilitates performance. Future work will need to test which of these features is more important for multiplication performance.

All the models that were presented in this chapter can explain the most basic empirical phenomena like the problem-size effect, for example. Yet, while the interacting neighbors model can even provide an explanatory description of mechanisms that account for more subtle effects like the tie effect or neighborhood effects, previous models struggle with a comprehensive explanation. Interestingly, the model includes a link to the mental magnitude representation and hence argues against a purely linguistic representation of arithmetic facts in long-term memory. Recent work has focused on the consequences that structural features of mental arithmetic problems and learning can have on performance like hypersensitivity to interference, for example. In sum, the interacting neighbors model provides a solid ground for understanding arithmetic performance.

THE ROLE OF SPATIAL PROCESSING FOR MENTAL ARITHMETIC

The ability to exactly (!) solve arithmetic problems such as 458×45, $10^3 + 5$, or even deciding whether $45 + 45$ equals 89, 90, or 91 is one of most important human achievements upon which an incredibly huge part of our daily lives is based. Just imagine if your bank would provide you with only an approximate amount of money in your account.

With respect to the time-scale of our evolutionary development, the breathtaking speed of cultural inventions during the last ~5000 years since the first written traces of arithmetic appeared in Mesopotamia is tremendous. Although modern humans have benefitted from a massive increase in brain volume, the evolutionary time frame was not sufficient to develop dedicated brain regions for mathematics. Hence, it has been proposed that during development, the neural implementation of mathematical concepts and operations is accomplished by occupying a "cortical niche" in the brain. In evolutionary biology, the term "exaptation" describes how a given system that emerged for a particular function is co-opted to subsequently serve another function. In cognitive neuroscience, related concepts of reuse have been proposed. *Neuronal recycling* (Dehaene & Cohen, 2007) assumes that cultural inventions are neurally implemented by co-opting cortical circuits that have evolved for evolutionary older functions. Neuronal recycling has been discussed as a basic mechanism that underlies functions in a variety of domains such as language, numerical reasoning, or social cognition (Parkinson, Liu, & Wheatley, 2014; Parkinson & Wheatley, 2013). The neural recycling hypothesis holds that a given brain circuit is co-opted by cultural functions that have not (yet) developed dedicated brain areas. High-level cultural functions (e.g. reading and mathematics) build from foundational concepts (e.g. face processing and space and number, respectively) by progressively co-opting cortical areas whose prior organization fits with the cultural need. Neuronal recycling does not co-opt existing cortical circuits by replacing their initial function. Instead, the initial functional scope is enlarged to the new culturally defined needs. This notion goes beyond the report of mere overlap between activations in functional imaging studies. Instead, the spatial pattern of activation that is elicited by different tasks in parietal and prefrontal areas manifests a high degree of ordered similarity and possesses predictive value across cognitive domains.

How can we identify the involvement of a particular neural system X and its original associated process x in a given process y? The following criteria were formulated with respect to the idea of neuronal recycling (Dehaene & Cohen, 2007, p. 385):

1   Variability in the cerebral representation of a cultural invention should be limited.
2   Cultural variability should also be limited.
3   The speed and ease of cultural acquisition in children should be predictable based on the complexity of the cortical remapping required.
4   Although acculturation often leads to massive cognitive gains, it might be possible to identify small losses in perceptual and cognitive abilities due to competition of the new cultural ability with the evolutionarily older function in relevant cortical regions.

Adopting these criteria, Dehaene and Cohen identified arithmetic as one candidate domain for the concept of cultural recycling. Mental arithmetic co-opts brain circuits that have evolved for spatial navigation, spatial perception, and acting in space. They demonstrated that numbers activate circumscribed areas in the horizontal aspect of the intraparietal sulcus (hIPS), irrespective of format, modality, or cultural background of the participants. As shown in Chapter 3, evolutionary precursors in putative homologue areas in the monkey have been described (criteria 1 and 2). Progressive change in the anatomical structure and functional scope of hIPS has been demonstrated during the acquisition of numerosity in children (criterion 3). Support for the fourth criterion comes from systematic biases in mental arithmetic that result from the involvement of spatial processes during mental arithmetic, and that will be described in the following.

SPATIAL ATTENTION

How is mental arithmetic implemented in the brain? I described the horizontal aspect of the bilateral intraparietal sulcus as the most probable host for a mental magnitude representation that may take the form of a mental number line. Hubbard and colleagues argued that mental arithmetic involves shifts of the locus of activation along the MNL (Hubbard, Piazza, Pinel, & Dehaene, 2005). These shifts of locus rely on a neural circuitry in a posterior superior parietal lobe (PSPL) shared with those involved in updating spatial information during saccadic eye movements. Knops and colleagues (Knops, Thirion, Hubbard, Michel, & Dehaene, 2009) set out to test this hypothesis by testing adult participants on two different tasks while recording their brain activity using a MR scanner. First, participants were presented with addition and subtraction problems in symbolic (i.e. Arabic digits) and non-symbolic notation (i.e. dot patterns). After a short calculation period, we presented participants with a number of response alternatives among which participants were asked to choose the one that appeared closest to the correct result. To encourage approximate calculation, the exact result was never presented. This had a surprisingly relaxing effect because participants realized that they would always be wrong in choosing an answer. In a second paradigm, participants were simply asked to follow with their gaze a white cross that moved along a horizontal axis on screen. To analyze the functional brain data, we employed a multivariate classifier to the PSPL activation to distinguish between leftward and rightward saccades. In this machine-learning approach, a statistical algorithm is trained to ideally distinguish between two or more data patterns. The training includes repeated analyses of different pieces of the data, where after each training step, the classifier predicts whether a given piece of data belongs to category A or category B and is told about the correctness of the classification. Then, after training, the classifier is presented with unknown parts of the data for which it "predicts" what category each was taken from. Without further training, the classifier that was trained on eye movement data from the PSPL successfully differentiated between addition and subtraction trials from the calculation task. That is, the classifier categorized addition trials as rightward saccades, for example. This generalization was observed with numbers presented either as Arabic symbols or as non-symbolic sets of dots, which implies shared cognitive processes – deployment of spatial attention – between both notations. The observed generalization implies that mental arithmetic utilizes a parietal circuitry originally associated with spatial coding. The results confirm the previous hypothesis that mental calculation can be likened to a spatial shift along a mental number line. In a certain sense, when a Western participant calculates $18 + 5$, the activation moves rightward on the MNL from 18 to 23. This spatial shift recycles neural circuitry in the PSPL shared with that involved in updating spatial information during saccadic eye movements. The PSPL area, perhaps because of its capacity for vector addition during eye movement computation (Pouget, Deneve, & Duhamel, 2002), appears to have a connectivity or internal structure relevant for arithmetic. This mechanism is likely at the heart of an interesting bias in mental arithmetic: the operational momentum effect. When participants are presented with non-symbolic addition and subtraction problems, the values chosen by the participants were not centered on the correct result but were influenced by the arithmetic operation. In addition problems, the estimated outcome was larger than the actual outcome, while it was smaller than the actual outcome in subtraction problems. This effect was observed with symbolic and non-symbolic quantities (Knops, Viarouge, & Dehaene, 2009) and was found to be independent from the acuity of the approximate number system (Knops, Dehaene, Berteletti, & Zorzi, 2014). McCrink and colleagues (McCrink, Dehaene, & Dehaene-Lambertz, 2007) argued that this bias showed similarity to a perceptual phenomenon called "representational momentum"

(Freyd & Finke, 1984). When they watch a moving object suddenly disappear, participants tend to misjudge its final position and report a position displaced in the direction of the movement (Halpern & Kelly, 1993; Hubbard, 2017). Analogously, McCrink et al. described their finding as an "operational momentum" (OM) because the mis-judgment was related to the arithmetic operation carried out and suggested that subjects were moving "too far" on the number line (McCrink et al., 2007). According to the spatial attention account, the OM reflects systematic biases from the deployment of the coordi-nate transformation system in the parietal cortex, which also mediates attentional shifts in space (Knops et al., 2014; Knops, Thirion, et al., 2009; Knops, Viarouge, et al., 2009; Knops, Zitzmann, & McCrink, 2013; Pinheiro-Chagas, Didino, Haase, Wood, & Knops, 2018). Men-tal arithmetic would hence be mediated by a dynamic interaction between positional codes on the MNL and an attentional system that shifts the spatial focus to the left or right.

These results support the idea that spatial attention is associ-ated with mental arithmetic. This raises several questions. (1) Is the co-occurrence of attentional shifts during mental arithmetic an epi-phenomenon without functional meaning? Or do attentional shifts play a functional role during mental arithmetic? (2) Is this associa-tion limited to approximate mental arithmetic? Or can we observe similar phenomena during exact mental arithmetic with symbolic numbers? (3) Is this association uni- or bi-directional? That is, does spatial attention influence mental arithmetic and vice versa?

A number of recent findings are in line with the idea that shifts of spatial attention substantially contribute to mental arithmetic. Masson and Pesenti (2014) found that the detection latency of lat-erally presented targets was systematically modulated by arithmetic operations that preceded target presentation. Addition led to faster detection of targets on the right, while subtraction led to faster detection of targets on the left. To determine the point in time when spatial attention "kicks in" during mental arithmetic, Liu and colleagues (Liu, Cai, Verguts, & Chen, 2017) intermingled the pre-sentation of lateral targets at different points during the presentation of arithmetic problems. In this dual-task situation, participants were asked to (a) detect the laterally presented targets as fast as possible and (b) solve addition and subtraction problems. Lateral targets were presented after the presentation of the operand, the presentation of the first operand, the second operand, or the results alternative that required validation. Again, addition led to faster detection of right-sided targets, while subtraction facilitated detection of left-sided targets. This association was observed both during the calculation process (i.e. after presentation of the second operand and – to a somewhat smaller degree – after presentation of the first operand) and at the end of the calculation process (i.e. immediately after presentation of the response). No bias was observed after presentation of the operator before the first operand. Horizontal shifts of attention are associated with solving symbolic addition and subtraction problems but not with multiplication (Mathieu, Gourjon, Couderc, Thevenot, & Prado, 2016). Katz and Knops (2014) observed an operational momentum effect in non-symbolic multiplication and division (multiplication results were over- and division results were underestimated) but not in symbolic multiplication and division. Hence, the association between attentional processes and arithmetic processing seems to be limited to situations that do not predominantly rely on the recall of arithmetic facts from MFM but rather require a semantic elaboration. While stronger operational momentum effects were observed with non-symbolic notations (e.g. sets of dots), the effect also was observed during semantic elaboration of symbolic problems, as first demonstrated by Knops, Viarouge, et al. (2009; see also Pinhas & Fischer, 2008).

The association between attention and mental arithmetic has also been demonstrated with optokinetic stimulation (OKS), a technique to orient spatial attention in space. Masson and colleagues showed that rightward OKS facilitates the solving of complex addition problems that contained a carry operation (i.e. the sum of the units is larger than 10), while no effect of OKS on subtraction was observed (Masson & Pesenti, 2016). Hence, it seems that the association between mental arithmetic and spatial attention is bi-directional: Mental arithmetic influences the orientation of spatial attention, and spatial attention interacts with mental arithmetic.

A straightforward test for a causal – rather than an epiphenomenal – role of spatial attention for mental arithmetic would be to find that patients suffering from attentional deficits would be specifically impaired in mental arithmetic. Indeed, a recent study showed that patients suffering from unilateral spatial neglect of objects in the left visual field made more errors when asked to solve subtraction problems in the two-digit number range compared to patients without spatial neglect and healthy controls (Dormal, Schuller, Nihoul, Pesenti, & Andres, 2014). Establishing a double dissociation, another patient who suffered from unilateral neglect of objects in the right visual field was impaired when solving addition problems but not subtraction problems (Masson, Pesenti, Coyette, Andres, & Dormal, 2017). In healthy participants, too, spatial attention appears to play a pivotal role during mental arithmetic. When being presented with lateral distractors while solving addition and subtraction problems, the impact (i.e. the degree to which distractors impaired performance) was a function of side of presentation and arithmetic operation. Left-sided targets exhibited stronger interference during subtraction, while right-sided targets interfered more strongly with addition (Masson & Pesenti, 2016). These results are particularly interesting since they go beyond previous studies that were merely correlational and establish a causal contribution of spatial attention to mental arithmetic. Spatial attention may be necessary to locate the result on a spatial numerical magnitude representation – the mental number line. In line with this assumption, Klein and colleagues suggest that the OM results from a "first rough spatial anticipation followed by an evaluation/correction process" (Klein et al., 2014).

Spatial transformations – imagery in the context of mathematics

From the previous results, we can conclude that spatial attention appears to play an important role during mental arithmetic. Yet, it is only one example from the spatial domain that has been shown to be associated with mathematical skills. Other spatial processes have been found to be predictive of mental arithmetic skills, too. One of the most prominent is the ability to mentally rotate an object. Mental rotation was introduced by Shepard and Metzler in the 1970s. Shepard and Metzler (1971) presented participants with cubic shapes or polygons that were rotated in a horizontal plane and asked them to decide whether they could be rotated such that they become identical with a standard (see Figure 4.3). The authors found that the time to answer this question was a linear function of the angular disparity (amount of rotation) between the rotated shape and the standard. The more the shape was rotated, the longer it took participants to provide the correct answer. When you try to align the right-most shape with the middle shape in Figure 4.3, for example, you will be slower the more the shape was rotated. In contrast, the left-most shape cannot be aligned with the middle shape since it is mirrored. Shepard and Metzler argued that this is due to an analogue transformation process by which participants mentally rotate the shape into its standard orientation. This transformation is analogue because it passes through all of the intermediate orientations between initial and standard orientation, akin to rotations in physical space.

Mental transformations such as rotations are correlated with arithmetic performance (Mix & Cheng, 2012 for a review) and can predict arithmetic performance later during development (Gunderson, Ramirez, Beilock, & Levine, 2012). Training mental rotation skills has been shown to improve children's mathematical abilities (Cheng & Mix, 2014). The question that arises here is: why do these abilities correlate with arithmetic performance? At least three mechanisms have been described. First, the association may result from the ease of creating mental models for a given problem. Mental models often have a strong spatial component and allow us to keep track of

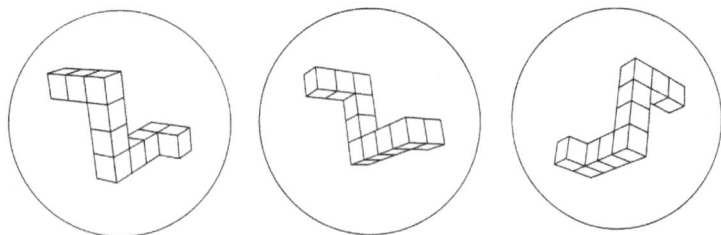

FIGURE 4.3 Example of original stimuli from Shepard and Metzler (1971). While the right-most figure can be rotated to match the standard in the middle, the left-most figure cannot because it is a rotated mirror image of the standard.

Source: Courtesy of Michael J. Tarr and Roger Shepard, who provided the figures for download on the CNBC wiki (http://wiki.cnbc.cmu.edu/Novel_Objects).

which terms should be grouped together, for example (Thompson, Nuerk, Moeller, & Cohen Kadosh, 2013). By helping to relate elements of a given problem to one another, mental models may render them easier. This ability, of course, would not be specific to mathematics but would apply to all sorts of reasoning problems. Ragni and Knauff (2013) show that a computational instantiation of mental models can indeed explain a number of empirical results – at least in the domain of spatial arrangement problems.

A second approach assumes that numerical concepts are grounded in space. The concept of the mental number line is a good example of how grounding a priori abstract concepts such as number in actual space can influence their processing. The SNARC effect (see Chapter 2) or the size congruency effect (participants take longer to decide which number is physically or numerically larger if physical relation is incongruent [e.g. 8_2] with the numerical one) can be understood as direct consequences of such grounding. It is less obvious, however, how mental rotation or mental transformation fits in this picture. Some authors argue that enhancing spatial mental transformation skills leads to improvement of imagery skills that can then be used to simulate the solution of arithmetic problems by mentally representing the problem with objects (Lourenco, Cheung, & Aulet, 2018). For a given problem such as $4 + 5 = ?$, children may imagine a set of 4 objects that needs to be added to the starting value 5 by counting up. Indeed, young children often represent arithmetic problems using their fingers. Training mental transformation and imagery skills may help children in forming slightly more abstract representations using mental objects instead of fingers (but see Hawes, Moss, Caswell, & Poliszczuk, 2015, for negative evidence).

The association between spatial transformations and mathematical processes may be driven by a shared third mental capacity. Working memory, for example, may drive both good performance in mental rotation or other transformation processes and mental arithmetic. Both mathematical competencies and mental rotation abilities correlate with working memory capacity (Mix, Levine, & Newcombe, 2016). The interaction between mental calculation and working memory has been the focus of a considerable amount of research (Menon, 2016). In particular, a number of studies sought to delineate the contribution of different WM components to particular arithmetic operations. One of the most influential models of WM, by Baddeley and Hitch (Baddeley, 2010), conceptualizes WM as a four-component construct: as a supervisory control instance, the central executive (CE) is responsible for allocating attentional resources to other slave systems. The CE also coordinates these systems. It is thought to be especially involved in arithmetic when keeping track of intermediate results is required (Fürst & Hitch, 2000). The visuospatial sketchpad (VSSP) processes visual and spatial information. This may entail, for example, information about an object's shape or location. In the context of mental arithmetic, the VSSP is pivotal because of the spatial nature of the mental number line. The phonological loop (PL) processes phonological material and comprises two subsystems: a phonological store and a rehearsal process. The PL is involved during verbally mediated calculation strategies such as decomposing complex problems into more simple ones or counting (Fürst & Hitch, 2000; Imbo & Vandierendonck, 2007). Finally, the episodic buffer has recently been added to the model to account for problems concerning the interaction of WM with long-term memory (Baddeley, 2000). It is thought to be a slave system dedicated to storage of pictorial or verbal episodic information that is integrated over time.

The contribution of these subsystems to mental arithmetic has been a topic of debate. It has been argued that different arithmetic operations might rely on different number codes that would – in turn – be differentially affected by concurrent load on the WM slave systems (Lee & Kang, 2002). Due to learning history, multiplication was argued to hinge on phonological codes, while operations that rely on semantic elaboration activate the MNL and hence rely on spatial codes (e.g. subtraction). Imbo and LeFevre (2010) found partial support for an interaction between visuospatial working memory (vsWM) and multiplication and between phonological working memory (pWM) and subtraction. They used one-digit × two-digit multiplications and two-digit minus two-digit subtractions. Participants had to keep in mind letter strings of four consonants for phonological suppression and a pattern of four asterisks arranged in a 4 × 4 array for visuospatial suppression. Moreover, they had two different participant groups (Canadian and Chinese) to investigate the effect of mathematical education and reading direction on the interaction. They found that differential suppression existed only for Chinese participants and only for multiplications presented horizontally for phonological load and vertically for visuospatial load. On the contrary, both types of calculations (subtraction and multiplication) were affected by both types of WM tasks (phonological and visuospatial) for Canadian participants. Others found that impairment due to concurrent WM load increased with arithmetic complexity (De Rammelaere, Stuyven, & Vandierendonck, 2001; Seitz & Schumann-Hengsteler, 2000; Seyler, Kirk, & Ashcraft, 2003). Inconsistencies in the results may partly result from the fact that a number of different secondary WM tasks were used in these psychophysical studies and the difficulty of phonological and visuospatial WM tasks was not balanced within and across participants. Therefore, the extent to which PL and VSSP were actually occupied by the secondary tasks differed, which might have affected the level of interaction between primary and secondary tasks (Fisk, Derrick, & Schneider, 1986).

To properly control for this, a recent study balanced task difficulty within and between participants by adaptive psychophysical staircase procedures to determine the individually appropriate span size for phonological and visuospatial WM tasks (Cavdaroglu & Knops, 2016). Through the use of two difficulty levels, Cavdaroglu and Knops investigated how task load affects interference. They found that when the difficulties of the WM tasks are controlled within and between participants, both types of arithmetic operations (i.e. multiplication and subtraction) were affected by both types of concurrent WM load (i.e. phonological and visuospatial). That is, no interaction between WM type and arithmetic operation was observed. Reciprocally, both types of WM tasks were affected by both types of concurrent arithmetic load. Moreover, the observed interference between calculations and WM tasks was more pronounced for WM trials with high load, emphasizing the significance of controlling for task difficulty. These results suggest that working memory (visuo-spatial or phonological) and different arithmetic operations share cognitive resources. This leads to reciprocal interference in dual-task situations. The more demanding one task (either arithmetic or working memory) is, the more the concurrent task will be affected. A systematic investigation of the mutual interferences of the cognitive triplet working memory, mental rotation, and mental arithmetic is still missing.

Finally, the idea that spatial attention is recycled in the context of mental arithmetic can be interpreted as one form of shared neural processes that is at the heart of the association between numerical and spatial transformations. According to this view, both numerical and spatial information share certain codes and are subject to identical cortically implemented transformations. For example, both numerical quantities and visual object representations are conceptualized as analogue. In support of this hypothesis, Bugden, Brannon, and colleagues recently demonstrated that symbolic and non-symbolic addition and subtraction tasks showed more similar overlapping activity in the parietal cortex compared to visually matched control tasks (Bugden, Woldorff, & Brannon, 2019). Together with the results from Knops and colleagues (Knops et al., 2014; Knops, Thirion, et al., 2009; Knops, Viarouge, et al., 2009), this points to a shared recruitment of parietal routines for (a) symbolic and non-symbolic arithmetic and (b) spatial processes and arithmetic in the parietal cortex.

To sum up, mental rotation and similar mental transformations are associated with mathematical abilities. This association emerges early in life and persists into adulthood. The exact mechanisms that give rise to this association have begun to be delineated but remain a matter of investigation. These results imply that transformation and maintenance of spatial information share resources and procedures with mental arithmetic at the cognitive and neural level.

SUMMARY

In this chapter, I described some of the most prominent effects that characterize arithmetic performance and how cognitive neuroscience models account for them. This includes the relation between language and mental arithmetic, the factors that render word problems difficult to solve, and how cognitive models account for the behavioral and neural characteristics of arithmetic fact retrieval. Mental arithmetic represents a major part of the school curriculum and certainly has the potential for frustrating experiences. From this point of view, knowing that humans in general show some very systematic errors and biases should be a starting point for rethinking our approach to mental arithmetic. In fact, humans are equipped with a cognitive and neural system that allows them to acquire and use arithmetic principles. The exciting question for the future will be how to efficiently build on that system when teaching (and learning) arithmetic.

- Counting as the initial arithmetic strategy is quickly replaced by other procedures, including direct retrieval from long-term memory.
- Tie problems (e.g. 5 × 5) are solved faster than non-tie problems.
- The problem-size effect describes the observation that reaction times and error rate when solving arithmetic problems increase with increasing numerical size of the outcome.
- Language and arithmetic are associated.
- The relation of language and arithmetic at the neural level is debated. Some argue for independent systems, while others see overlapping activity as evidence for common grounds.
- According to the interacting neighbors model, arithmetic facts are represented in a componential fashion in two different structures, following the syntax of the base-10 system.
- Multiplication problems contain features at the digit level that may lead to interference between arithmetic problems during learning. Problems learned earlier impede the acquisition of later problems.
- Spatial attention contributes to solving arithmetic problems due to the spatial nature of the mental number representation.
- Mental imagery is associated with mental arithmetic performance.

A description of the development of numerical competencies will be given in the next chapter.

REFERENCES

Amalric, M., & Dehaene, S. (2016). Origins of the brain networks for advanced mathematics in expert mathematicians. *Proc Natl Acad Sci USA*, *113*(18), 4909–4917. doi:10.1073/pnas.1603205113

Amalric, M., & Dehaene, S. (2017). Cortical circuits for mathematical knowledge: Evidence for a major subdivision within the brain's semantic networks. *Philos Trans R Soc Lond B Biol Sci*, *373*(1740). doi:10.1098/rstb.2016.0515

Ashcraft, M. H. (1987). Children's knowledge of simple arithmetic: A developmental model and simulation. In J. Bisanz, C. J. Brainerd, & R. Kail (Eds.), *Formal methods in developmental psychology: Progress in cognitive development research* (pp. 302–338). New York, NY: Springer New York.

Baddeley, A. (2000). The episodic buffer: A new component of working memory? *Trends in Cognitive Sciences, 4*(11), 417–423. doi:10.1016/S1364-6613(00)01538-2

Baddeley, A. (2010). Working memory. *Curr Biol, 20*(4), R136–R140. doi:10.1016/j.cub.2009.12.014

Blankenberger, S. (2005). Evaluation des COMP-Modells. In K. W. Lange, K.-H. Bäuml, M. W. Greenlee, M. Hammerl, & A. Zimmer (Eds.), *Experimentelle Psychologie* (p. 20). Lengerich: Pabst Science Publishers.

Bugden, S., Woldorff, M. G., & Brannon, E. M. (2019). Shared and distinct neural circuitry for nonsymbolic and symbolic double-digit addition. *Hum Brain Mapp, 40*(4), 1328–1343. doi:10.1002/hbm.24452

Butterworth, B., Zorzi, M., Girelli, L., & Jonckheere, A. R. (2001). Storage and retrieval of addition facts: The role of number comparison. *Q J Exp Psychol A, 54*(4), 1005–1029. doi:10.1080/713756007

Campbell, J. I. D. (1995). Mechanisms of simple addition and multiplication: A modified network-interference theory and simulation. *Math Cogn, 1*(2), 121–164.

Campbell, J. I. D., & Graham, D. J. (1985). Mental multiplication skill: Structure, process, and acquisition. *Can J Exp Psychol, 39*(2), 338–366. doi:10.1037/h0080065

Cavdaroglu, S., & Knops, A. (2016). Mental subtraction and multiplication recruit both phonological and visuospatial resources: Evidence from a symmetric dual-task design. *Psychol Res, 80*(4), 608–624. doi:10.1007/s00426-015-0667-8

Chen, Y., Loehr, J. D., & Campbell, J. I. D. (2019). Does the min-counting strategy for simple addition become automatized in educated adults? A behavioural and ERP study of the size congruency effect. *Neuropsychologia, 124*, 311–321. doi:10.1016/j.neuropsychologia.2018.11.009

Cheng, Y.-L., & Mix, K. S. (2014). Spatial training improves children's mathematics ability. *J Cogn Dev, 15*(1), 2–11. doi:10.1080/15248372.2012.725186

Daroczy, G., Wolska, M., Meurers, W. D., & Nuerk, H. C. (2015). Word problems: A review of linguistic and numerical factors contributing to their difficulty. *Front Psychol, 6*, 348. doi:10.3389/fpsyg.2015.00348

De Rammelaere, S., Stuyven, E., & Vandierendonck, A. (2001). Verifying simple arithmetic sums and products: Are the phonological loop and the central executive involved? *Mem Cognit, 29*(2), 267–273.

De Smedt, B., Holloway, I. D., & Ansari, D. (2011). Effects of problem size and arithmetic operation on brain activation during calculation in children with varying levels of arithmetical fluency. *Neuroimage, 57*(3), 771–781. doi:10.1016/j.neuroimage.2010.12.037

De Visscher, A., Berens, S. C., Keidel, J. L., Noël, M. P., & Bird, C. M. (2015). The interference effect in arithmetic fact solving: An fMRI study. *Neuroimage, 116*, 92–101. doi:10.1016/j.neuroimage.2015.04.063

De Visscher, A., & Noël, M. P. (2014). The detrimental effect of interference in multiplication facts storing: Typical development and individual differences. *J Exp Psychol Gen, 143*(6), 2380–2400. doi:10.1037/xge0000029

Dehaene, S., & Cohen, L. (1995). Towards an anatomical and functional model of number processing. *Math Cogn, 1,* 83–120.

Dehaene, S., & Cohen, L. (2007). Cultural recycling of cortical maps. *Neuron, 56*(2), 384–398. doi:10.1016/j.neuron.2007.10.004

Didino, D., Knops, A., Vespignani, F., & Kornpetpanee, S. (2015). Asymmetric activation spreading in the multiplication associative network due to asymmetric overlap between numerosities semantic representations? *Cognition, 141,* 1–8. doi:10.1016/j.cognition.2015.04.002

Domahs, F., Delazer, M., & Nuerk, H. C. (2006). What makes multiplication facts difficult. Problem size or neighborhood consistency? *Exp Psychol, 53*(4), 275–282. doi:10.1027/1618-3169.53.4.275

Dormal, V., Schuller, A. M., Nihoul, J., Pesenti, M., & Andres, M. (2014). Causal role of spatial attention in arithmetic problem solving: evidence from left unilateral neglect. *Neuropsychologia, 60,* 1–9. doi:10.1016/j.neuropsychologia.2014.05.007

Fisk, A. D., Derrick, W. L., & Schneider, W. (1986). A methodological assessment and evaluation of dual-task paradigms. *Current Psychological Research & Reviews, 5*(4), 315–327. doi:10.1007/BF02686599

Freyd, J. J., & Finke, R. A. (1984). Representational momentum. *J Exp Psychol Learn Mem Cogn, 10*(1), 126–132. doi:10.1037/0278-7393.10.1.126

Fürst, A. J., & Hitch, G. J. (2000). Separate roles for executive and phonological components of working memory in mental arithmetic. *Mem Cognit, 28*(5), 774–782. doi:10.3758/BF03198412

Galfano, G., Rusconi, E., & Umiltà, C. (2003). Automatic activation of multiplication facts: Evidence from the nodes adjacent to the product. *Q J Exp Psychol A, 56*(1), 31–61. doi:10.1080/02724980244000332

Grabner, R. H., Ansari, D., Koschutnig, K., Reishofer, G., Ebner, F., & Neuper, C. (2009). To retrieve or to calculate? Left angular gyrus mediates the retrieval of arithmetic facts during problem solving. *Neuropsychologia, 47*(2), 604–608. doi:10.1016/j.neuropsychologia.2008.10.013

Grabner, R. H., Ischebeck, A., Reishofer, G., Koschutnig, K., Delazer, M., Ebner, F., & Neuper, C. (2009). Fact learning in complex arithmetic and figural-spatial tasks: The role of the angular gyrus and its relation to mathematical competence. *Hum Brain Mapp, 30*(9), 2936–2952. doi:10.1002/hbm.20720

Groen, G. J., & Parkman, J. M. (1972). A chronometric analysis of simple addition. *Psychol Rev, 79*(4), 329–343.

Gunderson, E. A., Ramirez, G., Beilock, S. L., & Levine, S. C. (2012). The relation between spatial skill and early number knowledge: The role of the linear number line. *Dev Psychol, 48*(5), 1229–1241. doi:10.1037/a0027433

Halpern, A. R., & Kelly, M. H. (1993). Memory biases in left versus right implied motion. *J Exp Psychol Learn Mem Cogn, 19*(2), 471–484.

Hawes, Z., Moss, J., Caswell, B., & Poliszczuk, D. (2015). Effects of mental rotation training on children's spatial and mathematics performance: A randomized controlled study. *Trends Neurosci Educ, 4*(3), 60–68. doi:10.1016/j.tine.2015.05.001

Hecht, S. A., Torgesen, J. K., Wagner, R. K., & Rashotte, C. A. (2001). The relations between phonological processing abilities and emerging individual differences in mathematical computation skills: A longitudinal study from second to fifth grades. *J Exp Child Psychol, 79*(2), 192–227. doi:10.1006/jecp.2000.2586

Hubbard, E. M., Piazza, M., Pinel, P., & Dehaene, S. (2005). Interactions between number and space in parietal cortex. *Nat Rev Neurosci, 6*(6), 435–448. doi:10.1038/nrn1684

Hubbard, T. L. (2017). Toward a general theory of momentum-like effects. *Behav Processes, 141*(Pt 1), 50–66. doi:10.1016/j.beproc.2017.02.019

Imbo, I., & LeFevre, J. A. (2010). The role of phonological and visual working memory in complex arithmetic for Chinese- and Canadian-educated adults. *Mem Cognit, 38*(2), 176–185. doi:10.3758/MC.38.2.176

Imbo, I., & Vandierendonck, A. (2007). The role of phonological and executive working memory resources in simple arithmetic strategies. *Eur J Cogn Psychol, 19*(6), 910–933. doi:10.1080/09541440601051571

Ischebeck, A., Zamarian, L., Egger, K., Schocke, M., & Delazer, M. (2007). Imaging early practice effects in arithmetic. *Neuroimage, 36*(3), 993–1003. doi:10.1016/j.neuroimage.2007.03.051

Katz, C. & Knops, A. (2014). Operational momentum in approximate multiplication and division? *PLoS One, 9*(8), e104777. doi:10.1371/journal.pone.0104777

Klein, E., Huber, S., Nuerk, H. C., & Moeller, K. (2014). Operational momentum affects eye fixation behaviour. *Q J Exp Psychol* (Hove), *67*(8), 1614–1625. doi:10.1080/17470218.2014.902976

Knops, A., Dehaene, S., Berteletti, I., & Zorzi, M. (2014). Can approximate mental calculation account for operational momentum in addition and subtraction? *Q J Exp Psychol (Hove), 67*(8), 1541–1556. doi:10.1080/17470218.2014.890234

Knops, A., Thirion, B., Hubbard, E. M., Michel, V., & Dehaene, S. (2009). Recruitment of an area involved in eye movements during mental arithmetic. *Science, 324*(5934), 1583–1585. doi:10.1126/science.1171599

Knops, A., Viarouge, A., & Dehaene, S. (2009). Dynamic representations underlying symbolic and nonsymbolic calculation: Evidence from the operational momentum effect. *Atten Percept Psychophys, 71*(4), 803–821. doi:10.3758/APP.71.4.803

Knops, A., Zitzmann, S., & McCrink, K. (2013). Examining the presence and determinants of operational momentum in childhood. *Front Psychol, 4*, 325. doi:10.3389/fpsyg.2013.00325

Lee, K. M., & Kang, S. Y. (2002). Arithmetic operation and working memory: Differential suppression in dual tasks. *Cognition, 83*(3), B63–B68.

Liu, D., Cai, D., Verguts, T., & Chen, Q. (2017). The time course of spatial attention shifts in elementary arithmetic. *Sci Rep, 7*(1), 921. doi:10.1038/s41598-017-01037-3

Lourenco, S. F., Cheung, C.-N., & Aulet, L. S. (2018). Chapter 10 – Is visuospatial reasoning related to early mathematical development? A critical review. In A. Henik & W. Fias (Eds.), *Heterogeneity of function in numerical cognition* (pp. 177–210). Academic Press, London, UK.

Masson, N., & Pesenti, M. (2014). Attentional bias induced by solving simple and complex addition and subtraction problems. *Q J Exp Psychol (Hove), 67*(8), 1514–1526. doi:10.1080/17470218.2014.903985

Masson, N., & Pesenti, M. (2016). Interference of lateralized distractors on arithmetic problem solving: A functional role for attention shifts in mental calculation. *Psychol Res, 80*(4), 640–651. doi:10.1007/s00426-015-0668-7

Masson, N., Pesenti, M., Coyette, F., Andres, M., & Dormal, V. (2017). Shifts of spatial attention underlie numerical comparison and mental arithmetic: Evidence from a patient with right unilateral neglect. *Neuropsychology, 31*(7), 822–833. doi:10.1037/neu0000361

Mathieu, R., Gourjon, A., Couderc, A., Thevenot, C., & Prado, J. (2016). Running the number line: Rapid shifts of attention in single-digit arithmetic. *Cognition, 146*, 229–239. doi:10.1016/j.cognition.2015.10.002

McCloskey, M., Harley, W., & Sokol, S. M. (1991). Models of arithmetic fact retrieval: An evaluation in light of findings from normal and brain-damaged subjects. *J Exp Psychol Lear Mem Cogn, 17*(3), 377–397. doi:10.1037/0278-7393.17.3.377

McCrink, K., Dehaene, S., & Dehaene-Lambertz, G. (2007). Moving along the number line: Operational momentum in nonsymbolic arithmetic. *Percept Psychophys, 69*(8), 1324–1333.

Menon, V. (2016). Working memory in children's math learning and its disruption in dyscalculia. *Curr Opin Behav Sci, 10*, 125–132. doi:10.1016/j.cobeha.2016.05.014

Mix, K. S., & Cheng, Y. L. (2012). The relation between space and math: Developmental and educational implications. *Adv Child Dev Behav, 42*, 197–243.

Mix, K. S., Levine, S. C., & Newcombe, N. S. (2016). Chapter 1 – Development of quantitative thinking across correlated dimensions. In A. Henik (Ed.), *Continuous issues in numerical cognition* (pp. 1–33). San Diego: Academic Press.

Niedeggen, M., Rosler, F., & Jost, K. (1999). Processing of incongruous mental calculation problems: Evidence for an arithmetic N400 effect. *Psychophysiology*, *36*(3), 307–324.

Nuerk, H. C., Weger, U., & Willmes, K. (2001). Decade breaks in the mental number line? Putting the tens and units back in different bins. *Cognition*, *82*(1), B25–B33.

Oberauer, K., & Lange, E. B. (2009). Activation and binding in verbal working memory: A dual-process model for the recognition of nonwords. *Cogn Psychol*, *58*(1), 102–136. doi:10.1016/j.cogpsych.2008.05.003

Parkinson, C., Liu, S., & Wheatley, T. (2014). A common cortical metric for spatial, temporal, and social distance. *J Neurosci*, *34*(5), 1979–1987. doi:10.1523/JNEUROSCI.2159-13.2014

Parkinson, C., & Wheatley, T. (2013). Old cortex, new contexts: Re-purposing spatial perception for social cognition. *Front Hum Neurosci*, *7*, 645. doi:10.3389/fnhum.2013.00645

Pinhas, M., & Fischer, M. H. (2008). Mental movements without magnitude? A study of spatial biases in symbolic arithmetic. *Cognition*, *109*(3), 408–415. doi:10.1016/j.cognition.2008.09.003

Pinheiro-Chagas, P., Didino, D., Haase, V. G., Wood, G., & Knops, A. (2018). The developmental trajectory of the operational momentum effect. *Front Psychol*, *9*, 1062. doi:10.3389/fpsyg.2018.01062

Pouget, A., Deneve, S., & Duhamel, J. R. (2002). A computational perspective on the neural basis of multisensory spatial representations. *Nat Rev Neurosci*, *3*(9), 741–747. doi:10.1038/nrn914

Prado, J., Mutreja, R., Zhang, H., Mehta, R., Desroches, A. S., Minas, J. E., & Booth, J. R. (2011). Distinct representations of subtraction and multiplication in the neural systems for numerosity and language. *Hum Brain Mapp*, *32*(11), 1932–1947. doi:10.1002/hbm.21159

Ragni, M., & Knauff, M. (2013). A theory and a computational model of spatial reasoning with preferred mental models. *Psychol Rev*, *120*(3), 561–588. doi:10.1037/a0032460

Ranganath, C., & Ritchey, M. (2012). Two cortical systems for memory-guided behaviour. *Nat Rev Neurosci*, *13*(10), 713–726. doi:10.1038/nrn3338

Ritchey, M., Libby, L. A., & Ranganath, C. (2015). Cortico-hippocampal systems involved in memory and cognition: The PMAT framework. *Prog Brain Res*, *219*, 45–64. doi:10.1016/bs.pbr.2015.04.001

Seitz, K., & Schumann-Hengsteler, R. (2000). Mental multiplication and working memory. *Eur J Cogn Psychol*, *12*(4), 552–570. doi:10.1080/095414400750050231

Seyler, D. J., Kirk, E. P., & Ashcraft, M. H. (2003). Elementary subtraction. *J Exp Psychol Learn Mem Cogn*, *29*(6), 1339–1352. doi:10.1037/0278-7393.29.6.1339

Shepard, R. N., & Metzler, J. (1971). Mental rotation of three-dimensional objects. *Science, 171*(3972), 701–703.

Simon, O., Mangin, J. F., Cohen, L., Le Bihan, D., & Dehaene, S. (2002). Topographical layout of hand, eye, calculation, and language-related areas in the human parietal lobe. *Neuron, 33*(3), 475–487.

Stazyk, E. H., Ashcraft, M. H., & Hamann, M. S. (1982). A network approach to mental multiplication. *J Exp Psychol Learn Mem Cogn, 8*(4), 320–335. doi:10.1037/0278-7393.8.4.320

Thompson, J. M., Nuerk, H. C., Moeller, K., & Cohen Kadosh, R. (2013). The link between mental rotation ability and basic numerical representations. *Acta Psychol (Amst), 144*(2), 324–331. doi:10.1016/j.actpsy.2013.05.009

Tiberghien, K., Sahan, M. I., De Smedt, B., Fias, W., & Lyons, I. M. (2019). Disentangling neural sources of problem size and interference effects in multiplication. *J Cogn Neurosci, 31*(3), 453–467. doi:10.1162/jocn_a_01359

Verguts, T., & Fias, W. (2005a). Interacting neighbors: A connectionist model of retrieval in single-digit multiplication. *Mem Cogn, 33*(1), 1–16. doi:10.3758/bf03195293

Verguts, T., & Fias, W. (2005b). Neighbourhood effects in mental arithmetic. *Psychology Science, 47*(1), 132–140.

Woods, S. S., Resnick, L. B., & Groen, G. J. (1975). An experimental test of five process models for subtraction. *J Educ Psychol, 67*(1), 17–21. doi:10.1037/h0078666

Zamarian, L., Ischebeck, A., & Delazer, M. (2009). Neuroscience of learning arithmetic – Evidence from brain imaging studies. *Neurosci Biobehav Rev, 33*(6), 909–925. doi:10.1016/j.neubiorev.2009.03.005

5

THE DEVELOPMENT OF NUMERICAL COGNITION

Human numerical capacities undergo a massive development over the lifespan. This is mainly driven by formal education that imposes the acquisition of a number of structured and formalized mathematical procedures and concepts. But the development of numerical capacities is also driven by biological maturation of the underlying brain circuits that gives rise to increasing accuracy and allows establishing multiple cognitive associations and abstractions. As we move beyond adulthood, a number of cognitive functions decay (e.g. declarative memory, vigilance, . . .). We will see in this chapter whether this holds equally true for numerical capacities.

The chapter will give a brief overview of the following topics. First, I will have a closer look at the development of non-symbolic numerosity processing. At what age are infants sensitive to numbers? How does the accuracy of the ANS develop over the lifespan? I will then describe how children develop the ability to meaningfully use numerals (i.e. number words or Arabic digits). How do children learn to count? How do children acquire the meaning of number words? Does the underlying representation undergo a change in scaling from logarithmic to linear? Then, I will describe the development of a related concept and its relation to cardinality: ordinality. I will briefly reiterate the typical developmental trajectory for basic mental arithmetic and its neural correlates.

NUMEROSITY PERCEPTION

Immediately after birth, newborns possess a very limited set of cognitive and motor functions. Verbal expression is limited to a few variations of crying. Precise, target-oriented movements of the hand or other effectors are not possible. In fact, even the overall positioning of the body is not under willful control since newborns are unable to roll over until the age of approximately 6 months. Visual acuity is very low, too. Provided these (and other) limitations, it appears remarkable that newborns as young as 55 hours have been shown to be able to use their approximate number system to distinguish between different stimuli based on their numerosity. Babies that young are actually able to distinguish between numerosities if they are numerically separated by a ratio of 3:1 (Coubart, Izard, Spelke, Marie, & Streri, 2014). Coubart and colleagues (2014) familiarized babies during 60 seconds to sequences of auditory numerosities, comprising either 4 or 12 repeated syllables ("tuuuuuuuuuuuu – tuuuuuuuuuuu - tuuuuuuuuuuuu-tuuuuuuuuuuuu" or "tu-tu-tu-tu-tu-tu-tu-tu-tu-tu-tu-tu"). Then, babies were visually (!) presented with 4 test stimuli that either contained 12 items or 4 items. Coubart and colleagues found that babies would look longer at congruent stimuli (4 syllables – 4 items and 12 syllables – 12 items) compared to incongruent ones and interpreted this result as evidence for a cross-modal match of numerosities. Interestingly, babies showed neither differential performance for the same ratio that involved smaller numbers such as 2 vs. 6 nor for a ratio of 1:1.5 (2 vs. 3). Supposedly, babies were able to exploit their ANS to match between numerosities across modalities for stimuli with large numerosities and a 3:1 ratio. The results from this study also speak to an issue that I raised before. That is, in Chapter 2, I discussed the alternative explanation for human performance in numerosity discrimination tasks that draw on the combination of non-numerical cues. The results from Coubart and colleagues, however, provide compelling evidence for the idea that an amodal ANS gives rise to numerosity sensitivity.

Over the years that follow, infants' precision in discriminating numerosity increases. The ratios that can reliably be differentiated decrease from 1:3 in newborns (Izard et al., 2009) to 1:2 in 6-month-olds (Xu & Spelke, 2000; Lipton & Spelke, 2003) and 3:4 at the age of 3 to 4 years (Halberda & Feigenson, 2008). But how can we test this in babies who cannot provide verbal or motoric responses? Researchers exploit the fact that babies tend to look for longer periods of time at scenes and objects that contain new information and are hence deemed interesting. Consequently, researchers adapt babies to a given stimulus before presenting a deviant and measure for how long they fixate on the deviant. For example, infants are shown a sequence of displays, with each display containing a fixed number of items (e.g. 8 dots). The configuration of the dots varies across the displays so as not to habituate infants to non-numerical aspects such as circumference, individual dot size, or convex hull. The idea is that the cognitive system will adapt to the only constant feature of the displays: number. After the infants are habituated (e.g. after a series of 20 displays), a display with a deviating number of items is shown. For example, a display with 16 dots is shown to the infant. If the infants are sufficiently sensitive to the numerical deviation (ratio 1:2), the new display will actually be perceived as "new" and hence they will spend more time looking at it. Indeed, infants as young as 6 months have been shown to be sensitive to such a variation in ratio.

Another line of evidence has used a different paradigm in which infants are presented with non-symbolic addition and subtraction tasks. For example, Wynn (1992) presented 4- to 5-months-old infants with a sequence of events that can be described as addition and subtraction. In addition trials, infants were shown a single puppet in an empty display area. Then, a screen would turn up in front of the puppet, rendering it invisible. The experimenter then placed another puppet behind the screen. In subtraction trials, two puppets were placed in the display area before the screen comes up. Then, one of the puppets was removed from behind the screen in a way that was fully visible to the infants. If infants are sensitive to the numerical outcome, they will expect the presence of two items in addition trials and one in subtraction. Unbeknownst to the infants, in some trials, the experimenter removed one of the items in the addition trials (leaving only one item behind the screen) or added a second puppet in the subtraction condition (leaving two items behind the screen). Finally, the screen was moved away, allowing a free view of the display area. Wynn found that infants would spend more time looking at the "implausible" (e.g. $1 + 1 = 1$ and $2 - 1 = 2$) compared to the expected outcomes. However, one might argue that infants use their object tracking system OTS in this situation with low numerosities rather than relying on their ANS (Carey, 2009; Spelke, 2000). To test this hypothesis, McCrink and Wynn (2004) presented 9-months-old infants with a computerized variant of this task. Five (addition) or ten (subtraction) items would drop from the top of the screen and vanish behind an occluder. Subsequently, five additional items would drop down and vanish behind the occluder (addition), or five items would move out from behind the occluder and vanish from screen (subtraction). Hence, in addition trials, infants should expect ten items behind the occluder and five items in subtraction trials. Finally, the occluder would drop to reveal either five or ten items. Again, infants looked longer at "implausible" outcomes (e.g. five items in addition trials or ten items in subtraction trials) compared to expected outcomes, corroborating the assumption that infants were able to mentally add or subtract the approximate number of items over the sequence of events. Since the number of five items exceeds the capacity limit of the OTS that typically cannot track more than four items (Franconeri, Alvarez, & Cavanagh, 2013; Pylyshyn & Storm, 1988), these results provide conclusive evidence for the idea that infants at this early age are sensitive to numerical information and can use their ANS to mentally combine the approximate number representations.

These results demonstrate that humans are born with (or at least quickly develop after birth) a sensitivity to approximate numerical information. The acuity of the ANS increases over the preschool years. But how does the acuity of the ANS develop after children enter school? In a large cross-sectional study with ~10,000 participants, Halberda and colleagues (Halberda, Ly, Wilmer, Naiman, & Germine, 2012) showed that ANS acuity initially shows a rapid increase between 11 and 16 years. ANS acuity continuously increases throughout school-age years (at a slower pace) and peaks only at around 30 years of age. Finally, ANS acuity slowly declines in the age range 30 to 85 years. A part of the decline in the elderly can be explained by the decreasing ability to inhibit conflicting information (Cappelletti, Didino, Stoianov, & Zorzi, 2014). Cappelletti and colleagues found that dot discrimination capacities at an older range (age range: 60–75 years) was reduced only in trials where salient non-numerical features of the dot sets were in conflict with the numerical information but not when non-numerical and numerical information was jointly in favor of one particular response. Hence, while the ANS remained constant, inhibitory deficits led to reduced performance.

Halberda and colleagues also found that ANS acuity highly correlates with school achievement in maths. The better participants were at discriminating between two sets of dots, the better their math grades. This relationship remained unchanged across all age ranges. Subsequent studies found that ANS acuity not only predicts mathematical performance at the same time (i.e. when tested concurrently) but also pre- and postdicts mathematical performance (Halberda, Mazzocco, & Feigenson, 2008; Libertus, Feigenson, & Halberda, 2011; Odic et al., 2016).

In sum, the ANS is present very early on (55 hours after birth) and increases in accuracy as we grow older. The question whether the observed decay over the fourth to eighth decades of life is due to a decrease in core capacities or in domain-general abilities (e.g. inhibition) remains an issue of debate for the moment.

COUNTING AND THE MEANING OF NUMBER WORDS

One of the most natural things to adults is to count a (smaller) number of objects to make sure what the exact number is. This becomes important, for example, when a teacher accompanies a school class to a museum and needs to make sure no child gets lost on the way. In this situation, one can frequently see teachers counting the students, for example, when entering or leaving the metro or bus. Counting is the procedure that we use to establish the cardinality of a set of objects/persons. However, even if infants may be able to perfectly count up to a certain number, they have not necessarily understood that counting yields the cardinal number of objects in a set. In fact, over several years during development, there may exist this gap between procedural knowledge (i.e. reciting the count words) and conceptual knowledge (i.e. the understanding of numeral meaning). Typically, infants go through several "stages" or levels during the acquisition of a fully fledged counting system. These levels do not necessarily follow each other in the very same order as described here, and sometimes infants may go back and forth between them as they grow older. These levels should not be understood as a strictly hierarchical sequence of qualitatively separate steps that infants take. Rather, they are meant as labels of typical benchmark behaviors. Behaviors from different levels can be observed at the same time, and the acquisition of new strategies may lead to a developmental rollback. Another reason these levels should not be overestimated is that the observed age variance (i.e. at what age an infant reaches a given level) within a given level is often larger than the mean age difference between levels. Nevertheless, these labels provide a good overview of the different aspects that children may acquire.

Until the age of about 2 years, infants will predominantly sing-song numbers without attaching any meaning to them. Progressively, they will start to count objects with separate words that are not necessarily in the right order. By the age of 3, children can typically already count small sets of objects and recite the numbers until 10 or so. However, as we will see later, children struggle with larger sets (>3 or 4) and quickly lose track when pointing to members of a set. They may, for instance, assign two numbers to a single given member of a set. After the age of around 4 years, children progressively enlarge the range of sets that they can meaningfully count out. This progression often takes a serial form (count to three, count to four, count to five), and the time lags between these set sizes that can be reliably counted are surprisingly large. It may, for example, take a child 6 months to figure out how to count up to 4 items after having mastered counting up to 3. By the age of 5 to 6 years, children typically know how to count up to ten and find the number just before or after a number without counting up from one. Counting in a number range of 1 to 20 or even 30 becomes more and more flawless. At this age, children start being able to count backwards (e.g. 10–9–8–. . .).

But why is learning to count such a tedious process that takes several years? In fact, there are quite a few key concepts that children need to master in order to be able to attach some meaning to the counting words (Gelman & Gallistel, 1978). This includes learning the number word sequence, of course, and accepting that there is in fact a predefined and unchangeable sequence of number words (stable order principle). It is also important to understand that one should assign each item in a set only one number word, while at the same time it is important not to leave out any of the items (one-to-one principle). Hence, working memory is required to remember which items have already been counted and which ones still need to be counted. Children also need to understand that any set of items (or persons, puppets, animals, ideas, etc.) can be counted (abstraction principle). The order by which a given set is counted does not matter – the result is always the same (order invariance principle). Another cornerstone concept is the so-called "cardinality principle", which describes the idea that the last number in the count sequence describes the quantity of the set (i.e. how many items in the set).

Cardinality can be defined by establishing exact numeric equality (i.e. equinumerous). Two sets are said to be equinumerous if and only

BOX 5.1 GIVE-A-NUMBER OR GIVE-N TASK

In order to test whether children have understood the cardinality principle, they are often tested with the so-called "give a number task". The aim is to find out up to which number their counting behavior is actually conceptually related to the underlying cardinality of the number words. Put differently, to what extent do children understand that the last number word uttered when counting accurately refers to the cardinality of a counted set (given that no element was left out or counted more than once)? In the give a number task, the child is given a container with a larger number of small items (e.g. marbles). The experimenter then asks the child to give her (or another character in the setting) a defined number of items. The number of requested items varies between trials and is usually within the range 1–6. Typically, children who have fully understood the cardinality principle (CP-knowers) succeed for every requested number of items. So-called subset-knowers, however, only succeed for a subset of numbers (e.g. 3 items). If the requested number of items exceeds this limit (e.g. 4 or 5 items), they would give an arbitrary number of items to the experimenter. For example, they would simply grab a number of items or hand over all of the items. A two-knower, for example will succeed only for one and two requested items.

if there exists a bijection between the elements of the two sets. Put differently, two sets are equinumerous if and only if there is a one-to-one correspondence between the elements of the two sets. This set-theoretic definition is based upon three principles (Izard, Streri, & Spelke, 2014) that are easily understood when thinking in terms of transformations that can be applied to sets without affecting their cardinality:

First, when applying transformations that do not affect the identity of any member of either set, the sets remain equinumerous. This includes, for example, changing the position or the spatial configuration of the elements. We can dislocate the objects of either set without changing their numeric equivalence. This is referred to as the identity principle.

Second, adding to or subtracting from one set only changes their numeric equivalence – even if the change is ever so subtle. This is called the addition/subtraction principle.

Third, substituting one element of a set with any other element does not change the numeric equivalence of the sets. Ice hockey, volleyball, and football provide vivid examples of this substitution principle: Two teams remain equinumerous even if we substitute one player with another one.

What follows from these principles? Put simply, children can only be said to have fully understood the concept of cardinality (and hence the meaning of using a numeral to refer to any given set of items) when they subscribe to all three principles. During development, however, children are surprisingly unwilling (or better: unable) to commonly accept these principles. In his famous number conservation task, Piaget spread out two rows of marbles in front of children, each containing the same number of marbles (e.g. 4). When children agreed on the notion that both rows were "the same", that is, contained the same number of marbles, Piaget rearranged the elements of one row such that the marbles were spread further apart, hence forming a longer row but leaving cardinality unchanged. Piaget then asked children which row would contain more marbles. Until the age of about 5, children are prone to err and state that the longer row now contains more marbles. This would clearly be a misunderstanding of the identity principle. It should be noted that Piaget interpreted these results by assuming that children who erred had not reached a certain stage of development and had not yet learned what numbers were and what numerical quantifiers would mean. Several strands of later research, however, challenged this interpretation. First, we already saw in the beginning of this chapter and in previous chapters that infants and even newborns have a clear understanding of numerical quantities. Second, subsequent studies using variants of the number conservation task showed that Piaget's results may have been due to the pragmatics of the task. It was argued, for example, that children must assume that adults know better than they do and that the adult who asks the question also saw that the actual number of elements had not changed. Hence, children search for a stimulus dimension that would make sense in this context and allow for a more or less comparison. Hence, they resort to the length of the rows to comply with the adult and provide the answer (s)he was probably hoping for. If, on the other hand, the rearrangement was done by a third party (e.g. a "naughty" teddy bear) in such a way that the adult would indeed not know which row had more, children were able to correctly answer this question (McGarrigle & Donaldson, 1974). Others have argued that Piaget's task is actually an interference task where children need to actively inhibit alternative visuo-spatial strategies in order to make the right decision (Borst, Poirel, Pineau, Cassotti, & Houdé, 2012). Finally, a seminal study by Mehler and Bever (Mehler & Bever, 1967) demonstrated that children do possess a good understanding of quantifiers such as more and less – when they are sufficiently motivated. In a first experiment, Mehler and Bever asked children at different ages (2 years 4 months [2;4] to 4;7) if they agreed that two rows of four clay pellets each were identical. Then, the experimenter added two clay pellets to one row while at the same time shortening the length of this row such that it would be shorter than the row that still contained four clay pellets. Mehler and Bever found a non-linear pattern of performance, with 100% of the youngest children choosing the more numerous row. With age, performance dropped to a minimum of 13% at the age of 3 years 8 months to 3 years 11 months before it soared again for the oldest age groups. In the second experiment, Mehler and Bever replaced the clay pellets with candy-coated chocolate pellets and asked children to pick the row that they would like to eat. Again, they found a slightly U-shaped performance pattern across age, where children performed worse at the age of 3 years 8 months to 3 years 11 months. But overall, children's performance was much better than in the first experiment. All age groups performed better than chance (>50% correct). Hence, Piaget's assumption that development occurs as progressing in stages cannot explain this pattern of performance. In addition, these results imply that children at this age actually do have a notion of the identity principle.

In another situation, children may respect identity and substitution principles but may be unable to perceive the consequences of addition/subtraction of a single element and hence erroneously continue to perceive numerical equivalence. For instance, even for adults, it is impossible to visually distinguish between two large sets of objects that contain 999 and 1001 elements. Since the estimates in this situation rely on the ANS and go far beyond its discrimination accuracy, they appear equally numerous, and this impression will not change when adding or subtracting a single element – hence contradicting the second principle.

The substitution principle can be violated in situations where a given set is made up of particular members that cannot simply be replaced. A family would be one example where the spatial layout can change and one can add or subtract members (grandparents, for example), but no single member can simply be replaced by a foreign person.

Izard and colleagues (Izard et al., 2014) tested to what extent children (2.5–2.9 years) used one-to-one-correspondence when judging exact numerical equality without referring to verbal labels (i.e. number words). They found that subset-knowers were exploiting one-to-one correspondence cues for sets of five or six objects (i.e. exceeding the limits of the object tracking system). This held true, though, only for situations that did not involve addition or subtraction of items. In such transformational contexts, children did not show any sign of using the one-to-one correspondence for reconstructing the exact quantity. These results indicate that even subset-knowers have an understanding of exact cardinality beyond the subset limits. But this understanding critically hinges on the presence of correspondence cues. Without these cues, performance drops. Also, performance dropped once the experimenter manipulated the set by adding or subtracting one element. Hence, children did not fully understand the successor function at this age. The understanding of cardinality at this age is thus going beyond what the ANS would predict but falls short of a full-blown understanding of numerical equality.

THE SYMBOL GROUNDING PROBLEM

This leads to the interesting question: how do children come to grasp the meaning of number words? This question is often referred to as the symbol-grounding problem. There are several theoretical positions that differ, for example, with respect to the role that language plays in this context. At one extreme, researchers assume that "the human number faculty [is] essentially an 'abstraction' from human language" (Chomsky, 1988). According to this view, the rules that govern the evolution of language systems also produce number knowledge. One key concept is the idea that words largely differ in meaning as a function of their position in a sentence. For example, "The financier dazzled the actress" is very different from "The actress dazzled the financier" (example taken from Rips, Bloomfield, & Asmuth, 2008). This means that the position of a word in a given system determines its meaning. The same is true for numbers. The meaning of the number word three is defined by its position in the entire system of number words. However, the observation described in Chapter 3 are hard (if not impossible) to reconcile with this assumption: we saw that the Mundurukú do not possess words that describe exact cardinal values larger than four. If language is sufficient for the emergence of a number system, we need to explain why one is present (language) without the other (number) in Mundurukú.

Others assume that mathematics and number represent a cognitive primitive, a natural category with a dedicated network in the brain that is largely independent from language (Amalric & Dehaene, 2016; Dehaene & Cohen, 2007; Piazza, 2010). Under this assumption, numerals acquire their meaning by being mapped onto the ANS. This is referred to as the ANS mapping account. The ANS mapping account argues that children are correct in mapping numerals to numerosities only to the degree that the ANS allows to reliably distinguish between two numerosities. Hence, the previously described succession of subset knowledge would actually result from and reflect the increasing precision of the ANS. For example, children can only map the numeral "three" to a set of three items if this set can be distinguished from sets of two and sets of four items; that is, when children become sensitive to the ratio 3:4. As we saw before, this occurs – by and large – at the age of 3 to 4 years (Le Corre & Carey, 2007). This account is built on several observations (see Chapters 2 and 3). First, the ANS can be found in multiple species, as discussed previously. Second, in humans, the ANS is present from birth. Third, the behavioral patterns that characterize non-symbolic magnitude processing can be found in symbolic number processing, too – in particular, the distance and size effects. Furthermore, the overlapping neural correlates of non-symbolic numerosities and numerals have been taken as evidence for a shared number system and the idea that numerals acquire meaning by mapping them to non-symbolic numerosities (Piazza, 2010). Fourth, numerical processing relies on a dedicated network of parietal, prefrontal, and temporal regions that is independent from numerical format, reasoning, and language. Fifth, ANS acuity correlates with (future) mathematical achievement and can hence be understood as a foundational basis for symbolic mathematical abilities. The idea is that the ANS, an evolutionary ancient system, is co-opted by cultural requirements (i.e. mathematics and symbolic, exact number) because its mechanisms and architecture are well suited for the culturally new behavior (Dehaene & Cohen, 2007). For having a foundational role, this system needs to meet two requirements. (a) The integrity should be a necessary condition for efficient learning. As we will see in the next chapter, the evidence for the first requirement is mixed at best. (b) The second requirement alludes to the overlapping activity patterns for symbolic and non-symbolic quantity information (e.g. distance effect) and arithmetic in the parietal cortex: The computational constraints should limit and determine the ease of learning and the functional characteristics of performance.

Several weaknesses of this proposition have been pointed out over the years. While the presence of the ANS in infants and other species is fascinating, it does not directly speak to the question of how human number words acquire meaning for two reasons. Humans are the only species with highly developed language facility. Since other species lack this facility, the findings from these species may not be generalized to the symbol-grounding problematic. The other reasoning is that the ANS is inherently noisy. Numbers, however, refer to a very exact cardinality. Hence, the ANS may be essentially useless in distinguishing between 4 and 5 and even more so to distinguish between 122 and 123, for example. It has further been questioned whether the resemblance of distance and size effects in symbolic and non-symbolic notation actually results from the exploitation of a common analogue magnitude representation. Rather, the distance effect may have its origin in system properties that are outside the mental number representation. The locus depends on the system architecture. One example is the mapping between decision and output units. This has been implemented by Verguts and Fias (2004) in a computational model that successfully reproduces a number of important behavioral effects (distance and size effect) without assuming approximate and overlapping representations. Further support against this idea comes from experiments that observe distance effects on dimensions that do not have approximate and overlapping representations (e.g. military ranks). Finally, two recent studies (Bulthe, De Smedt, & Op de Beeck, 2014; Lyons, Ansari, & Beilock, 2015) have failed to observe a common underlying neural substrate for symbolic and non-symbolic quantity information and demonstrated format-dependent coding of non-symbolic (dot patterns) and symbolic (Arabic digits) numerals (see Chapter 2 for more details). Together, this body of evidence casts some doubt on the ANS mapping account.

Alternatively, it has been argued that children acquire number meaning through a process that is called conceptual rule bootstrapping (Carey, 2009, 2011; Quine, 1960). During conceptual rule bootstrapping, learners first acquire a placeholder structure. In the beginning, the placeholders are void of content – they are meaningless. Over time, however, the learner begins to fill symbols with meaning. According to this view, learners systematically pass through a series of knowledge levels that start at the level of "pre-number-knowers". At this level, children have no idea of the differentiation between different numerals. For example, in a give-N task, they would perform randomly even for N = 1. That is, they would give a random number of objects when asked to give one only. This is followed by the levels of subset-knowers. These learners know the meaning of some (a subset) but not all numerals. This level comprises one-knowers, two-knowers, three-knowers, and four-knowers. A crucial test for establishing the different levels is the give-N task. According to their performance in this task, children are able to accurately give N objects from a set but fail at higher numbers (see Box 5.1). Importantly, Lee and Sarnecka (2011) found that children tend to overshoot in their responses. That is, when asked to give N and N is beyond their current level, they would tend to give a number larger than N (Lee & Sarnecka, 2011). This is incompatible with the idea that errors would be due to counting errors because erroneous counting would lead to symmetrical errors around the target number (if anything, undershooting should be more probable). According to the bootstrapping account, the level of four-knowers is then followed by cardinal principle knowers (CP-knowers). Children at that level have understood the cardinality principle. In support of this account, it has been found that performance in the give-N task positively correlates with chronological age. Moreover, it has been found that the transition from subset-knower to CP-knower indeed entails a mastery of different cardinality principles, including the understanding of the successor function. Sarnecka and Carey (2008) presented children aged 24 to 48 months with two tasks that tested their understanding of cardinality. First, children (all of whom were able to count to ten) were shown two plates with six items each. The experimenter then picked up one item from one plate and moved it to the other plate. The critical test question was "Now there's a plate with five and one with seven. Which plate has five?" As expected, CP-knowers succeeded in this task while two- and three-knowers failed. The fact that four-knowers also succeeded was explained with the notion that they were at the verge of understanding cardinality. More conclusive, in the second experiment, children were shown a box that contained a certain number of items (e.g. toy apples). The experimenter would name the number, for example saying "There are five apples in this box". Then the experimenter added one or two items and asked "Now how many? Is it six or seven items?" In this task, only CP-knowers succeeded, suggesting that the transition to this level entails the understanding of the successor function.

The bootstrapping account assumes that the critical boundary of four-knowers to CP-knowers occurs at four items because of the limitations that the object tracking system imposes. Hence, the object tracking system that gives rise to the subitizing phenomenon also determines the numerical quantity at which children move from subset- to CP-knowers. However, it has been found that the OTS limit quickly develops during the first year of life. By the age of 12 months, infants already display a tracking limit of three to four items, very similar to adults. If the OTS is indeed responsible for the conceptual change from subset-knowers to CP-knowers, the subsets should extend to two, three, or four very early in life and simultaneously. This is, however, not the case. Also, a recent longitudinal study found that the ANS but not the OTS predicts acquisition of the cardinality principle (vanMarle et al., 2018).

Finally, Reynvoet and Sasanguie (2016) argued for a variant of the bootstrapping model where the initial symbols (i.e. number words) might be first mapped onto a precise representation of numerosity. This mapping crucially relies on the OTS. The symbolic number system, in turn, results from the combination of the initial mapping with relational inference principles such as the successor function and language (i.e. counting routines). By the end of this process, a separate system has evolved, in which numbers are rank-associated with other numbers (symbol-symbol associations). Hence, the ordinal relationship between numbers plays an important role according to this approach. In support of this idea, Davidson and colleagues (Davidson, Eng, & Barner, 2012) recently demonstrated that 3- to 5-year-olds can correctly compare verbal numbers that exceed their subset range and for which they merely know the order in the list of number words.

Taken together, a solution for the symbol grounding problem is not in sight for the moment being. This discussion may appear highly theoretic and academic. However, the solution of the symbol-grounding problem has important implications for the way children are taught about numbers and what training measures should be adopted. According to the ANS mapping account, it makes sense to train numerosity discrimination in order to improve symbolic number understanding. Indeed, recent training studies in which students were trained to add or subtract non-symbolic numerosities have shown improvements in symbolic mathematics that exceeded the changes in an active control group (Hyde, Khanum, & Spelke, 2014; Park & Brannon, 2013). To date, no study has demonstrated similar findings with younger children, though. The bootstrapping approach, on the other side, would stipulate that training the OTS may lead to a better or faster acquisition of symbolic number knowledge. To the best of my knowledge, no study has attempted to improve number knowledge via training parallel object individuation. The trainings that may be considered closest have aimed at improving spatial skills in general, such as mental rotation, for example (Cheng & Mix, 2014). These trainings have been found to show not only close but also far transfer to untrained domains such as arithmetic (Cheung, Sung, & Lourenco, 2019). For example, a single session of mental rotation training improved performance on missing term problems (e.g. $5 +\_\_\_ = 12$) in 6- to 8-year-olds. It should be mentioned, however, that while such training has repeatedly been shown to improve math skills (Hawes, Moss, Caswell, Naqvi, & MacKinnon, 2017; Lowrie, Logan, & Ramful, 2017), others did not find any far transfer (Cornu, Schiltz, Pazouki, & Martin, 2017; Hawes, Moss, Caswell, & Poliszczuk, 2015).

NUMBER LINE TASK

A popular tool for teaching numbers is the number line, where numbers occupy specific positions on a regularly spaced and left-to-right–oriented continuum. The number line has also received massive attention from researchers in the field who have used it to investigate the understanding of symbolic number processing. Siegler and Opfer (2003) presented second graders, fourth graders, sixth graders, and undergraduates with horizontal lines that were labeled with 1 at the left and 100 or 1000 at the right. Participants were then presented with a number that was randomly taken from a predefined list (e.g. 2, 3, 6, 25, 67, and 86). Participants were asked to indicate the position of the presented number on the line. Therefore, this task is referred to as "number line task" or "number position task". Ideally, the relation between estimated position and actual position on the number line should be linear. When plotting the estimated position against the actual position, ideal performance should resemble a straight line with an origin at position [0,0] and a slope that equals 1 (see grey dashed line in Figure 5.1). However, Siegler and Opfer observed a systematic deviation. Second and fourth graders assigned more space to the smaller number range compared to the larger number range. For example, they placed the number 6 where the number

25 should go. Sixth graders and undergraduates, however, showed on average a very linear mapping of numbers to positions. Siegler and Opfer interpreted these results as reflecting the scaling of the internal numerical magnitude representation. For a known number range, children would predominantly rely on a linear representation. For unknown number ranges, however, they rely on a logarithmically compressed representation. Siegler and Booth (2004) followed up on these findings and showed how the mapping becomes increasingly linear from Kindergarten to second grade as children gain numerical proficiency within the numerical range. The average results from Kindergarteners, first graders, and second graders are shown in Figure 5.1. When looking at the black line in Figure 5.1, one can readily see that Kindergarteners initially estimate the actual number 25 to be located at the position where 55 should go. In contrast, larger numbers are squeezed into a limited range of positions. For example, the actual number 86 is assigned to the position of 73. By second grade, however, the mapping has become largely linear, albeit showing some regression to the mean (avoidance of the extremes). Interestingly, the degree to which the mapping deviates from linearity correlates with math achievement. The less the mapping diverges from linearity, the better the math achievement (Schneider et al., 2018). This correlation holds across a wide age range and is somewhat stronger for fractions ($r \approx .5$) than for whole-number arithmetic ($r \approx .4$).

Some researchers challenge the assumption that the result of the number line task indexes the internal representation. They argue that

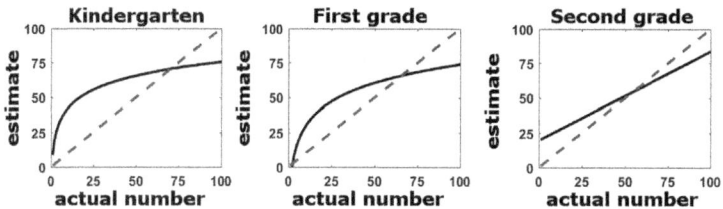

FIGURE 5.1 Regression function that best fit the median estimation data of Kindergarteners and first and second graders. Reproduced after the results in Siegler and Booth (2004). Dashed line shows theoretically ideal, linear mapping performance.

Source: Adapted from Siegler and Booth (2004).

the strategies that children (and adults) use in this task vary substantially. Some strategies rely on proportional reasoning abilities in combination with spatial skills. That is, participants may actually divide the space and the numbers proportionally and use anchor points (e.g. quartiles) to place the number on the line. The non-linearity may then merely reflect the lack of familiarity in a given number range rather than a logarithmic scaling of the underlying representation. In line with this critique, Simms and colleagues found that visuomotor integration and visuospatial skills fully explain the often-replicated negative correlation between deviance from linearity and mathematical skills (Simms, Clayton, Cragg, Gilmore, & Johnson, 2016).

ORDINALITY

As we saw at the beginning of Chapter 2, numbers can convey different meanings, cardinality being the most frequent one. Yet, understanding the ordinal information that – bluntly put – answers the question "What rank?" has recently been argued to be another important stepping stone for the development of numerical and mathematical capacities (Lyons, Vogel, & Ansari, 2016). A very prominent ritual in Germany, for example, consists of the weekly announcement of the winning 6 lottery numbers that have been drawn from the numbers 1–49. A winning series may be 1, 4, 12, 24, 25, 38. Here, 1 is the first number (ordinal and cardinal information are consistent), but 4 is the second and 12 is the third number. This demonstrates that cardinal and ordinal meaning do not necessarily coincide. To measure ordinal processing capacities, participants are typically presented with number triplets (e.g. 2_4_8 or 3_1_8) and are asked to decide whether they appear in ascending order (first triplet) or not (second triplet).

But is this distinction between the cardinal and ordinal quality of numbers relevant to the brain? Recent neuroimaging studies indeed revealed that ordinal processing of numbers relies on brain networks that partially deviate from those that are recruited for the processing of cardinality. Lyons and Beilock (2013) presented participants with numbers and dot sets in four different task settings. Participants were either asked to judge whether the given triplet (either numbers or dot sets) was in ascending (1) numerical or (2) luminance order or

which of two dot sets was numerically larger (3) or (4) more luminous. Luminance judgments served as a high-level control in this
experiment. The authors observed a predominantly right-lateralized
network of the parietal and dorsolateral prefrontal cortex, as well as
anterior cingulum that was activated for both cardinal and ordinal
processing of non-symbolic quantities. This implies that judging the
ordinality of dot sets relies on the same network that is involved in
judging the cardinality of number symbols. For numerals, no such
overlapping network was observed. This implies that symbolic and
non-symbolic ordinality judgments do not share the same network. In
particular, the authors argue that the judgment of symbolic ordinality
relies on different mental processes. This is consistent with neuropsychological findings. Here, a double dissociation between ordinal and
cardinal processing was observed. Delazer and Butterworth (1997)
reported the case of a patient who was able to answer questions such
as "Which number comes next?" and was able to count elements.
However, this patient was impaired in comparing two numbers in
terms of numerical magnitude. Hence, the left frontal lesion in this
patient impaired cardinal processing but spared ordinal processing.
On the other side, Turconi and Seron (2002) reported the case of a
patient who suffered from lesions in the left posterior parietal cortex
and the right parietal occipital junction. This patient was unable to
process ordinal information in multiple contexts (numbers, days of
the week, months of the year). However, his cardinal capacities were
unimpaired and he was perfectly able to compare the magnitude of
two numbers or place a number on a spatial continuum. According
to classical neuropsychological interpretation, this double dissociation
is proof of a modular and independent organization of cardinal and
ordinal number meaning at the brain level. Further evidence for the
idea that ordinality and cardinality are two conceptually independent dimensions comes from the finding that one of the hallmark
effects of number processing, the distance effect, is reversed when
participants are asked to judge ordinality (Franklin & Jonides, 2009;
Lyons & Beilock, 2013; Turconi, Campbell, & Seron, 2006). That
is, participants are faster in judging the order of two stimuli in a
sequence when they are closer. Franklin and Jonides found that it
is the reverse distance effect in order judgments that gives rise to
increased parietal activity (2009). However, the reverse distance effect

is highly task dependent. Marshuetz and colleagues (Marshuetz, Smith, Jonides, DeGutis, & Chenevert, 2000) observed a canonical distance effect when asking participants to judge whether two members (e.g. D K) of a previously learned list (e.g. {L D M N K}) appeared in the previously learned order or not. Items that were more remote in the list were responded to faster and with higher accuracy. Together, these results show that ordinality is – to some extent – independent from cardinality. Yet the underlying cognitive mechanism for judging order is still a matter of debate (Marshuetz, 2005). I will come back to this question later.

DEVELOPMENT OF ORDER PROCESSING

We saw earlier that the approximate number system emerges very early in life. How does ordinal processing develop? Early studies used a task in which children were presented with two sets of objects (e.g. two sets of two toys each) that were then covered by putting a box over them. Then, the experimenter added one toy to one of the boxes or took away one of the toys from within one of the boxes (Sophian & Adams, 1987). Sophian and Adams showed that infants as young as 14 months were able to choose the box with more toys after a toy had been added. They failed, however, until the age of 24 months to choose the correct box when one toy had been taken away. These results are often cited in support of an early representation of ordinal relations (e.g. Brannon, 2002). It is, however, conceivable that infants simply kept track of the objects and merely perceived the qualitative difference between the contents of the two boxes. That is, infants may perceive the twoness and threeness inside these boxes as different without necessarily putting them in any ordinal relation. Even the opposite interpretation is possible according to which infants use the cardinal difference between the boxes as a cue to answer the question of where more toys would be. Hence, these results are not very conclusive. More conclusively, researchers have used an adaptation procedure to habituate participants to sequences of events that were characterized by ordinal relations. For example, Cooper (1984) habituated infants to pairs of displays. Each pair consisted of sequentially presented displays that had an ordinal relationship which was maintained throughout the pairs (e.g. pair 1: 1 → 2, pair 2: 2 → 3, pair

3: 1 → 4, . . .). Hence, cardinal values (and their ratios) changed but the ordinal relationship was maintained (here: smaller precedes larger). Upon the test, children were then shown pairs with either identical numbers of objects (e.g. test pair: 2 → 2) or pairs in which the ordinal relationship was reversed (e.g. test pair: 4 → 2). Infants at the age of 14–16 months dishabituated (i.e. looked longer) at both types of ordinal deviants (constant or reversed). Younger (10–12 months) infants, however, only dishabituated to pairs of equal number, not when ordinal relationship changed (from smaller → larger to larger → smaller). While inconclusive for the younger age group, these results imply that infants by the age of 14–16 months already perceive changes in ordinal relationship. Later studies employed three-item series that made the ordinal relationship more salient and showed that order sensitivity can already be observed by the age of 11 (Brannon, 2002), 7 (Macchi Cassia, Picozzi, Girelli, & de Hevia, 2012), or even 4 months (Picozzi, de Hevia, Girelli, & Macchi Cassia, 2010) when physical size and not numerosity was the relevant ordinal dimension.

Given that ordinal processing represents an independent psychological dimension and emerges early in infants, what relevance does it have for the development of numerical and mathematical competencies? Lyons and colleagues measured cardinal and ordinal processing of symbolic and non-symbolic quantities in the same participants. While in first and second grade, cardinal processing of symbolic number still accounted for the lion's share of variance in arithmetic scores, the unique variance captured by ordinal processing of numbers increased over the years and became the most important predictor of arithmetic performance (Lyons, Price, Vaessen, Blomert, & Ansari, 2014). In this particular cross-sectional study (children in each grade were tested in the same and unique testing period), a number of non-symbolic and symbolic measures were included. This comprised standard non-symbolic tasks such as dot comparison (see Chapter 2) and dot estimation ("How many dots are on screen?"). Symbolic tasks included ordering, counting, number comparison, number line estimation, and a task that required matching between auditorily (e.g. "/three/") and visually (e.g. "4") presented numbers. Non-verbal intelligence, reading ability, and basic stimulus–response processing were measured as domain-general control variables. In stark contrast to the assumed key role of non-symbolic numerosity processing, non-symbolic measures did not prove predictive of concurrent arithmetic competencies. Even though only three non-symbolic measures were included in this study, none of them turned out to be predictive of arithmetic competencies in any of the tested grades (Lyons et al., 2014). Based on these results, Sasanguie and Vos (2018) studied the developmental dynamics of the relation between number comparison, ordinal processing of numbers, and mental arithmetic in first and second graders. In line with the results by Lyons and colleagues, Sasanguie and Vos found that in first grade, number comparison (indexing cardinal processing of numbers) was a significant predictor of arithmetic abilities. Number comparison also mediated the relation between ordinal processing and arithmetic at this age. In second grade, however, the relation between number comparison and arithmetic was mediated by ordinal processing, which was a significant predictor of arithmetic competencies at this stage. Hence, the predictive value of cardinal and ordinal processing for arithmetic switches between first and second grade, potentially indexing a stronger impact of declarative knowledge that relies on item–item associations (see subsequently for mechanisms underlying order judgments).

How does order processing relate to the ANS, which has been proposed as a neurocognitive start-up tool for symbolic number understanding (Piazza, 2010)? Order processing has been found to mediate the relationship between approximate number sense and arithmetic performance (Lyons & Beilock, 2011). Knops and Willmes (2014) found a right-lateralized network of regions in the anterior and posterior parietal cortex that was active both during order judgments on number triplets and during symbolic addition and subtraction. Beyond a mere overlap of activity, the patterns of activity in these regions resembled each other in both tasks, and we argued that functional and anatomical characteristics of this network make it a candidate for linking the ANS to mental arithmetic. Analyzing the pattern of activity is important since the mere overlap between two or more conditions may cover up underlying differences between these conditions. For example, Fias and colleagues observed that judging the order of letters and numbers activated similar regions in the IPS (Fias, Lammertyn, Caessens, & Orban, 2007). They concluded that the IPS is similarly engaged in processing numerical and non-numerical order information. Later, however, Zorzi, Di Bono, and Fias (2011) re-analyzed these data and found that letters and numbers gave rise to distinct patterns of activity in these regions that were distinguishable with multi-variate supervised machine learning techniques (i.e. support vector classification).

In sum, the existing evidence suggests that order is not only a theoretical mathematical feature of numbers that may restrict the number of meaningful operations in the case of ordinal scaling. Rather, order appears as a separate and important dimension of numbers that triggers distinguishable cognitive effects and is characterized by neural mechanisms that are separate from cardinality. But what mechanisms underlie order processing? One of the earliest mechanisms that has been proposed relies on pairwise item-to-item associations, also known as associative chaining. Under this view, each item is memorized via its associations with neighboring items. In a series such as A-B-C-D, for example, the ordinal position of C is defined as "comes before D and after B". Such a mechanism can, for example, explain why Sternberg (1967) found that "When Subjects name the item that follows a test item in a short recently memorized list, their mean reaction-time [. . .] increases linearly with list length" (p. 55). It cannot explain the results by Marshuetz and colleagues (2000), however, who found faster reaction times when items were more remote in a list. Others have added that the successful recollection of an item did not depend on the retrieval of the item previous in the list (Baddeley, 1968; Kahana & Jacobs, 2000). Hence, item-to-item associations may not be the best candidate mechanism for coding ordinal relations.

Another class of models that was proposed for the coding of ordinal information is referred to as magnitude models (Marshuetz, 2005). Since describing all the existing models would go beyond the scope of the current book, I will focus on two recently developed models that were also applied to numerical order tasks. What is common to both models is the notion of (cardinal) magnitude that is used to code for the ordinal information. In a sense, these models bridge the conceptual and empirical distinction between ordinal and cardinal processing by including both within a joint model framework.

Watanabe and Botvinick (Botvinick & Watanabe, 2007) described a model that is based on three assumptions that determine its empirical foundation. First, single-unit recordings from the prefrontal cortex of macaques have revealed neurons that code for ordinal and item information at the same time. The so-called conjunctive code reflects the fact that neurons specifically respond to particular items, but their response depends on the ordinal position at which these items appear. That is, a given neuron may respond maximally to an apple that appeared in the third position of a sequence of items. This neuron's response will decrease gradually as either ordinal position or item similarity changes (or both). Second, the way the brain computes conjunctive codes has been identified in single-unit recording studies and computationally implemented. The crucial idea is that a certain class of neurons integrate two sources of incoming information in an additive fashion. The parietal cortex hosts coordinate transformation processes that help to transform information from different reference frames to guide action and navigation. For example, to compute the position of an object in space with respect to the head position, the sensory system combines eye-centered information with the information about the eyes' posture (Beck, Latham, & Pouget, 2011; Brotchie, Andersen, Snyder, & Goodman, 1995). These mechanisms have been shown to generalize to other domains, such as object recognition and sensorimotor mapping (Pouget & Snyder, 2000; Salinas & Abbott, 2001; Salinas & Thier, 2000). Third, Nieder has demonstrated that neurons in the parietal cortex provide a graded, compressive coding of count information. In particular, Nieder, Diester, and Tudusciuc (2006) demonstrated that neurons in the parietal cortex responded maximally to particular sequential numerosities and that the response of these neurons decreased gradually as the presented sequence diverged numerically from the preferred value (see Chapter 3). For example, a given neuron may respond maximally when five items have been shown to the monkey. This neuron thus codes for the fifth presentation of a given stimulus. Botvinick and Watanabe's model combines these three principles in stating that the ordinal information that is directly coded in parietal neurons is transmitted to the prefrontal cortex. Here, neurons that exhibit conjunctive coding integrate this information with item information through gain modulation.

A second model has been proposed by Brown, Neathe, and Chater (2007) as a memory model. The SIMPLE (scale independent memory, perception, and learning) model assumes that

> (a) episodic memories in multidimensional psychological space are located along a dimension representing temporal distance from the point of retrieval, (b) the retrievability of an item is inversely proportional to its summed confusability with other items in memory, and (c) the confusability of items along a temporal dimension is given by the ratio of the temporal distances of those items at the time of recall.
>
> (p. 539)

Hence, the model places temporal ratios at its heart and assumes that memory traces can be located and individuated according to their position on a (logarithmically compressed) temporal continuum. The difficulty of retrieving an item is defined by (1) its discriminability from neighboring items in psychological space and (2) by the ratio of the temporal distances from recall between the item and its neighbors. Put differently, the less an item suffers from interference from neighboring items, the better it can be recalled. Interference can be due to the previously mentioned two factors: psychological similarity along multiple stimulus feature dimensions and temporal vicinity. By including psychological similarity in their model, Brown, Neathe and Chater, too, include semantic number features (i.e. cardinality) in their explanation for ordinal processing.

Few empirical studies have aimed at putting these models to a test in the domain of numerical cognition. A recent neuroimaging study might be interpreted as lending empirical support for the idea that a fronto-parietal network is involved in coding ordinal information (Botvinick & Watanabe, 2007). Matejko and colleagues (Matejko, Hutchison, & Ansari, 2019) found that compared to 7-to-10 year-old children, adults exhibited a more pronounced reversed distance effect in the left parietal cortex when judging the order of a number triplet. However, no overlapping region in the PFC was observed for both groups where the model predicts activity of conjunctive neurons. These results need to be interpreted with caution since the authors used an active task that included response selection and preparation, two cognitive stages that in and by themselves can lead to parietal activity (Gobel, Johansen-Berg, Behrens, & Rushworth, 2004), even if Matejko and colleagues used a high-level control task (luminance judgments).

In sum, order processing turns out to be an important stepping stone during the development of mathematical competencies. At present, we neither understand the cognitive or neural mechanisms involved nor their developmental trajectories over the lifespan. For example, it remains a matter of debate whether the understanding of ordinality precedes cardinality (Colomé & Noël, 2012; Wiese, 2007) and what cognitive models underlie the coding or ordinal information.

DEVELOPMENT OF MENTAL ARITHMETIC AND ITS NEURAL UNDERPINNINGS

The mechanisms underlying mental arithmetic were introduced in the previous chapter. Here, I will particularly focus on the developmental trajectories of mental arithmetic. At the same time, I will show that these changes do not only appear at the behavioral level but are accompanied by a profound change at the neural level.

Generally speaking, mental arithmetic undergoes a change from procedural to retrieval strategies (Geary, 2011; Jordan, Hanich, & Kaplan, 2003). In addition, for example, many children start out with a simple counting strategy. For example, to solve $4 + 2$, children will count 1, 2, 3, 4, 5, 6 and provide 6 as the correct answer. In a next step, children may figure out that it is advantageous to start counting onward starting from the largest number ($4 + 2 \rightarrow 4, 5, 6 \rightarrow 6$) (Geary, Bow-Thomas, & Yao, 1992). As children become more proficient with number decomposition (e.g. $12 = 10 + 2$ or $6 + 6$, etc.), this provides an additional strategy that is utilized to solve addition problems. Children might, for example, decompose $8 + 6$ into $8 + 2 = 10, 6 - 2 = 4, 10 + 4 = 14 \rightarrow 14$. In the final stage, it is often assumed that children retrieve the results of simple problems from long-term memory (see previous chapter). Memory retrieval is most often used when solving multiplication and division problems.

Children dispose of a number of different strategies that they flexibly use to solve a given problem. According to the overlapping waves theory of development (Siegler, 1996), the shift from one strategy to another is not abrupt but should be understood as a gradual shift of frequency with which a given strategy is used. This also implies that different strategies may overlap over a period of time. Under this perspective, it is of ample importance that children learn to choose the most efficient strategy. Hence, routine-based problem solving needs to be differentiated from an adaptive use of solution strategies. This competency is referred to as adaptive expertise (Verschaffel, Luwel, Torbeyns, & Dooren, 2009). Interestingly, a U-shaped relation has been observed between knowledge/understanding and variety of strategy use (Dowker, 1996; Siegler & Jenkins, 1989). The highest variety of strategies is observed in novices and experts, albeit for different reasons. While novices try out different strategies – among them many inefficient ones – to find the most appropriate one to solve a given problem, experts may use their extensive knowledge of procedures and concepts to invent new strategies (Dowker, 1996).

In adults, mental arithmetic relies on the orchestrated cooperation of a number of brain regions that are organized in different networks (e.g. attention network; default mode network, task-positive network). These regions include bilateral prefrontal areas, bilateral superior and inferior parietal cortex, temporo-parietal regions (e.g. angular gyrus, supramarginal gyrus), and occipito-temporal regions (e.g. fusiform gyrus). The activity of these regions is modulated by a number of task-related factors (e.g. task difficulty, operation type, format) and individual strategies (Tschentscher & Hauk). Ischebeck and colleagues, for example, demonstrated that increasing familiarity with a given multiplication problem led to a shift of activity from the bilateral parietal cortex to the angular gyrus over the course of a single scanning session (Ischebeck, Zamarian, Egger, Schocke, & Delazer, 2007). While this has initially been interpreted as evidence for the involvement of the angular gyrus in arithmetic fact retrieval, subsequent studies revealed that the increasing activity in angular gyrus did not reflect number-specific fact retrieval but rather is a general signature of learning that can be found with various contents (Grabner, Ansari, et al., 2009; Grabner, Ischebeck, et al., 2009). Nevertheless, these studies pointed out that different strategies at the behavioral level (retrieval vs. procedural) are reflected by differential neural activation patterns.

In 10-to-12-year-old children, a similar distinction has been observed between more complex problems that require the application of arithmetic procedures (e.g. large addition or subtraction problems) on one hand and simple problems that can be solved by memory retrieval on the other hand (De Smedt, Holloway, & Ansari, 2011). While solving complex problems was associated with activity in a large fronto-parietal network, retrieval was associated with activity in the left hippocampus. Later studies confirmed the crucial role of the hippocampus in arithmetic fact retrieval (Cho et al., 2012; Cho, Ryali, Geary, & Menon, 2011; Menon, 2016). In a longitudinal design, Qin and colleagues observed a decrease of activity in the bilateral DLPFC, left superior parietal lobule, and right posterior occipito-parietal areas that was accompanied by an increase in activity in the bilateral hippocampus (Qin et al., 2014). Together, these studies indicate that increasing proficiency in arithmetic fact retrieval that is characterized by increasing reliance on retrieval from memory and decreasing involvement of working memory and executive control leads to a massive change in the neural resources that are recruited. The hippocampus is particularly important during early periods of arithmetic fact acquisition (approximately grades 1–5), where it shows a massive increase of activity compared to adolescents or adults. Hence, arithmetic fact acquisition is not associated with special neural networks but recruits domain-general circuits that subserve learning in many domains. Qin and colleagues showed that individual improvement in arithmetic fact retrieval was associated with increased functional connectivity between the hippocampus on one hand and frontal as well as parietal areas on the other.

In sum, we begin to understand how the development of numerical competencies maps onto the underlying neural networks. However, more longitudinal data are required that target the development and acquisition of specific and circumscribed numerical and mathematical skills.

SUMMARY

- Starting a few hours after birth, humans show remarkable numerical competencies that allow them to differentiate numerical quantities across different modalities.

- The acuity of the approximate number system increases with age.
- The question how children acquire the understanding of the cardinality of numerical symbols remains debated. Neither the bootstrapping nor the ANS mapping account can fully explain the current body of empirical data.
- Order processing appears to be an important ingredient of numerical development, but a thorough theoretical account is still missing.
- The development of arithmetic skill has been shown to be associated with a shift of neural activity from frontal to parietal and hippocampal sites, following the change of procedural solution to retrieval strategies.

A thorough understanding of the neurocognitive mechanisms underlying the acquisition of numerical skills will be an important future endeavor. This is particularly important before the background of the lack of understanding of the origins of dysfunctional numerical cognition, which I will describe in the next chapter.

FURTHER READINGS

An interesting discussion on the principles that guide the acquisition of cardinality can be found in Rips and colleagues (2008). A more detailed description of the development of neural underpinnings of numerical cognition can be found in Iuculano and Menon (2018) or Peters and De Smedt (2018). A more detailed overview of higher mathematical functions can be found in Gilmore, Göbel, and Inglis (2018), or in Rittle-Johnson and Schneider (2015) for an overview of the development of conceptual and procedural knowledge.

REFERENCES

Amalric, M., & Dehaene, S. (2016). Origins of the brain networks for advanced mathematics in expert mathematicians. *Proc Natl Acad Sci U S A*, *113*(18), 4909–4917. doi:10.1073/pnas.1603205113

Baddeley, A. (1968). How does acoustic similarity influence short-term memory? *Q J Exp Psychol (Hove)*, *20*, 249–264.

Beck, J. M., Latham, P. E., & Pouget, A. (2011). Marginalization in neural circuits with divisive normalization. *J Neurosci*, *31*(43), 15310–15319. doi:10.1523/JNEUROSCI.1706-11.2011

Borst, G., Poirel, N., Pineau, A., Cassotti, M., & Houdé, O. (2012). Inhibitory control in number-conservation and class-inclusion tasks: A neo-Piagetian intertask priming study. *Cogn Dev*, *27*(3), 283–298. https://doi.org/10.1016/j.cogdev.2012.02.004

Botvinick, M., & Watanabe, T. (2007). From numerosity to ordinal rank: A gainfield model of serial order representation in cortical working memory. *J Neurosci*, *27*(32), 8636–8642. doi:10.1523/JNEUROSCI.2110-07.2007

Brannon, E. M. (2002). The development of ordinal numerical knowledge in infancy. *Cognition*, *83*(3), 223–240.

Brotchie, P. R., Andersen, R. A., Snyder, L. H., & Goodman, S. J. (1995). Head position signals used by parietal neurons to encode locations of visual stimuli. *Nature*, *375*(6528), 232–235. doi:10.1038/375232a0

Brown, G. D., Neath, I., & Chater, N. (2007). A temporal ratio model of memory. *Psychol Rev*, *114*(3), 539–576. doi:10.1037/0033-295X.114.3.539

Bulthe, J., De Smedt, B., & Op de Beeck, H. P. (2014). Format-dependent representations of symbolic and non-symbolic numbers in the human cortex as revealed by multi-voxel pattern analyses. *Neuroimage*, *87*, 311–322. doi:10.1016/j.neuroimage.2013.10.049

Cappelletti, M., Didino, D., Stoianov, I. P., & Zorzi, M. (2014). Number skills are maintained in healthy ageing. *Cogn Psychol*, *69*, 25–45. doi:10.1016/j.cogpsych.2013.11.004

Carey, S. (2009). *The origin of concepts*. New York: Oxford University Press.

Carey, S. (2011). Precis of "The Origin of Concepts". *Behav Brain Sci*, *34*(3), 113–124; discussion 124–162. doi:10.1017/S0140525X10000919

Cheng, Y.-L., & Mix, K. S. (2014). Spatial training improves children's mathematics ability. *J Cogn Dev*, *15*(1), 2–11. doi:10.1080/15248372.2012.725186

Cheung, C. N., Sung, J. Y., & Lourenco, S. F. (2019). Does training mental rotation transfer to gains in mathematical competence? Assessment of an at-home visuospatial intervention. *Psychol Res*. doi:10.1007/s00426-019-01202-5

Cho, S., Metcalfe, A. W. S., Young, C. B., Ryali, S., Geary, D. C., & Menon, V. (2012). Hippocampal-prefrontal engagement and dynamic causal interactions in the maturation of children's fact retrieval. *J Cogn Neurosci*, *24*(9), 1849–1866. http://dx.doi.org/10.1162/jocn_a_00246

Cho, S., Ryali, S., Geary, D. C., & Menon, V. (2011). How does a child solve 7 + 8? Decoding brain activity patterns associated with counting and retrieval strategies. *Dev Sci*, *14*(5), 989–1001. http://dx.doi.org/10.1111/j.1467-7687.2011.01055.x

Chomsky, N. (1988). *Language and Problems of Knowledge. The Managua Lectures.* Cambridge, MA, MIT Press.

Colomé, À., & Noël, M.-P. (2012). One first? Acquisition of the cardinal and ordinal uses of numbers in preschoolers. *J Exp Child Psychol, 113*(2), 233–247. https://doi.org/10.1016/j.jecp.2012.03.005

Cooper, R. G. (1984). Early number development: Discovering number space with addition and subtraction. In C. Sophian (Ed.), *Origins of cognitive skills* (pp. 157–192). Hilsdale, NJ: Erlbaum.

Cornu, V., Schiltz, C., Pazouki, T., & Martin, R. (2017). Training early visuo-spatial abilities: A controlled classroom-based intervention study. *Appl Dev Sci, 23*, 1–21.

Coubart, A., Izard, V., Spelke, E. S., Marie, J., & Streri, A. (2014). Dissocia-tion between small and large numerosities in newborn infants. *Dev Sci, 17*(1), 11–22. doi:10.1111/desc.12108

Davidson, K., Eng, K., & Barner, D. (2012). Does learning to count involve a semantic induction? *Cognition, 123*(1), 162–173. doi:10.1016/j.cognition.2011.12.013

De Smedt, B., Holloway, I. D., & Ansari, D. (2011). Effects of problem size and arithmetic operation on brain activation during calculation in children with varying levels of arithmetical fluency. *Neuroimage, 57*(3), 771–781. doi:10.1016/j.neuroimage.2010.12.037

Dehaene, S., & Cohen, L. (2007). Cultural recycling of cortical maps. *Neuron, 56*(2), 384–398. doi:10.1016/j.neuron.2007.10.004

Delazer, M., & Butterworth, B. (1997). A dissociation of number meanings. *Cogn Neuropsychol, 14*(4), 613–636.

Dowker, A. (1996). Estimation strategies of four groups. *Math Cogn, 2*(2), 113–135. doi:10.1080/135467996387499

Fias, W., Lammertyn, J., Caessens, B., & Orban, G. A. (2007). Processing of abstract ordinal knowledge in the horizontal segment of the intraparietal sul-cus. *J Neurosci, 27*(33), 8952–8956. doi:10.1523/JNEUROSCI.2076-07.2007

Franconeri, S. L., Alvarez, G. A., & Cavanagh, P. (2013). Flexible cognitive resources: Competitive content maps for attention and memory. *Trends Cogn Sci, 17*(3), 134–141. doi:10.1016/j.tics.2013.01.010

Franklin, M. S., & Jonides, J. (2009). Order and magnitude share a com-mon representation in parietal cortex. *J Cogn Neurosci, 21*(11), 2114–2120. doi:10.1162/jocn.2008.21181

Geary, D. C. (2011). Cognitive predictors of achievement growth in mathemat-ics: A 5-year longitudinal study. *Dev Psychol, 47*(6), 1539–1552. doi:10.1037/a0025510

Geary, D. C., Bow-Thomas, C. C., & Yao, Y. (1992). Counting knowledge and skill in cognitive addition: A comparison of normal and mathematically dis-abled children. *J Exp Child Psychol, 54*(3), 372–391.

Gelman, R., & Gallistel, C. R. (1978). *The children's understanding of number.* Cambridge, MA: Harvard University Press.

Gilmore, C., Göbel, S. M., & Inglis, M. (2018). *An introduction to mathematical cognition.* Abingdon, Oxon and New York, NY: Routledge.

Gobel, S. M., Johansen-Berg, H., Behrens, T., & Rushworth, M. F. (2004). Response-selection-related parietal activation during number comparison. *J Cogn Neurosci, 16*(9), 1536–1551. doi:10.1162/0898929042568442

Grabner, R. H., Ansari, D., Koschutnig, K., Reishofer, G., Ebner, F., & Neuper, C. (2009). To retrieve or to calculate? Left angular gyrus mediates the retrieval of arithmetic facts during problem solving. *Neuropsychologia, 47*(2), 604–608. doi:10.1016/j.neuropsychologia.2008.10.013

Grabner, R. H., Ischebeck, A., Reishofer, G., Koschutnig, K., Delazer, M., Ebner, F., & Neuper, C. (2009). Fact learning in complex arithmetic and figural-spatial tasks: The role of the angular gyrus and its relation to mathematical competence. *Hum Brain Mapp, 30*(9), 2936–2952. doi:10.1002/hbm.20720

Halberda, J., Ly, R., Wilmer, J. B., Naiman, D. Q., & Germine, L. (2012). Number sense across the lifespan as revealed by a massive internet-based sample. *Proc Natl Acad Sci U S A, 109*(28), 11116–11120. doi:10.1073/pnas.1200196109

Halberda, J., Mazzocco, M. M., & Feigenson, L. (2008). Individual differences in non-verbal number acuity correlate with maths achievement. *Nature, 455*(7213), 665–668. doi:10.1038/nature07246

Hawes, Z., Moss, J., Caswell, B., Naqvi, S., & MacKinnon, S. (2017). Enhancing children's spatial and numerical skills through a dynamic spatial approach to early geometry instruction: Effects of a 32-week intervention. *Cogn Instruct, 35*, 1–29.

Hawes, Z., Moss, J., Caswell, B., & Poliszczuk, D. (2015). Effects of mental rotation training on children's spatial and mathematics performance: A randomized controlled study. *Trends Neurosci Educ, 4*(3), 60–68. doi:10.1016/j.tine.2015.05.001

Hyde, D. C., Khanum, S., & Spelke, E. S. (2014). Brief nonsymbolic, approximate number practice enhances subsequent exact symbolic arithmetic in children. *Cognition, 131*(1), 92–107.

Ischebeck, A., Zamarian, L., Egger, K., Schocke, M., & Delazer, M. (2007). Imaging early practice effects in arithmetic. *Neuroimage, 36*(3), 993–1003. doi:10.1016/j.neuroimage.2007.03.051

Iuculano, T., & Menon, V. (2018). *Development of mathematical reasoning* (S. Ghetti, Ed., Vol. 4). Hoboken, NJ: John Wiley & Sons.

Izard, V., Sann, C., Spelke, E. S., & Streri, A. (2009). Newborn infants perceive abstract numbers. *Proc Natl Acad Sci USA, 106*(25), 10382–10385. doi:10.1073/pnas.0812142106

Izard, V., Streri, A., & Spelke, E. S. (2014). Toward exact number: Young children use one-to-one correspondence to measure set identity but not numerical equality. *Cogn Psychol, 72*, 27–53. doi:https://doi.org/10.1016/j.cogpsych.2014.01.004

Jordan, N. C., Hanich, L. B., & Kaplan, D. (2003). Arithmetic fact mastery in young children: A longitudinal investigation. *J Exp Child Psychol, 85*(2), 103–119.

Kahana, M. J., & Jacobs, J. (2000). Interresponse times in serial recall: Effects of intraserial repetition. *J Exp Psychol Learn Mem Cogn, 26*(5), 1188–1197.

Knops, A., & Willmes, K. (2014). Numerical ordering and symbolic arithmetic share frontal and parietal circuits in the right hemisphere. *Neuroimage, 84*, 786–795. doi:10.1016/j.neuroimage.2013.09.037

Le Corre, M., & Carey, S. (2007). One, two, three, four, nothing more: An investigation of the conceptual sources of the verbal counting principles. *Cognition, 105*(2), 395–438. doi:10.1016/j.cognition.2006.10.005

Lee, M. D., & Sarnecka, B. W. (2011). Number-knower levels in young children: Insights from Bayesian modeling. *Cognition, 120*(3), 391–402. doi:10.1016/j.cognition.2010.10.003

Libertus, M. E., Feigenson, L., & Halberda, J. (2011). Preschool acuity of the approximate number system correlates with school math ability. *Dev Sci, 14*(6), 1292–1300. doi:10.1111/j.1467-7687.2011.01080.x

Lipton, J. S., & Spelke, E. S. (2003). Origins of number sense. Large-number discrimination in human infants. *Psychol Sci, 14*(5), 396–401. doi:10.1111/1467-9280.01453

Lowrie, T., Logan, T., & Ramful, A. (2017). Visuospatial training improves elementary students' mathematics performance. *Br J Educ Psycholo, 87*, 170–186.

Lyons, I. M., Ansari, D., & Beilock, S. L. (2015). Qualitatively different coding of symbolic and nonsymbolic numbers in the human brain. *Hum Brain Mapp, 36*(2), 475–488. doi:10.1002/hbm.22641

Lyons, I. M., & Beilock, S. L. (2011). Numerical ordering ability mediates the relation between number-sense and arithmetic competence. *Cognition, 121*(2), 256–261. doi:10.1016/j.cognition.2011.07.009

Lyons, I. M., & Beilock, S. L. (2013). Ordinality and the nature of symbolic numbers. *J Neurosci, 33*(43), 17052–17061. doi:10.1523/JNEUROSCI.1775-13.2013

Lyons, I. M., Price, G. R., Vaessen, A., Blomert, L., & Ansari, D. (2014). Numerical predictors of arithmetic success in grades 1–6. *Dev Sci, 17*(5), 714–726. doi:10.1111/desc.12152

Lyons, I. M., Vogel, S. E., & Ansari, D. (2016). On the ordinality of numbers: A review of neural and behavioral studies. *Prog Brain Res, 227*, 187–221. doi:10.1016/bs.pbr.2016.04.010

Macchi Cassia, V., Picozzi, M., Girelli, L., & de Hevia, M. D. (2012). Increasing magnitude counts more: Asymmetrical processing of ordinality in 4-month-old infants. *Cognition, 124*(2), 183–193. doi:10.1016/j.cognition.2012.05.004

Marshuetz, C. (2005). Order information in working memory: An integrative review of evidence from brain and behavior. *Psychol Bull, 131*(3), 323–339. doi:10.1037/0033-2909.131.3.323

Marshuetz, C., Smith, E. E., Jonides, J., DeGutis, J., & Chenevert, T. L. (2000). Order information in working memory: fMRI evidence for parietal and prefrontal mechanisms. *J Cogn Neurosci, 12*(2), 130–144. doi:10.1162/08989290051137459

Matejko, A. A., Hutchison, J. E., & Ansari, D. (2019). Developmental specialization of the left intraparietal sulcus for symbolic ordinal processing. *Cortex, 114*, 41–53. doi:10.1016/j.cortex.2018.11.027

McCrink, K., & Wynn, K. (2004). Large-number addition and subtraction by 9-month-old infants. *Psychol Sci, 15*(11), 776–781. doi:10.1111/j.0956-7976.2004.00755.x

McGarrigle, J., & Donaldson, M. (1974). Conservation accidents. *Cognition, 3*(4), 341–350. doi:10.1016/0010-0277(74)90003-1

Mehler, J., & Bever, T. G. (1967). Cognitive capacity of very young children. *Science, 158*(3797), 141–142. doi:10.1126/science.158.3797.141

Menon, V. (2016). Working memory in children's math learning and its disruption in dyscalculia. *Curr Opin Behav Sci, 10*, 125–132. doi:10.1016/j.cobeha.2016.05.014

Nieder, A., Diester, I., & Tudusciuc, O. (2006). Temporal and spatial enumeration processes in the primate parietal cortex. *Science, 313*(5792), 1431–1435. doi:10.1126/science.1130308

Odic, D., Lisboa, J. V., Eisinger, R., Olivera, M. G., Maiche, A., & Halberda, J. (2016). Approximate number and approximate time discrimination each correlate with school math abilities in young children. *Acta Psychol (Amst), 163*, 17–26. doi:10.1016/j.actpsy.2015.10.010

Park, J., & Brannon, E. M. (2013). Training the approximate number system improves math proficiency. *Psychol Sci, 24*(10), 2013–2019. doi:10.1177/0956797613482944

Peters, L., & De Smedt, B. (2018). Arithmetic in the developing brain: A review of brain imaging studies. *Dev Cogn Neurosci, 30*, 265–279. doi:10.1016/j.dcn.2017.05.002

Piazza, M. (2010). Neurocognitive start-up tools for symbolic number representations. *Trends Cogn Sci, 14*(12), 542–551. doi:10.1016/j.tics.2010.09.008

Picozzi, M., de Hevia, M. D., Girelli, L., & Macchi Cassia, V. (2010). Seven-month-olds detect ordinal numerical relationships within temporal sequences. *J Exp Child Psychol, 107*(3), 359–367. doi:10.1016/j.jecp.2010.05.005

Pouget, A., & Snyder, L. H. (2000). Computational approaches to sensorimotor transformations. *Nat Neurosci, 3*(Suppl), 1192–1198. doi:10.1038/81469

Pylyshyn, Z. W., & Storm, R. W. (1988). Tracking multiple independent targets: Evidence for a parallel tracking mechanism. *Spat Vis, 3*(3), 179–197.

Qin, S., Cho, S., Chen, T., Rosenberg-Lee, M., Geary, D. C., & Menon, V. (2014). Hippocampal-neocortical functional reorganization underlies children's cognitive development. *Nat Neurosci, 17*(9), 1263–1269. doi:10.1038/nn.3788

Quine, W. V. O. (1960). *Word and object.* Cambridge: MIT Press.

Reynvoet, B., & Sasanguie, D. (2016). The symbol grounding problem revisited: A thorough evaluation of the ANS mapping account and the proposal of an alternative account based on symbol-symbol associations. *Front Psychol, 7,* 1581. doi:10.3389/fpsyg.2016.01581

Rips, L. J., Bloomfield, A., & Asmuth, J. (2008). From numerical concepts to concepts of number. *Behav Brain Sci, 31*(6), 623–642; discussion 642–687. doi:10.1017/S0140525X08005566

Rittle-Johnson, B., & Schneider, M. (2015). Developing conceptual and procedural knowledge of mathematics. In R. Cohen Kadosh & A. Dowker (Eds.), *The Oxford Handbook of Numerical Cognition.* Oxford, UK: Oxford University Press.

Salinas, E., & Abbott, L. F. (2001). Coordinate transformations in the visual system: How to generate gain fields and what to compute with them. *Prog Brain Res, 130,* 175–190.

Salinas, E., & Thier, P. (2000). Gain modulation: A major computational principle of the central nervous system. *Neuron, 27*(1), 15–21.

Sarnecka, B. W., & Carey, S. (2008). How counting represents number: What children must learn and when they learn it. *Cognition, 108*(3), 662–674. doi:10.1016/j.cognition.2008.05.007

Sasanguie, D., & Vos, H. (2018). About why there is a shift from cardinal to ordinal processing in the association with arithmetic between first and second grade. *Dev Sci, 21*(5), e12653. doi:10.1111/desc.12653

Schneider, M., Merz, S., Stricker, J., De Smedt, B., Torbeyns, J., Verschaffel, L., & Luwel, K. (2018). Associations of number line estimation with mathematical competence: A meta-analysis. *Child Dev, 89*(5), 1467–1484. doi:10.1111/cdev.13068

Siegler, R. S. (1996). *Emerging minds: The process of change in children's thinking.* Oxford: Oxford University Press.

Siegler, R. S., & Booth, J. L. (2004). Development of numerical estimation in young children. *Child Dev, 75*(2), 428–444. doi:10.1111/j.1467-8624.2004.00684.x

Siegler, R. S., & Jenkins, E. A. (1989). *How children discover new strategies.* Hillsdale, NJ: Erlbaum.

Siegler, R. S., & Opfer, J. E. (2003). The development of numerical estimation: Evidence for multiple representations of numerical quantity. *Psychol Sci, 14*(3), 237–243. doi:10.1111/1467-9280.02438

Simms, V., Clayton, S., Cragg, L., Gilmore, C., & Johnson, S. (2016). Explaining the relationship between number line estimation and mathematical achievement: The role of visuomotor integration and visuospatial skills. *J Exp Child Psychol, 145,* 22–33. doi:10.1016/j.jecp.2015.12.004

Sophian, C., & Adams, N. (1987). Infants' understanding of numerical transformations. *Br J Dev Psychol, 5,* 257–264.

Spelke, E. S. (2000). Core knowledge. *Am Psychol*, *55*(11), 1233–1243.

Sternberg, S. (1967). Retrieval of contextual information from human memory. *Psychonomic Science*, *8*, 55–56.

Turconi, E., Campbell, J. I. D., & Seron, X. (2006). Numerical order and quantity processing in number comparison. *Cognition*, *98*(3), 273–285. doi:10.1016/j. cognition.2004.12.002

Turconi, E., & Seron, X. (2002). Dissociation between order and quantity meanings in a patient with Gerstmann syndrome. *Cortex*, *38*, 911–914.

vanMarle, K., Chu, F. W., Mou, Y., Seok, J. H., Rouder, J., & Geary, D. C. (2018). Attaching meaning to the number words: Contributions of the object tracking and approximate number systems. *Dev Sci*, *21*(1). doi:10.1111/desc.12495

Verguts, T., & Fias, W. (2004). Representation of number in animals and humans: A neural model. *J Cogn Neurosci*, *16*(9), 1493–1504. doi:10.1162/0898929042568497

Verschaffel, L., Luwel, K., Torbeyns, J., & Dooren, W. V. (2009). Conceptualizing, investigating, and enhancing adaptive expertise in elementary mathematics education. *Eur J Psychol Educ*, *24*, 335–359.

Wiese, H. (2007). The co-evolution of number concepts and counting words. *Lingua*, *117*, 758–772.

Wynn, K. (1992). Addition and subtraction by human infants. *Nature*, *358*(6389), 749–750. doi:10.1038/358749a0

Xu, F., & Spelke, E. S. (2000). Large number discrimination in 6-month-old infants. *Cognition*, *74*(1), B1–B11. doi:10.1016/s0010-0277(99)00066-9

Zorzi, M., Di Bono, M. G., & Fias, W. (2011). Distinct representations of numerical and non-numerical order in the human intraparietal sulcus revealed by multivariate pattern recognition. *Neuroimage*, *56*(2), 674–680. doi:10.1016/j. neuroimage.2010.06.035

6

DEVELOPMENTAL DYSCALCULIA

Over the previous five chapters, I described the cognitive and neurofunctional mechanisms underlying the perception and processing of numerical information. It has become evident that numerical information is ubiquitous in our everyday life and that processing it involves a complex interaction of multiple cognitive systems that rely on a multitude of brain regions. We cannot spend a single day without coming across any numerical information. In fact, as soon as we open our eyes, we perceive the number of items in our visual field as soon as we categorize what constitutes an item. Beyond this "natural" numerosity information, symbolic numbers constitute an important part of our daily life. Before this background, it becomes clear how much of a problem it can be if we struggle with numerical information. Life instantly becomes more tedious, and a huge number of work-arounds are needed to make up for this deficit.

Developmental dyscalculia (DD) is a specific learning disorder that prevents the acquisition of basic arithmetic and numerical skills. DD symptoms include severe difficulties in solving arithmetic and mathematical problems. But persons with dyscalculia will also find it difficult to read the time from an analog clock face, have poor memory for number-related facts and dates, will show inappropriate money-related behavior (e.g. handing over a 100 € note when paying €1.49), or mixing up the order of things (Morsanyi, van Bers, O'Connor, & McCormack, 2018). This can have severe effects on daily life, for example, when it comes to financial issues. Dyscalculics will find it difficult to even compare two numbers with each other since these terms do not convey any meaning to them.

DD develops during childhood but often persists into adulthood. Repeated failure in math-related tasks leads to a negative attitude that in some children turns into a specific math anxiety (Ma & Xu, 2004). As children develop math anxiety, their negative emotional state in turn impedes future performance in mathematical contexts. This can create a negative dynamic that is difficult to break up. Not only does this have dramatic consequences for the emotional and psychological development of the affected persons, it also diminishes their chances for succeeding in their professional career, often causing economic issues like higher risk for mortgage default, for example (Gerardi, Goette, & Meier, 2013). In general, lower numeracy levels (i.e. the ability to solve basic mathematical problems) have been shown to result in lower income (Estrada-Mejia, de Vries, & Zeelenberg, 2016) and affect medical decision-making (Reyna, Nelson, Han, & Dieckmann, 2009).

Developmental dyscalculia is a developmental disorder that affects between 4% and 7% of the population, comparable to dyslexia (deficit in reading and writing; Butterworth, Varma, & Laurillard, 2011). Often authors adopt slightly more lenient thresholds for including children in a group with mathematical difficulties. In this case, the term mathematical learning difficulties (MLD) is often used to characterize children in the lower 20% of the distribution on mathematical skills in a given sample or population. However, this threshold can vary between studies from 5% to 25%.

DIAGNOSIS

According to the latest Diagnostic and Statistical Manual of Mental Disorders (DSM-5), dyscalculia is classified as a specific learning disorder. A person must meet the following four criteria to be diagnosed with dyscalculia.

1   Difficulties with understanding number concepts, number facts or calculation, or with mathematical reasoning (e.g. applying math concepts or solving math problems) despite targeted help.

2   Academic skills that are substantially below what is expected for the child's age and cause problems in school, work, or everyday activities.
3   Difficulties start during school age, even if some people don't experience significant problems until adulthood.
4   Learning difficulties are not due to other conditions, such as intellectual disability, vision or hearing problems, a neurological condition (e.g. pediatric stroke), adverse conditions such as economic or environmental disadvantage, lack of instruction, or difficulties in speaking/understanding the language.

As clear-cut as these criteria appear, in particular criterion four can lead to difficulties. This is due to the required discrepancy between general intelligence and number-related performance. The problem is that most multi-faceted intelligence tests (e.g. WISC-V; Wechsler, 2014) also include subscales for numerical performance or use numbers to test working memory. If a child fails at these sub-tests, he or she may receive a below-average IQ that in turn causes the child to fail meeting the fourth criterion. This may, in some cases, prevent the child from being admitted to suited training programs because he or she has not been diagnosed with DD but a general intellectual deficit.

When testing for dyscalculia, we need to differentiate between tests that are based on the country-specific curriculum on one hand and tests that are inspired by neurocognitive models on the other. The first class of tests allows testing of whether a child has met the grade-specific learning objectives. On the downside, these tests are mainly inspired by the curriculum and hence do not allow a fine-grained analysis of the particular difficulties that is needed for the planning of any kind of intervention. This is the main objective of the second class of tests. Neurocognitive tests do allow establishment of a functional profile of the numerical abilities that may then be addressed by tailored interventions.

In a joint effort, 20 German associations and societies (e.g. German Psychological Association, Professional Association of Pediatricians, German Teachers Association) recently published the world's first evidence- and consensus-based S3 guideline on the diagnosis and treatment of dyscalculia (Haberstroh & Schulte-Körne, 2019). In this guideline, the associations reviewed and evaluated existing literature on the diagnosis and treatment of DD. Applying transparent scientific criteria, they agreed on a consensus concerning symptoms, diagnosis, treatment, and comorbidities. This guideline represents an excellent starting point for readers who are interested in more details on DD, in particular (but not limited to) German-speaking readers.

The guideline recommends that testing for dyscalculia needs to be accompanied by a thorough clinical examination to exclude other potential causes of failure in the mathematical context (Haberstroh & Schulte-Körne, 2019). This includes physical and neurological examinations where factors such as brain damage, impaired hearing, or the effects of neurogenetic disorders need to be evaluated. A psychosocial assessment is required that excludes potential factors such as negative learning environment at home, sleep deprivation, prolonged school absence, and socioeconomic status of the family.

There are a number of tests in different languages that allow a detailed analysis of the strengths and weaknesses in several numerical tasks and domains across a wide range of ages. This chapter does not allow delving into the details of the different tests. The interested reader may have a look at the guideline (Haberstroh & Schulte-Körne, 2019) that lists a number of (curriculum-based) tests that are ranked according to their methodological quality. For French-speaking readers, the TEDI-Math and TEDI-Math Grands (Noël & Grégoire, 2015; Van Nieuwenhoven & Noël, 2001) provide a detailed profile of mathematical and numerical competences from preschool to sixth grade. It has been adapted and translated into German and Spanish. In Italian, there is the Numerical Intelligence Battery (Molin, Poli, & Lucangeli, 2007). English-speaking readers could go for the Test of Early Mathematics Ability – 3rd Edition or the Preschool Early Numeracy Scales (Ginsburg & Baroody, 2003; Purpura & Lonigan, 2015). Often subtests and number-specific scales from the Woodcock-Johnson tests of achievement are used to identify DD (Woodcock, McGrew, & Mather, 2001). Caution is required when interpreting single items or subscales since they may not always have been validated according to psychometric standards.

DYSCALCULIA AND OTHER DIFFICULTIES – RELATED OR INDEPENDENT?

Developmental dyscalculia often is diagnosed alongside other difficulties. As research is only emerging, the empirical data remain scant for the moment. Existing data suggest joint occurrence of domain-general as well as domain-specific deficits with DD. Domain-general deficits that have been reported in children with DD include attentional deficits and emotional reactions such as math and test anxiety (Haberstroh & Schulte-Körne, 2019). Dyslexia represents the most prominent domain-specific deficit that is often diagnosed together with DD. The prevalence rate of both dyslexia and dyscalculia are comparably high, with 4–7 out of 100 children being affected. Reformulated as probability, both would have a prevalence between .04 and .07, or an average prevalence rate of .055 $((.04 + .07)/2)$. If both disorders were strictly independent, we would expect an average prevalence rate of .055 × .055 = .003, which corresponds to 3 children in 1000. Instead, roughly 4 children in 100 are diagnosed with both dyscalculia and dyslexia at the same time. This rate is about 13 times higher than would be expected on the basis of independent disorders, providing a strong implication for an association between both disorders. It is important to note that both disorders are not due to low overall intelligence or a generalized learning disorder. Rather, impaired phonological processing may provide a better explanation of this comorbidity (see previous chapters for association between language and math).

ETIOLOGY – WHAT ARE THE UNDERLYING MECHANISMS OF DEVELOPMENTAL DYSCALCULIA?

Different models have been proposed to account for the emergence of developmental dyscalculia. Roughly speaking, the models reflect the ideas that were described in the context of the development of numerical skills (Chapter 5). We can differentiate between models that assume a representational deficit on one side and models that assume a deficit in accessing numerical representations on the other.

THE CORE DEFICIT HYPOTHESIS

One hypothesis that has received massive attention over the last years is the core deficit assumption. The core deficit assumption comes in two flavors. One postulates that DD originates from an impairment in the approximate number system (Piazza, 2010). According to this hypothesis, DD emerges from the impaired scaffold that the ANS provides to the acquisition of numerical skills. In children suffering from DD, the ANS is comparably more imprecise and hence provides only limited support during the acquisition of numerical skills. Butterworth (2010), on the other side, postulates a deficit in a so-called number module that does not allow children to represent exact numerosities. In turn, this prevents children from performing correct arithmetic computations. In support of this hypothesis, researchers found that children with mathematical learning deficits show considerably worse numerosity discrimination performance compared to typically developing children (Mazzocco, Feigenson, & Halberda, 2011; Piazza, 2010). Mussolin, Mejias, and Noël (2010) asked 10-to-11-year-old children with and without DD to compare numerical quantities in symbolic (i.e. Arabic digits, number words, canonical dot sets) and non-symbolic format (i.e. sets of dots). Irrespective of the to-be-compared format, children with DD showed a larger numerical distance effect compared to typically developing children. Overall reaction times of both groups did not differ, speaking against a general deficit in processing speed or comparison processes in and of themselves. Rather, these results provide support for the idea that DD is associated with (or results from) deficits in the ANS. Piazza and colleagues demonstrated that children who suffered from DD were delayed in their refinement of the ANS (Piazza et al., 2010). They assessed ANS acuity by determining the Weber fraction in a numerosity comparison task and found that 10-year-old children suffering from DD showed a Weber fraction that was comparable to 5-year-old typically developing children. Further support for this idea comes from neuroimaging studies that found structural and functional abnormalities in the parietal cortex during numerical processing. Price and colleagues (Price, Holloway, Räsänen, Vester-inen, & Ansari, 2007), for example, compared brain activation of children with DD to typically developing (TD) children who decided which of two numerosities was larger. While TD children showed a standard distance effect in the right parietal cortex, no such effect was observed in children suffering from DD. On the behavioral level, DD children showed a stronger distance effect when response accuracy was analyzed. Hence, a stronger impact of numerical distance on performance is associated with a lack of modulation of parietal activity in the same children. Others have found decreased gray matter volume in right intraparietal sulcus, the anterior cingulum, the left inferior frontal gyrus, and the bilateral middle frontal gyri when comparing DD children with TD children (Rotzer et al., 2008).

Overall, these results are in line with the core deficit hypothesis. There exist, however, a number of findings that are hard to reconcile with this idea. As pointed out by Noël and Rousselle (2011), the temporal cascade of deficits that occur in DD children is not in line with the assumptions of the core deficit hypothesis. Noël and Rousselle analyzed studies that report the results of numerical quantity comparison in both symbolic and non-symbolic notations. They observed that in younger children (<8), TD children did not differ from DD children when comparing non-symbolic numerosities. They did, however, demonstrate impaired *symbolic* number comparison performance. Only in older children (8 years and older), DD children were worse than TD children in comparing both symbolic and non-symbolic quantities. This pattern of results stands in striking contrast to the assumption of the core deficit hypothesis. Why would a symbolic deficit precede a non-symbolic deficit if the ANS is the origin of difficulties in symbolic arithmetic?

Others have pointed out that the Weber fraction is subject to various influences that go beyond the numerical features of the stimuli. That is, multiple studies observed an association between Weber fraction and math skills only for a part of the data set. As described previously, when varying numerosity, non-numerical features automatically and inevitably covary with number. Gilmore and colleagues found a correlation between ANS acuity and arithmetic skills only in incongruent stimulus pairs where the smaller numerosity covered the larger stimulus area (Gilmore et al., 2013). Fuhs and McNeil (2013) found that ANS proficiency only correlated with arithmetic proficiency in trials where surface area was incongruent with numerosity (smaller numerosities cover a larger number of pixels). Similar findings have been reported by Bugden and Ansari (2016). One way to interpret these findings is that this association between ANS acuity and arithmetic is mediated by domain-general executive skills, such as inhibition. Executive skills may be relevant to filter the irrelevant stimulus dimensions and thereby help in attending to the relevant numerical content. De Smedt (De Smedt, Noël, Gilmore, & Ansari, 2013) reviewed 25 studies and only found significant correlations between ANS acuity and arithmetic performance in 11 studies (7 of 18 in children, 4 of 7 in adults). A recent meta-analysis of the association between ANS acuity as measured by Weber fraction and symbolic arithmetic skills estimate the correlation to be r = .20 in cross-sectional studies (Chen & Li, 2014). In prospective studies, ANS acuity predicts arithmetic skills with a correlation of r = .24.

When it comes to brain imaging, the results are equally mixed. While the previously mentioned studies report altered activations and structural parameters for regions that are key to the ANS (i.e. IPS), other studies found diverging results. For example, Iuculano and colleagues (Iuculano et al., 2015) observed increased (rather than decreased) IPS activation in DD children compared with TD children. Aberrant brain activation was also observed in bilateral prefrontal cortices including the dorsolateral and ventrolateral prefrontal cortices, the bilateral anterior insular cortices, the bilateral superior frontal gyri, and the right orbitofrontal cortex (Iuculano et al., 2015). Interestingly, these increased activations normalized after an intervention that provided 8 weeks of one-to-one math tutoring (see subsequently for more details). Similar patterns of compensatory (i.e. increased) parietal activity in DD have been reported by other authors, too (Kaufmann et al., 2009; Rosenberg-Lee et al., 2015). A recent study investigated the brain dynamics of adults with DD during a quantity (symbolic and non-symbolic number) comparison task and compared it to a carefully matched group of controls (Bulthe et al., 2019). They observed no univariate activity differences between the DD group and the control group. Adopting a multivariate approach, they observed less distinguishable neural correlates of non-symbolic quantities in adults with DD. The differential patterns emerged in the anterior parietal cortex and frontal and temporal lobes. No differences were observed for symbolic numbers. These results can be interpreted as supporting the idea that adults suffering from DD exhibit stronger representational overlap between numerosities, leading to reduced discriminability (i.e. impaired ANS). Yet these results were partly observed outside core regions dedicated to the processing of numerosity.

Taken together, the idea that an impaired ANS is responsible for the emergence of DD may not provide a comprehensive explanation for all empirical data available. Nevertheless, the ANS may represent an important stepping stone during numerical development, and its precise functional association with DD needs to be refined in future studies.

ACCESS DEFICIT HYPOTHESIS

A second explanation for the emergence of DD is the so-called access deficit hypothesis (Rousselle & Noël, 2007). According to this idea, children who suffer from DD do have intact numerical core capacities, but they cannot properly access them. Number symbols remain unconnected to their semantic signification.

Support for this idea comes from studies that find children with mathematical learning difficulties in second to fourth grade only were impaired when comparing numerical symbols in terms of numerical magnitude. Numerosity comparison was intact and did not differ from TD children (Rousselle & Noël, 2007). De Smedt and Gilmore (2011) reported that this pattern was already present in first graders with mathematical learning difficulties. MLD children showed deficits in symbolic number comparison and approximate calculation tasks with symbols but no deficits when those tasks were presented in a non-symbolic notation. If DD is associated with deficits in processing numerical symbols rather than non-symbolic numerosities, there should be a correlation of symbolic but not non-symbolic quantity processing with mathematical achievement in the entire population. Indeed, Ansari and colleagues repeatedly observed correlations between symbolic number processing (number knowledge) and mathematical achievement (Holloway & Ansari, 2009; Vanbinst, Ansari, Ghesquiere, & De Smedt, 2016) but failed to find such correlation with numerosity comparison.

Neurofunctional studies also support this idea. What does it mean if we talk about an access deficit at the neural level? One basic idea is to look at how brain regions that are known to be crucial for magnitude processing are interconnected to other parts of the functional network that is involved in arithmetic thinking (e.g. hippocampus, prefrontal cortex, left-hemispheric language areas). The results by Rosenberg-Lee and colleagues can be interpreted in this way since they observed an increased functional connectivity of the IPS with frontal regions in 7-to-9-year-old children who were in the lowest quartile (lowest 25%) of a standardized math test compared to control children. In detail, Rosenberg-Lee and colleagues found bilateral IPS to exhibit stronger functional connectivity with bilateral middle, superior and left inferior frontal gyri, bilateral supramarginal and angular gyri, as well as ventral medial prefrontal cortex and anterior and posterior cingulate cortex (Rosenberg-Lee et al., 2015). These brain regions can be classified as being part of two large-scale functional networks in the brain, the default mode network (DMN) and the task-positive network (TPN). The DMN comprises a number of regions that are tightly interconnected during rest but deactivate as soon as a person engages in a cognitively demanding activity. The TPN, in turn, is the network that becomes active as soon as a person engages in a cognitive task. Interestingly, stronger functional connectivity during solving of subtraction and addition problems was not associated with successful behavioral performance. That is, despite a greater neural effort (hyper-connectivity and hyperactivation of IPS), low-achieving children displayed poorer performance in symbolic arithmetic. Aberrant connectivity of IPS with these two networks implies that children with mathematical difficulties (a) have trouble disengaging the DMN and (b) engage in compensatory activation in the TPN during arithmetic quantity processing.

Finally, the previously mentioned study by Bulthé and colleagues (2019) reported increased functional connectivity between occipital and temporal brain regions during the processing of Arabic number symbols that might reflect compensatory Arabic symbol deciphering processes in adults with DD.

The access deficit hypothesis provides an interesting alternative explanation for some of the data that are inconsistent with the core deficit hypothesis. The main problems with this hypothesis are: (1)

the difficulties in measuring directional connectivity patterns in fMRI that would allow establishing a causal role for deficient IPS connectivity in the emergence of DD. The neural hypotheses and the access deficit idea also assume a localized number module in IPS, which may be an overly simplistic assumption. (2) The lack of longitudinal data from children with DD that include indices for both non-symbolic and symbolic number understanding.

SYSTEMIC MODELS OF DD

Both approaches (core deficit hypothesis and access deficit hypothesis) can be characterized as domain-specific models of DD. Both focus on either the representation of numerical quantities or deficient access via symbols to explain DD. However, mental arithmetic is a complex cognitive process that recruits a variety of domain-specific and domain-general processes. These rely, in turn, on a variety of brain systems inside and outside the parietal cortex. Most of the hitherto cited studies focus on areas that have been shown to be crucially involved in numerical cognition, therefore adopting a domain-specific approach to explain DD.

Adopting a systemic approach, Menon and Iuculano propose that DD may arise from deficits in various brain systems that jointly contribute to mathematical cognition (Iuculano, 2016; Iuculano & Menon, 2018; Iuculano, Padmanabhan, & Menon, 2018). In line with the interactive specialization framework of development (Johnson, Halit, Grice, & Karmiloff-Smith, 2002), "developmental disorders follow a different developmental trajectory from typical development and thus are characterized by subtle, but diffuse, rather than gross and focal, functional (and structural) abnormalities" (p. 316). This includes systems that represent numerical content, higher-order visual symbols, and their interaction that mediates the association between symbols and semantic representation. Deficits in domain-general cognitive modules that orchestrate the learning of rules and principles such as working memory or attentional processing can potentially contribute to the development of DD. Finally, alterations in the medial temporal lobe (hippocampus) may lead to difficulties in acquiring and maintaining arithmetic facts in memory.

The results of a recent intervention study are in line with this view. Iuculano and colleagues (2015) used a variety of math games in a one-on-one tutoring program for children with mathematical learning difficulties. These games included:

> Math Bingo in which the child has to calculate the sum of a given problem and verify whether the answer is on their Bingo card, Math War in which the child competes with the tutor to get the highest sum from their decks of cards, and Treasure Hunt in which the child has to calculate the answer of a given problem, and write down both the equation and its correct solution on the stepping stones of the 'treasure map' to get to the treasure chest.
>
> (p. 3)

While MLD children were considerably worse than TD children in solving arithmetic problems, there were no accuracy differences after tutoring between both groups. As described previously, the pre-training fMRI data revealed significantly stronger activation in a widespread network of regions important for arithmetic problem solving when comparing MLD to TD children. After interventions, this hyperactivation disappeared. The tutoring led to a normalization of brain activation in MLD children whose patterns of brain activation were indistinguishable from TD children after tutoring – even at a fine-grained multivariate pattern level of analysis. To sum up, this study reveals that deviations in a widespread network of brain regions normalize after tutoring.

In general, this view might explain the heterogeneity of the observed functional and structural deviations that were observed in children and adults with DD. Focused analysis of the central regions in number processing did not reveal a unanimous picture, showing hyperactivations (DD > TD) as well as hypoactivations (DD < TD) in the IPS and other parietal regions. A similar picture holds true for structural deviations, where some studies observed lower gray and white matter volume in parietal cortex (Rotzer et al., 2008; Rykhlevskaia, Uddin, Kondos, & Menon, 2009), while others did not. Structural connectivity deficits (i.e. reduced fractional anisotropy of fiber tracts) involving the parietal cortex have sometimes been reported (Kucian et al., 2014) and sometimes were absent in the examined samples

(Moreau, Wilson, McKay, Nihill, & Waldie, 2018). This points to a complex picture of altered balance between multiple brain systems that need to be well orchestrated during complex cognitive activities such as numerical cognition. Hypo- or hyperactivity in any of the brain circuits involved may lead to an overall dysfunction at the behavioral level. Hence, understanding how different brain systems contribute to numerical cognition will be key in understanding the origins of DD.

Compared to accounts that focus on parietal (dys)function, the systemic view is a more realistic approach that respects the complexity of the relation between brain activation patterns and the behavioral phenotype. The comorbidity of DD with other dysfunctions such as dyslexia or ADHD also points to origins outside the core numerical domain, including learning circuits of the hippocampus (Skeide, Evans, Mei, Abrams, & Menon, 2018).

On the downside, our understanding of the specific interaction between different brain circuits is still emerging and far from complete. There is, for example, an important gap in spatial resolution between the accurate recordings of single units and the functional data from fMRI studies, where a single voxel can easily contain 100,000 neurons whose activity is only roughly estimated at a global level. Only with a comprehensive understanding of the neurofunctional underpinnings of numerical and mathematical cognition can we develop specific hypotheses about the subtle dysbalances that may lead to DD.

When considering the correlation between structural brain parameters and cognitive functions, one should always keep in mind the correlational character of the associations. That is, a given difference in brain structure between TD and DD children may well represent the cause of the functional difference that emerges at the behavioral level. However, it may also be possible that the structural deviance is a consequence of an altered cognitive dynamic that recruits different brain circuits (Jolles et al., 2016).

In sum, there is progress in identifying the cognitive and neural mechanisms leading to DD, but we are still a long way from having a comprehensive understanding of the origins of this disorder. The development of a coherent theoretical framework for the emergence of DD is crucial for designing targeted interventions that successfully remedy DD.

TREATMENT OF DEVELOPMENTAL DYSCALCULIA

DD is a learning disorder that persists if not treated adequately. For the moment being, it remains unclear, however, what treatment is the most promising. We are only beginning to systematically examine the different programs in a way that fulfills established scientific standards. To conclusively evaluate the effects of a given intervention, the minimal study design requires (a) a test group who is assigned to a standardized intervention program, (b) a control group who receives a comparable intervention targeting a different cognitive function that is ideally not related to the function aimed at by the test group, and (c) a pre–post design in which the performance of both groups is measured before (pre) and after (post) the intervention using standardized tests. Ideally, the persistence of the effect of the intervention is measured in a follow-up testing session after several weeks, months, or even years.

The number of studies that systematically investigated the effects of specific interventions on DD is extremely small due to the relatively low prevalence rate of 3% to 7%. In order to include a group of 50 children with DD, one would have to potentially screen as many as 1700 children. Hence, researchers included children with mathematical learning difficulties in their studies. With this more lenient definition, Monei and Pedro (2017) identified 11 studies. Dennies and colleagues (2016) identified 25 studies published between 2000 and 2014 that report the effects of specific interventions on children (Kindergarten–fifth grade) with mathematical difficulties. They found an average effect size of g = 0.53 (95% CI = 0.36–1.07). This is generally classified as a medium effect size and means that children's performance improved by roughly half a standard deviation. Interventions at the elementary level were more effective compared to those at Kindergarten level. Children with a percentile rank (PR) below 35 (i.e. they were among the lowest 35% of the sample) benefitted more from intervention. Interventions that were provided by researchers or researcher-trained graduate assistants had a higher impact compared to computer-based training or teachers. This represents a particular challenge when considering the up-scaling of interventions, that is, expanding the number of schools and/or districts using an intervention and holding everything else constant. The estimated effect size varied as a function of the dependent measure employed. Interventions measuring early numeracy only had an effect size of g = 0.36 (95% CI = 0.26–0.46), while interventions that measured algebra (g = 0.73; 95% CI = 0.53–0.93) or computation (g = 0.75; 95% CI = 0.48–1.01) were found to be more effective.

Mononen et al. (Mononen, Aunio, Kopnonen, & Aro, 2014) reviewed the effects of 19 interventions for very young children in Kindergarten or first years of school (4 to 7 years) at risk for DD. They differentiated between core interventions and supplemental interventions. Core interventions target all children in a given classroom setting, usually during schooling hours (e.g. replacing regular teaching hours). Supplemental interventions are given in small groups or individually in addition to the regular curriculum. The average effect sizes for 19 studies were g = 0.76 and g = 0.62 for comparisons to active and passive control groups, respectively. However, the studies only unsystematically provided information about whether the program succeeded in reducing or even eliminating the performance gap between at-risk children and TD children. At the moment of writing this chapter, a number of review articles on this issue are due, notably by Sarah Powell and colleagues.

Two classes of interventions can be identified in the literature. First, interventions target multiple arithmetic and numerical skills by practicing tasks and elaborating procedures. Second, basic core numerical capacities are trained in order to foster the putative underlying numerical concepts at a basic level (e.g. ANS). While the number of studies remains limited, I cannot describe all of the studies in detail here. I will focus on recent examples for each of these two categories.

MULTIPLE SKILL PROGRAMS

One recent study investigated the effects of a program that intended to increase early numerical skills in low-performing Kindergartners (Toll & Van Luit, 2012). Although not formally diagnosed with DD, these 25 children were in the lowest quartile on the standardized Early Numeracy Test (Van Luit & Van de Rijt, 2009) and at risk for DD since Kindergarten numeracy has been shown to be predictive of later math performance (Mazzocco & Thompson, 2005).

The Road To Mathematics (TRTM) program consists of exercises in nine domains of numerical skills, covering math language use (number words, ordinal position words), reasoning skills (e.g. comparison), verbal counting, concrete counting, structures (dice, fingers), number symbols, measuring (distance estimation), number lines, and simple calculations (addition and subtraction). TRTM was administered over the duration of sixteen 30-minute sessions, administered twice a week outside classroom. TRTM was administered to small groups (three to four children) by trained supervisors. TRTM was also administered to a group of children who performed just below average (25th–50th PR). Two control groups with equally low or below-average performance did not receive any additional training. Finally, there was a group of typically achieving children in this study. TRTM adopts a concrete–representational–abstract (CRA) scheme, according to which internalization is facilitated by a sequence of three levels during which children first ("doing") use tangible objects (e.g. blocks, fingers), then ("seeing") visually represent the problem with semi-concrete symbols (e.g. dice, tallies) or pictures. In the final step ("symbolic"), the problem is represented using abstract symbols (e.g. numbers, mathematical symbols, letters). Results showed that children in the intervention group achieved the largest performance gains when comparing pre- to post-test scores. However, the difference between very low-performing children in the intervention group and those in the control group did not reach statistical significance, contrary to the below-average groups. Hence, the TRTM program was effective only for children who performed just below average – not for those at risk due to very low performance (< 25th PR). These results illustrate the difficulties in designing and evaluating the impact of standardized programs. In fact, only very few programs report the results from randomized controlled trials and even fewer show positive effects that persist over time.

The group around Lynn and Doug Fuchs has developed a number of math interventions for different topics and grades (see link to their website at the end of the chapter). One of them is Pirate Math that focuses on "single-digit and double-digit word problems of three types: total problems (where parts are combined to result in a total), difference problems (where quantities are compared to result in a difference), and change problems (where an event happens to change a starting amount, which results in an ending amount)." To evaluate Pirate Math, Fuchs and colleagues (Fuchs et al., 2010) trained children with MLD with strategic counting strategies (counting from the max in addition or missing addend strategy in subtraction) in order to improve number combination (NC) skills (i.e. simple addition and subtraction word problems). One hundred fifty students were stratified according to their MD status (MD alone or MD with reading difficulties) and then randomly assigned to control (no tutoring) or one of two variants of NC remediation procedures (with and without deliberate practice). The training procedures were part of Pirate Math. In the variant without practice, the focus on NCs was limited to a single lesson on strategic counting. The variant with deliberate practice involved additional 4 to 6 minutes of practice per session. The training covered 16 weeks, three 20- to 30-minute sessions a week. The additional practice variant group improved compared to the no tutoring control group ($d = 0.67$) but also outperformed the intervention group without deliberate practice ($d = 0.22$). This underlines the additional value of deliberate practice over and above training procedures. Looking from a different angle, the group without deliberate practice received only a single session of instruction on the counting strategies. "After this lesson, tutors did not review the strategies; they did not demonstrate the strategies; they did not provide practice to contextualize the use of the strategies; they did not prompt students to use counting strategies to correct NC errors" (p. 97). Nevertheless, this intervention group improved by almost half a standard deviation compared to the control group.

Other interventions from this group focus on fluency in addition and subtraction in first graders (Number Rocket), or fraction understanding in fourth graders (Fraction Face-Off!). Fuchs and colleagues (Fuchs, Malone, Schumacher, Namkung, & Wang, 2017) summarize the findings from five randomized controlled trials on "Fraction Face-Off!" targeting children at risk as defined by being in the lowest 35% at the beginning of fourth grade in the Wide Range Achievement Test – 4 (Wilkinson & Robertson, 2006). The intervention mainly focused on fostering the understanding of fraction magnitude, for example, by using a number line task where children have to place a fraction on a labeled line. The control condition mainly focused on a part-whole interpretation of fractions, which involves understanding a fraction as one or more equal parts of a single object (e.g. in a pie chart). Children in the control condition were also less often required to explicitly explain work. Fractions Face-Off! sessions occurred three times per week for 12 weeks with pairs of children. Fuchs and colleagues (Fuchs et al., 2016) describe the intervention as follows:

> tutors modeled a 4-step problem-solving sequence, gradually transferring responsibility to students while scaffolding to ensure understanding. In the first step, students wrote whether the fractions had the same denominator ("same D"), the same numerator ("same N"), or different numerators and denominators ("both diff"). In the second step, students explained why a good drawing shows two units of the same size, with each unit divided into the correct number of parts, with all parts in each unit the same size, and with the correct number of parts shaded. In the third step, students labeled each drawing of a fraction with its numerical value and described how the parts in the fractions compared ("same size parts" to indicate each unit was divided into the same number of parts or "bigger parts" to indicate the fraction with fewer parts had bigger parts). When numerators and denominators both differed, students rewrote ½ so both fractions had the same denominator and updated the picture to show how ½ is equivalent to the original fraction and how finding a common denominator allowed them to compare two fractions with the same size parts. Then students circled the larger fraction. In the final step, students wrote a short sentence or phrase to explain why the circled fraction was greater [. . .]. Tutors provided corrective feedback as needed. [. . .] Later lessons focused on discriminating between viable explanations for same denominator versus same numerator problems. Tutors solved a same denominator and same numerator problem side by side. Students highlighted and discussed important distinctions between the problem types. Note, however, that we did not incorporate schema-based instruction into self-explaining (i.e. students did not classify problems into problem types prior to formulating explanations).

Children who received training on fraction magnitude understanding outperformed children from the control group on a number line task (g = 0.94) that was not part of the training, illustrating some near transfer. The intervention also improved children's performance on addition and subtraction of fractions (g = 1.72). This improvement narrowed the achievement gap between at-risk children and TD children by 0.99 SD at post-test. Authors also report that the intervention was successful in most but not all students. In particular, those children who performed below 13th PR did not catch up entirely and failed to show normalized performance in the National Assessment of Educational Progress (NAEP).

Re and colleagues (Re, Pedron, Tressoldi, & Laucangeli, 2014) assigned 35 children from third to fifth grade with MLD and 19 children with DD either to an individualized (10 DD; 17 MLD) training condition or a control condition (9 DD; 18 MLD). Children were assessed with a standardized test battery for arithmetic performance that included mental calculation (addition, subtraction), written calculation (addition, subtraction, multiplication, division), number comparison, digit transcoding (e.g. "Write as Arabic digit: We have 3 tens, 8 units, and 2 hundreds!"), and number ordering. Children who scored below 1.5 SD in four or more (three or less) out of six subtests but had IQ in the normal range were diagnosed as DD (MLD). In the individualized training, children were trained according to an individual profile. Improvement was assessed in four fundamental calculation skills: number concepts, arithmetic fact retrieval, mental calculation, and written calculation. In addition, metacognitive skills were trained, for example, by asking the children to summarize what they had learned at the end of a given lesson. Children in the control condition worked on the same topics but less tailored to individual strengths and weaknesses. Rather, activities were adapted to the grade-specific curriculum. Compared to the control group, the intervention had clinically relevant effects in both children with DD and MLD. The strongest effect sizes (improvement from pre- to post-test, compared to control group) were observed in written calculation and numerical knowledge (all ds > 1.22). Calculation time in DD did not improve (d = 0.06), while mental calculation errors decreased in both DD (d = 0.32) and MLD (d = 0.95). This study demonstrates that individually tailored training intervention has a more positive effect than additional (i.e. outside regular class) general training of curriculum-relevant issues. This underlines the importance of a detailed assessment of the child's mathematical profile as the basis for subsequent interventions.

There exist a large number intervention programs that target multiple numerical and arithmetic skills. However, most of the programs have not undergone scientific evaluation in randomized controlled trials. To evaluate which programs work and which were subject to scientific testing, interested readers may visit the What Works Clearinghouse (WWC) website (http://whatworks.ed.gov/). WWC describes and evaluates the scientific evidence for the effect of a number of programs in various areas such as mathematics (https://ies.ed.gov/ncee/wwc/FWW/Results?filters=,Math), literacy, or science. Programs are evaluated as having "positive or potentially positive" or "mixed" effects. Unfortunately, the list is not exhaustive and shows the tremendous lack of empirical evidence for the various listed programs.

INTERVENTIONS TARGETING CORE NUMERICAL SKILLS

In line with the core deficit hypothesis, some programs focus on enhancing the core capacities, such as the ANS.

Räsänen and colleagues tested the effects of a computer-assisted intervention program (Number Race; https://sourceforge.net/projects/numberrace/) on 30 Kindergartners with low numeracy skills. The Number Race "trains children on an entertaining numerical comparison task. [. . .] The child is instructed to select more from two options presented either as dots, numbers or as addition or subtraction tasks. When the number symbols or calculations are presented, they are at first accompanied with dot patterns" (p. 457). To enhance the ANS, number comparison is the main component of the adaptive program that adapts difficulty such that children always perform around 75% correct. The children in the control group engaged in a computerized intervention that focused on matching of verbal labels to visual patterns and symbols (Graphogame Math). Children from the intervention groups performed – on average – one SD below TD children in various mathematical tests (counting, subitizing, number comparison, arithmetic). The effects of the intervention were small and relatively short lived. Both interventions led to response time improvements on a number comparison task that reduced the gap between TD and low numeracy children. None of the groups did, however, catch up with the TD children. The Number Race had a stronger effect on number comparison items with a large numerical distance compared to Graphogame. This differential improvement was present only at post-intervention assessment and had vanished 3 weeks later. Compared to pre-intervention performance, the Number Race had only a small effect on arithmetic performance immediately after intervention ($g = 0.22$; 95% CI = -0.40–0.85) and even a slightly detrimental effect 3 weeks later ($g = -0.64$; 95% CI = -1.27–0.0). The same tendency was observed for the Graphogame intervention (immediate effect: $g = -0.12$; 95% CI = -0.74–0.51; 3 weeks later: $g = -0.22$; 95% CI = -0.85–0.4). Hence, the Number Race only had small and short-lived effects on number comparison performance that did not transfer to arithmetic performance.

Hellstrand and colleagues (Hellstrand, Korhonen, Linnanmäki, & Aunio, 2019) tested the effect of a more recent version of the Number Race (continuous number line, updated graphical design, focus on counting on rather than counting from the start; www.thenumberrace.com/nr/home.php) on low-performing first-graders ($n = 29$). The study comprised two control groups, a low-performing control group ($n = 27$) and a TD control group ($n = 334$), both of which did not receive additional training besides standard schooling. Differences in math performance between low-achieving groups and TD group persisted throughout the study (pre- and post-intervention). No difference was found between low-achieving groups – neither before nor after intervention. Hence, this study failed to observe any significant intervention effect on mathematical performance.

These results contrast with the benefits that have been observed in a study with low-achieving children (Szkudlarek & Brannon, 2018) and typically achieving children who received training on approximate number understanding (Obersteiner, Reiss, & Ufer, 2013; Park, Bermudez, Roberts, & Brannon, 2016; Sella, Tressoldi, Lucangeli, & Zorzi, 2016) or adult students (Park & Brannon, 2013, 2014). From the description of the Number Race, it also becomes clear that it affects more than only the core ANS. Displaying number symbols alongside non-symbolic quantities may as well improve the association between a given numerosity and its associated symbolic representation.

The Swiss computer-based intervention program Calcularis (https://dybuster.com/de/calcularis/) targets both core numerical competencies and arithmetic skills from first grade to adulthood. It adopts a personalized approach (student model), and progress is adapted to the individual learning rate. In an fMRI study (Kucian et al., 2011), DD children were tested before and after training with a precursor version of Calcularis. Before intervention, DD children exhibited less parietal and increased prefrontal activity during mental arithmetic. Training induced a decrease in frontal and parietal activity in both control and intervention groups. In a follow-up measurement after 5 weeks, an increase of parietal activity was observed in DD children. Behaviorally, the training showed positive effects in standardized tests and variance in the number line task (Kaser et al., 2013).

Finally, in direct comparison of the core deficit hypothesis and the access deficit hypothesis, Van Herwegen and colleagues (Van Herwegen, Costa, Nicholson, & Donlan, 2018) pitted the impact of symbolic versus non-symbolic training against each other. They randomly assigned low-achieving preschoolers who were below chance in a numerosity comparison task to either a program that focused on non-symbolic abilities (numerosity estimation; numerosity comparison/matching) or on symbolic number skills (digit ordering; counting; digit detection in a text). Non-symbolic training improved ANS abilities as well as symbolic abilities. Likewise, symbolic training improved both symbolic abilities and ANS abilities.

As is the case for studies that target multiple number skills, more research and randomized controlled trials are necessary to understand these discrepancies and the determinants of successful intervention effects.

SUMMARY

Although the number of published studies on DD increased over the last 10 years, there is still a dramatic lack of empirical studies on this topic. This holds true for all of the mentioned areas of research (diagnosis, etiology, intervention). It is still unclear, for example, whether there exist different subtypes of DD or whether it is a unitary disorder. The current models for the etiology of DD are not yet able to explain the entire pattern of empirical findings. One issue that makes research in math more arduous than in reading, for example, is that the curriculum is more rich and includes a large variety of different topics from place-value system to fractions and algebra. Without a good model that guides the development of remediation programs, it remains unclear which factors determine success or failure of existing interventions. Empirical data from randomized controlled studies are required to evaluate the effect of a given intervention. Unfortunately, most of the existing programs have been developed by practitioners without adopting an empirical evaluation approach. This makes it difficult for teachers or parents to choose adapted programs or develop targeted exercises. The National Center on Intensive Intervention at the American Institutes for Research provides some guidelines that may be useful in this context (https://intensiveintervention.org/intensive-intervention-math-course).

- Developmental dyscalculia is a specific learning disorder that prevents the acquisition of basic arithmetic and numerical skills.
- Four criteria determine the diagnosis of DD:
  - o Difficulties with understanding number concepts
  - o Low academic skills
  - o Onset of difficulties during school age
  - o Learning difficulties are not due to other conditions, such as intellectual disability
- The core deficit hypothesis postulates that DD results from a deficient core number understanding (ANS or number module).
- The access deficit hypothesis assumes that core number understanding is intact but cannot be associated with numerical symbols.
- The systemic view assumes that DD results from a dysbalance of cortical systems that contribute to mental arithmetic.
- There is a lack of controlled studies that evaluate the success of intervention programs.
- Programs that individually determine deficits and target those in a systematic fashion showed positive effects.
- Programs that target core deficits show mixed effects. The factors that determine a successful intervention remain to be identified.

FURTHER READINGS AND RESOURCES

The review by Kucian and von Aster (2015), as well as the recently published paper by Haberstroh and Schulte-Körne (2019), provide a good first overview.

The International Handbook of Dyscalculia and Mathematical Learning Difficulties contains some interesting chapters for a more in-depth view on selected topics (Quinn, 2015).

The website www.dyscalculia.org provides information about DD, its symptoms, diagnosis, and remediation programs. The websites of Sarah Powell (www.sarahpowellphd.com/home.html) and the Fuchs laboratory (https://frg.vkcsites.org/) by Lynn and Doug Fuchs provide useful information on various training programs for children with difficulties in math or reading.

REFERENCES

Bugden, S., & Ansari, D. (2016). Probing the nature of deficits in the 'approximate number system" in children with persistent developmental dyscalculia. *Dev Sci, 19*(5), 817–833. doi:10.1111/desc.12324

Bulthe, J., Prinsen, J., Vanderauwera, J., Duyck, S., Daniels, N., Gillebert, C. R., . . . De Smedt, B. (2019). Multi-method brain imaging reveals impaired representations of number as well as altered connectivity in adults with dyscalculia. *Neuroimage, 190*, 289–302. doi:10.1016/j.neuroimage.2018.06.012

Butterworth, B. (2010). Foundational numerical capacities and the origins of dyscalculia. *Trends Cogn Sci, 14*(12), 534–541. doi:10.1016/j.tics.2010.09.007

Butterworth, B., Varma, S., & Laurillard, D. (2011). Dyscalculia: From brain to education. *Science, 332*(6033), 1049–1053. doi:10.1126/science.1201536

Chen, Q., & Li, J. (2014). Association between individual differences in non-symbolic number acuity and math performance: A meta-analysis. *Acta Psychol (Amst), 148*, 163–172. https://doi.org/10.1016/j.actpsy.2014.01.016

De Smedt, B., & Gilmore, C. K. (2011). Defective number module or impaired access? Numerical magnitude processing in first graders with mathematical difficulties. *J Exp Child Psychol, 108*(2), 278–292. doi:10.1016/j.jecp.2010.09.003

De Smedt, B., Noël, M.-P., Gilmore, C., & Ansari, D. (2013). How do symbolic and non-symbolic numerical magnitude processing skills relate to individual differences in children's mathematical skills? A review of evidence from brain and behavior. *Trends Neurosci Educ, 2*(2), 48–55. doi:10.1016/j.tine.2013.06.001

Dennis, M. S., Sharp, E., Chovanes, J., Thomas, A., Burns, R. M., Custer, B., & Park, J. (2016). A meta-analysis of empirical research on teaching students with mathematics learning difficulties. *Learn Disab Res Pract, 31*(3), 156–168. doi:10.1111/ldrp.12107

Estrada-Mejia, C., de Vries, M., & Zeelenberg, M. (2016). Numeracy and wealth. *J Econ Psychol, 54*, 53–63. doi:10.1016/j.joep.2016.02.011

Fuchs, L. S., Malone, A. S., Schumacher, R. F., Namkung, J., Hamlett, C. L., Jordan, N. C., . . . Changas, P. (2016). Supported self-explaining during fraction intervention. *J Educ Psychol, 108*, 493–508.

Fuchs, L. S., Malone, A. S., Schumacher, R. F., Namkung, J., & Wang, A. (2017). Fraction intervention for students with mathematics difficulties: Lessons learned from five randomized controlled trials. *J Learn Disabil, 50*(6), 631–639. doi:10.1177/0022219416677249

Fuchs, L. S., Powell, S. R., Seethaler, P. M., Cirino, P. T., Fletcher, J. M., Fuchs, D., & Hamlett, C. L. (2010). The effects of strategic counting instruction, with and without deliberate practice, on number combination skill among students with mathematics difficulties. *Learn Individ Differ, 20*(2), 89–100. doi:10.1016/j.lindif.2009.09.003

Fuhs, M. W., & McNeil, N. M. (2013). ANS acuity and mathematics ability in preschoolers from low-income homes: Contributions of inhibitory control. *Dev Sci, 16*(1), 136–148. doi:10.1111/desc.12013

Gerardi, K., Goette, L., & Meier, S. (2013). Numerical ability predicts mortgage default. *Proc Natl Acad Sci USA, 110*(28), 11267–11271. doi:10.1073/pnas.1220568110

Gilmore, C., Attridge, N., Clayton, S., Cragg, L., Johnson, S., Marlow, N., . . . Inglis, M. (2013). Individual differences in inhibitory control, not non-verbal number acuity, correlate with mathematics achievement. *PLOS ONE, 8*(6), e67374. doi:10.1371/journal.pone.0067374

Ginsburg, H. P., & Baroody, A. J. (2003). *TEMA – Test of Early Mathematical Abilities* (3rd ed.). Austin, TX: Pro-ed.

Haberstroh, S., & Schulte-Körne, G. (2019). The diagnosis and treatment of dyscalculia. *Dtsch Arztebl International, 116*(7), 107–114. doi:10.3238/arztebl.2019.0107

Hellstrand, H., Korhonen, J., Linnanmäki, K., & Aunio, P. (2019). The Number Race – Computer-assisted intervention for mathematically low-performing first graders. *Eur J Spec Need Educ*, 1–15. doi:10.1080/13488678.2019.1615792

Holloway, I. D., & Ansari, D. (2009). Mapping numerical magnitudes onto symbols: The numerical distance effect and individual differences in children's mathematics achievement. *J Exp Child Psychol, 103*(1), 17–29. doi:10.1016/j.jecp.2008.04.001

Iuculano, T. (2016). Neurocognitive accounts of developmental dyscalculia and its remediation. *Prog Brain Res, 227*, 305–333. doi:10.1016/bs.pbr.2016.04.024

Iuculano, T., & Menon, V. (2018). *Development of mathematical reasoning* (S. Ghetti, Ed., Vol. 4). Hoboken, NJ: John Wiley & Sons.

Iuculano, T., Padmanabhan, A., & Menon, V. (2018). Chapter 15 – Systems neuroscience of mathematical cognition and learning: Basic organization and neural sources of heterogeneity in typical and atypical development. In A. Henik &

W. Fias (Eds.), *Heterogeneity of function in numerical cognition* (pp. 287–336). Academic Press, London, UK.

Iuculano, T., Rosenberg-Lee, M., Richardson, J., Tenison, C., Fuchs, L., Supekar, K., & Menon, V. (2015). Cognitive tutoring induces widespread neuroplasticity and remediates brain function in children with mathematical learning disabilities. *Nat Commun, 6*, 8453. doi:10.1038/ncomms9453

Johnson, M. H., Halit, H., Grice, S. J., & Karmiloff-Smith, A. (2002). Neuroimaging of typical and atypical development: A perspective from multiple levels of analysis. *Dev Psychopathol, 14*(3), 521–536. doi:10.1017/S0954579402003073

Jolles, D., Ashkenazi, S., Kochalka, J., Evans, T., Richardson, J., Rosenberg-Lee, M., . . . Menon, V. (2016). Parietal hyper-connectivity, aberrant brain organization, and circuit-based biomarkers in children with mathematical disabilities. *Dev Sci, 19*(4), 613–631. doi:10.1111/desc.12399

Kaser, T., Baschera, G. M., Kohn, J., Kucian, K., Richtmann, V., Grond, U., . . . von Aster, M. (2013). Design and evaluation of the computer-based training program Calcularis for enhancing numerical cognition. *Front Psychol, 4*, 489. doi:10.3389/fpsyg.2013.00489

Kaufmann, L., Vogel, S. E., Starke, M., Kremser, C., Schocke, M., & Wood, G. (2009). Developmental dyscalculia: Compensatory mechanisms in left intraparietal regions in response to nonsymbolic magnitudes. *Behav Brain Funct, 5*, 35. doi:10.1186/1744-9081-5-35

Kucian, K., Ashkenazi, S. S., Hänggi, J., Rotzer, S., Jäncke, L., Martin, E., & von Aster, M. (2014). Developmental dyscalculia: A dysconnection syndrome? *Brain Struct Funct, 219*(5), 1721–1733. doi:10.1007/s00429-013-0597-4

Kucian, K., Grond, U., Rotzer, S., Henzi, B., Schonmann, C., Plangger, F., . . . von Aster, M. (2011). Mental number line training in children with developmental dyscalculia. *Neuroimage, 57*(3), 782–795. doi:10.1016/j.neuroimage.2011.01.070

Kucian, K., & von Aster, M. (2015). Developmental dyscalculia. *Eur J Pediatr, 174*(1), 1–13. doi:10.1007/s00431-014-2455-7

Ma, X., & Xu, J. M. (2004). The causal ordering of mathematics anxiety and mathematics achievement: A longitudinal panel analysis. *J Adolesc, 27*(2), 165–179. doi:10.1016/j.adolescence.2003.11.003

Mazzocco, M. M., Feigenson, L., & Halberda, J. (2011). Preschoolers' precision of the approximate number system predicts later school mathematics performance. *PLOS ONE, 6*(9), e23749. doi:10.1371/journal.pone.0023749

Mazzocco, M. M., & Thompson, R. E. (2005). Kindergarten predictors of math learning disability. *Learn Disabil Res Pract, 20*(3), 142–155. doi:10.1111/j.1540-5826.2005.00129.x

Molin, A., Poli, D., & Lucangeli, D. (2007). *BIN – Batteria intelligenza numerica*. Trento, Italy: Erickson.

Monei, T., & Pedro, A. (2017). A systematic review of interventions for children presenting with dyscalculia in primary schools. *Educ Psychol Practic, 33*(3), 277–293. doi:10.1080/02667363.2017.1289076

Mononen, R., Aunio, P., Kopnonen, T., & Aro, M. (2014). A review of early numeracy interventions for children at risk in mathematics. *International Journal of Early Childhood Special Education, 6*(1), 25–54.

Moreau, D., Wilson, A. J., McKay, N. S., Nihill, K., & Waldie, K. E. (2018). No evidence for systematic white matter correlates of dyslexia and dyscalculia. *Neuroimage Clin, 18,* 356–366. doi:10.1016/j.nicl.2018.02.004

Morsanyi, K., van Bers, B. M. C. W., O'Connor, P. A., & McCormack, T. (2018). developmental dyscalculia is characterized by order processing deficits: Evidence from numerical and non-numerical ordering tasks. *Dev Neuropsychol, 43*(7), 595–621. doi:10.1080/87565641.2018.1502294

Mussolin, C., Mejias, S., & Noël, M. P. (2010). Symbolic and nonsymbolic number comparison in children with and without dyscalculia. *Cognition, 115*(1), 10–25. doi:10.1016/j.cognition.2009.10.006

Noël, M. P., & Grégoire, J. (2015). *TediMath Grands, Test diagnostique des compétences de base en mathématiques du CE2 à la 5e.* Pearson, Montreuil, France.

Noël, M. P., & Rousselle, L. (2011). Developmental changes in the profiles of dyscalculia: An explanation based on a double exact-and-approximate number representation model. *Front Hum Neurosci, 5,* 165. doi:10.3389/fnhum.2011.00165

Obersteiner, A., Reiss, K., & Ufer, S. (2013). How training on exact or approximate mental representations of number can enhance first-grade students' basic number processing and arithmetic skills. *Learn Instr, 23,* 125–135. doi:10.1016/j.learninstruc.2012.08.004

Park, J., Bermudez, V., Roberts, R. C., & Brannon, E. M. (2016). Non-symbolic approximate arithmetic training improves math performance in preschoolers. *J Exp Child Psychol, 152,* 278–293. doi:10.1016/j.jecp.2016.07.011

Park, J., & Brannon, E. M. (2013). Training the approximate number system improves math proficiency. *Psychol Sci, 24*(10), 2013–2019. doi:10.1177/0956797613482944

Park, J., & Brannon, E. M. (2014). Improving arithmetic performance with number sense training: An investigation of underlying mechanism. *Cognition, 133*(1), 188–200. doi:10.1016/j.cognition.2014.06.011

Piazza, M. (2010). Neurocognitive start-up tools for symbolic number representations. *Trends Cogn Sci, 14*(12), 542–551. doi:10.1016/j.tics.2010.09.008

Piazza, M., Facoetti, A., Trussardi, A. N., Berteletti, I., Conte, S., Lucangeli, D., . . . Zorzi, M. (2010). Developmental trajectory of number acuity reveals a severe impairment in developmental dyscalculia. *Cognition, 116*(1), 33–41. doi:10.1016/j.cognition.2010.03.012

Price, G. R., Holloway, I., Räsänen, P., Vesterinen, M., & Ansari, D. (2007). Impaired parietal magnitude processing in developmental dyscalculia. *Curr Biol*, *17*(24), R1042–R1043. doi:10.1016/j.cub.2007.10.013

Purpura, D. J., & Lonigan, C. J. (2015). Early numeracy assessment: The development of the preschool early numeracy scales. *Early Educ Dev*, *26*(2), 286–313. doi:10.1080/10409289.2015.991084

Quinn, S. (2015). *The Routledge international handbook of dyscalculia and mathematical learning difficulties* (S. Quinn, Ed.). New York: Routledge.

Re, A. M., Pedron, M., Tressoldi, P. E., & Laucangeli, D. (2014). Response to specific training for students with different levels of mathematical difficulties. *Except Child*, *80*(3), 337–352.

Reyna, V. F., Nelson, W. L., Han, P. K., & Dieckmann, N. F. (2009). How numeracy influences risk comprehension and medical decision making. *Psychol Bull*, *135*(6), 943–973. doi:10.1037/a0017327

Rosenberg-Lee, M., Ashkenazi, S., Chen, T., Young, C. B., Geary, D. C., & Menon, V. (2015). Brain hyper-connectivity and operation-specific deficits during arithmetic problem solving in children with developmental dyscalculia. *Dev Sci*, *18*(3), 351–372. doi:10.1111/desc.12216

Rotzer, S., Kucian, K., Martin, E., von Aster, M., Klaver, P., & Loenneker, T. (2008). Optimized voxel-based morphometry in children with developmental dyscalculia. *Neuroimage*, *39*(1), 417–422. doi:10.1016/j.neuroimage.2007.08.045

Rousselle, L., & Noël, M. P. (2007). Basic numerical skills in children with mathematics learning disabilities: A comparison of symbolic vs non-symbolic number magnitude processing. *Cognition*, *102*(3), 361–395. doi:10.1016/j.cognition.2006.01.005

Rykhlevskaia, E., Uddin, L. Q., Kondos, L., & Menon, V. (2009). Neuroanatomical correlates of developmental dyscalculia: Combined evidence from morphometry and tractography. *Front Hum Neurosci*, *3*, 51. doi:10.3389/neuro.09.051.2009

Sella, F., Tressoldi, P., Lucangeli, D., & Zorzi, M. (2016). Training numerical skills with the adaptive videogame "The Number Race": A randomized controlled trial on preschoolers. *Trends Neurosci Educ*, *5*(1), 20–29. doi:10.1016/j.tine.2016.02.002

Skeide, M. A., Evans, T. M., Mei, E. Z., Abrams, D. A., & Menon, V. (2018). Neural signatures of co-occurring reading and mathematical difficulties. *Dev Sci*, *21*(6), e12680. doi:10.1111/desc.12680

Szkudlarek, E., & Brannon, E. M. (2018). Approximate arithmetic training improves informal math performance in low achieving preschoolers. *Front Psychol*, *9*, 606. doi:10.3389/fpsyg.2018.00606

Toll, S. W. M., & Van Luit, J. E. H. (2012). Early numeracy intervention for low-performing kindergartners. *J Early Interv*, *34*(4), 243–264. doi:10.1177/1053815113477205

Van Herwegen, J., Costa, H. M., Nicholson, B., & Donlan, C. (2018). Improving number abilities in low achieving preschoolers: Symbolic versus non-symbolic training programs. *Res Dev Disabil*, 77, 1–11. doi:10.1016/j.ridd.2018.03.011

Van Luit, J. E. H., & Van de Rijt, B. A. M. (2009). *Utrechtse getalbegrip toets – Revised. [Early Numeracy Test – Revised]*. Doetinchem, Netherlands: Graviant.

Van Nieuwenhoven, C., & Noël, M. P. (2001). *TEDI-Math. Test diagnostique des apprentissages de base en mathématiques*. Paris: Pearson.

Vanbinst, K., Ansari, D., Ghesquiere, P., & De Smedt, B. (2016). Symbolic numerical magnitude processing is as important to arithmetic as phonological awareness is to reading. *PLOS ONE*, *11*(3), e0151045. doi:10.1371/journal.pone.0151045

Wechsler, D. (2014). *Wechsler intelligence scale for children-fifth edition*. Bloomington, MN: Pearson.

Wilkinson, G. S., & Robertson, G. J. (2006). *Wide Range Achievement Test – 4 professional manual*. Lutz, FL: Psychological Assessment Resources.

Woodcock, R., McGrew, K. S., & Mather, N. (2001). *Woodcock-Johnson tests of achievement* (3rd ed.). Itasca, IL: Riverside.

INDEX